30 DAYS TO THE ACT ASSESSMENT®

30 DAYS TO THE ACT ASSESSMENT®

Margaret Moran

THOMSON
™
ARCO

Australia • Canada • Mexico • Singapore • Spain • United Kingdom • United States

Introduction

Consider these scenarios:

Student X in San Diego knows he has to take the ACT Assessment because all of his colleges of choice require it. So he signs up to take it early in the second semester of his junior year. He buys one of those 800-page test-prep books and every day for fifteen weeks he spends the prescribed time studying.

Student Y in Boston knows she has to take the ACT Assessment because all of her colleges of choice require it. But she hates to take those fill-in-the-oval tests. She procrastinates until she has no choice about when to take it. She registers and procrastinates some more until she has thirty-one days left to prepare for the test.

Which one is you?

If Student Y were standing where you are today—in a bookstore with this book in her hands—she would be smart to buy this book and begin tomorrow studying for the ACT Assessment. Since you *will* be that smart, welcome to *30 Days to the ACT Assessment*.

The purpose of this book is to

- prepare you to become a great test-taker,
- help you develop strategies to boost your confidence

and, above all,

- help you master test-taking strategies in a short period of time—thirty days.

Doing well on the ACT Assessment requires familiarity with the tests as much as subject-area knowledge of English, math, reading, and science reasoning. Using a full-length practice ACT Assessment, we walk you through the format of the four subject-area tests and offer strategies for answering each one. In this way, you will become familiar with the four parts of the ACT Assessment—and help relieve any anxiety. Just set aside the necessary time each day and you can improve your score.

Good luck.

THE 30-DAY PROGRAM

Day 1 to **Day 11**

Test Structure and Strategies

Day 1

Get to Know the ACT Assessment

Assignments for Today:

- Learn the structure of the ACT Assessment.
- Learn how the ACT Assessment is scored.
- Learn how to and when to register for the ACT Assessment.

THE STRUCTURE OF THE ACT ASSESSMENT

The developers of the ACT Assessment state that it is an achievement test that follows typical high school curricula. They are quite clear that it's not an intelligence test. The ACT Assessment has four parts, or tests: English, Math, Reading, and Science Reasoning. The test is divided as follows:

Test	Number of Items	Time in Minutes
English	75	45
Math	60	60
Reading	40	35
Science Reasoning	40	35

In total, the test has 215 items and the time allotted is 2 hours and 50 minutes.

When the test begins, the test proctor will tell you when to open the test booklet and when to begin. During the time allotted for a particular section, you may work in that section only. If you finish a section before time is called, you may not go forward to the next section or turn back to a previous section. You may, however, move backward and forward within the section in which you are working. This is important to remember because you can turn it into a test-taking strategy to help you answer more questions on test day!

Types of Questions on the Test

You will read more about the types of information tested on each test and the question formats later in this book, but the following provides an overview.

The English Test (75 Questions)

There are two basic areas tested: usage and mechanics and rhetorical skills. These are divided according to the following categories:

- Usage and mechanics (40 of the 75 items)
  - Punctuation, 10 items
  - Basic grammar and usage, 12 items

- Sentence structure, 18 items
- Rhetorical skills (35 of the 75 items)
  - Strategy, 12 items
  - Organization, 11 items
  - Style, 12 items

The 75 items are scattered across five passages. The passages combine question types; that is, the questions in a single passage will not be all punctuation or all grammar or all style.

The Math Test (60 Questions)

The Math Test has the following six categories of information tested:

- Pre-Algebra, 14 items
- Elementary algebra, 10 items
- Intermediate algebra, 9 items
- Coordinate geometry, 9 items
- Plane geometry, 14 items
- Trigonometry, 4 items

As you can see, most of the test items focus on Algebra I and geometry topics. You also need to know basic operations and principles of pre-algebra, but don't worry if you have never taken trigonometry. There are only four questions on the test that require knowledge of trigonometric functions. If you've never had trig, you can ignore those four and still do well.

Reading Test (40 Questions)

The content of the Reading Test is taken from four areas:

- Prose fiction, 10 items
- Humanities, 10 items
- Social studies, 10 items
- Natural science, 10 items

The humanities refer to the visual arts, music, philosophy, dance, and theater. The natural sciences are the physical sciences, biology, chemistry, and physics. Don't lose heart at this point about

the test. The purpose of the natural science passage is to test how well you read and understand a passage about a topic in science, not what you know about that topic.

This is a good time to talk about an important issue for the Reading and Science Reasoning Tests. Everything you need to know to answer a question on either of these tests is on the page in front of you. You don't need to know the content of the subject matter to read a passage closely, think critically about what the question is asking you, and then choose the correct answer.

Science Reasoning Test (40 Questions)

The subject matter of the Science Reasoning Test is tested in three different formats. The subject matter is drawn from the following areas:

- Biology
- Earth and space science
- Chemistry
- Physics

The item formats are set up as follows:

- Conflicting viewpoints, 7 items
- Research summaries, 18 items
- Data representation, 15 items

The data representation questions use graphs and tables as the basis for questions. The research summaries ask questions about the designs and results of experiments, and the conflicting viewpoints questions ask you to understand and compare different hypotheses about scientific subject matter.

Again, the purpose of these questions is to test your ability to interpret and analyze problems, not to test your prior knowledge of the subject matter.

HOW THE ACT ASSESSMENT IS SCORED

You will receive a series of scores for the ACT Assessment that you take: (1) a set of subscores for the

English, Math, and Reading Tests; (2) a subject test score for each test; (3) a composite score for all four tests; and (4) a percentile ranking. The last is not really a score, but rather a comparison of where you stand among all the other students who took the test. It uses your composite score as the basis for the percentile comparison.

But First: A Word About Raw Scores and Scaled Scores

The raw score is the number of correct answers out of the total number of items for each test. The ACT Assessment scorers convert the raw scores to scaled scores using a conversion table. This conversion table in effect "levels the playing field." It makes all scores equal, regardless of which version of the test you take. Some versions given on a particular day may be more difficult than others.

You should also know that the ACT Assessment provides a 4-point spread as a margin of error. That is, the test developers consider 2 points above and 2 points below the scaled score as the "standard error of measurement." The "ACT Student Assessment Report" that you receive after you take the test will show you the range for each test, subscore, and the overall ACT Assessment.

> Remember, incorrect or unanswered questions don't count against you on the ACT Assessment. You can use this to your benefit when you take the test!

Test Subscores

Certain categories are combined on the English, Math, and Reading Tests to provide you with a set of scaled subscores. The Science Reasoning Test does not break down content or skill areas.

- English Test
  - Usage and mechanics
  - Rhetorical skills
- Math Test
  - Pre-algebra and elementary algebra
  - Intermediate algebra and coordinate geometry

- Plane geometry and trigonometry
- Reading Test
  - Arts and literature (humanities and prose fiction)
  - Social studies and Sciences (social studies and natural sciences)

Remember that the ACT Assessment bills itself as an achievement test and a tool to help you "evaluate your readiness for college work." These subscores can help you pinpoint areas for improvement.

The subscores range from 1, being the lowest, to 18, being the highest.

Subject Test Score

You will also receive a scaled score for each test. These range from 1, being the lowest, to 36, being the highest. In recent years, the average score for each test has been 21.

Composite ACT Assessment Score

The composite ACT Assessment scaled score is the average of the four test scores. It, too, ranges from 1, being the lowest, to 36, being the highest.

Percentile Ranking

The percentile score is based on the scale of 1 to 100 and indicates the number of people below that level. A percentile of 80 for Usage/Mechanics means that 80 percent of the test-takers scored less well on the section than you did. You will receive a percentile ranking for each subscore on the test, each test, and for the overall ACT Assessment.

REGISTERING FOR AND TAKING THE ACT ASSESSMENT

The ACT Assessment is given on five Saturdays during the school year—February, April, June, October, and December. Your school may be one of the 5,000 locations in the United States that serve as administration sites. It is also possible to take the test on a day other than Saturday, if Saturday presents a problem for you because of your religious beliefs.

Most high school guidance offices have registration forms, or you can contact ACT, Inc., directly for a form:

- Call 319-337-1270 from 8 a.m. to 8 p.m. Central time.
- Write to ACT Assessment Registration, P.O. Box 414, Iowa City, IA 52243-0414.
- Register on line at www.act.org/aap/. You will need a credit card to register on line.

Check the registration information for the current fee. There is a basic fee for taking the test and reporting your scores to up to four colleges. Each additional college is an additional fee. Registering late incurs an additional fee, as do registering by phone, asking to have your scores reported to you before having them sent to colleges, and rushing processing—taking the ACT Assessment so late that you just make the cut-off date for your colleges.

If you miss the late cut-off date for registering for the ACT Assessment, you may still register for standby testing for a steeper fee, but there is no guarantee that a seat will come open the day of the test. You may still miss taking the test. Procrastination has its costs—in money and anxiety.

When Should You Take the ACT Assessment?

It generally takes four weeks to score and process scores after you have taken the test. In calculating when you should take the ACT Assessment, add time for mailing and then catching up the scores with your admissions file at your colleges of choice. Don't cut it close. It's not worth the anxiety of worrying whether your scores will make it in time for the admissions committee. Take the test *at least* eight weeks before your first college-filing deadline.

Consider taking the test twice. Many students do and then choose which set of scores to send to their colleges. However, you have to use a complete set of scores. You can't use the best tests from the two ACT Assessment administrations, mixing and matching Math and Natural Science from the first ACT Assessment administration with Reading and English from the second.

Most students take their first ACT Assessment some time in the second semester of junior year. If you take it early enough, you can take a second one either later that spring or at the beginning of senior year.

Remember, too, that if you decide to do early admissions, you will need your scores in mid-fall of your senior year.

General Strategies for Taking the ACT Assessment

Assignment for Today:

- Learn ten important strategies for taking the ACT Assessment.

There are specific strategies for approaching each test on the ACT Assessment, and you will be learning them in subsequent days. Today, your task is to learn ten general strategies that will work for all the tests. Don't groan. You don't need to memorize them, because they aren't long, involved *rules*. They are common-sense ways to make taking the ACT Assessment less anxiety-producing.

As you take each test section in this book, practice these strategies and see how quickly you can apply them without having to think about it.

ACT ASSESSMENT STRATEGY 1: KNOW THE DIRECTIONS.

Every test-prep book you'll ever read will tell you to save time and not read the directions. This is true. Even if omitting reading the directions saves you only 20 seconds—and it will save you more time than that—you could have read the answers to a question in that amount of time.

However, you also have to know what the directions say in order to answer the questions. For obvi-

ous copyright reasons, the directions in this book are not word-for-word as they appear on the tests, but they present the basic information about question formats and what you are supposed to do. Days 3, 5, 10, and 11 walk you through the directions for each test.

ACT ASSESSMENT STRATEGY 2: SKIM THE PASSAGES AND ITEMS AND PLAN THE ORDER IN WHICH TO ANSWER THEM.

Trig not your thing? Cross off those four questions right away.

Love painting but not sure about quarks? Order the Reading passages so that the one on painting is the first one you read and answer and the one on the property of quarks is the last one you tackle.

Skimming the problems and passages gives you an idea of what to expect so that when you turn the page of the test booklet with 10 minutes to go, you don't find a really easy-to-understand passage after having just slogged through one on your least favorite topic. You can't move back and forth from test to test, but you can move around within a test.

See what's on the test. Where you have passages to read, mark 1, 2, 3, etc., on the passages and answer them in the order that's best for you. There's less flexibility on the Math Test, but even there you can get a fairly good idea of which items are about the kinds of math you're most comfortable with.

ACT ASSESSMENT STRATEGY 3: PACE YOURSELF.

One of the most frequent complaints from students about the ACT Assessment is that it's too long—there are too many questions to answer in the amount of time given. These students didn't pace themselves.

You can work out a pacing schedule for yourself now because the test times and item numbers are always the same. Consider breaking your time into groups of minutes and questions. Consider that there are 60 items on the Math Test and you have 60 minutes to complete the test. Subtract, say, 5 minutes from the total to save for checking answers at the end. That leaves 55 minutes and 60 items. You could worry about answering 1 question every 55 seconds, but it's easier to set a pace of 10 questions every 9 minutes or so. That translates into 20 questions at the end of 18 minutes, 30 questions at the end of 27, and so on, until you've dealt with all 60 questions at the end of about 54 minutes.

Having markers such as 10 questions in 9 minutes and 20 questions in 18 minutes means that as you work, you can check how quickly or how slowly you're going. If you've completed—read, answered, or moved on without answering—25 questions in 18 minutes, you might want to slow down. If you've only considered 10 items in 18 minutes, you might want to speed up.

You can work a pacing schedule for the English Test, too. Figuring 75 items and 45 minutes, subtract 5 minutes for reviewing at the end. Then think in terms of about 20 items every 10 minutes, 40 items in 20 minutes, 60 items in 30 minutes, and 75 items in 40 minutes.

Work out your pacing for the Reading and Science Reasoning Tests here:

• Reading:

4 passages/40 items/35 minutes

$35 - 3 = 32 \div \_\_ = \_\_$ minutes for each passage and question

__ minutes for reading each passage

__ minutes for answering the accompanying questions

• Science Reasoning

7 passages/40 items/35 minutes

$35 - 3 = 32 \div \_\_ = \_\_$ minutes for each passage and question

__ minutes for reading each passage

__ minutes for answering the accompanying questions

Remember that some passages will be easier for you than others, but these time frames will give you a basis for working the two tests.

There is one important fact to remember in working out your pacing schedule. The degree of difficulty for items on the English, Reading, and Science Reasoning Tests is consistent from first question to last. The Math Test is the only test in which the questions become more difficult as you work through the test. You might want to factor that into figuring out pacing for the Math Test.

ACT ASSESSMENT STRATEGY 4: ANSWER THE EASY ITEMS FIRST.

In the discussion about pacing, did you notice the words and phrases *considered, dealt with,* and *moved on without answering*? This relates back to ACT Assessment Strategy 2. Tackle the easiest passages first. Then answer the easiest questions about those passages.

Remember that only correct answers count, but you want to answer as many questions as you can. If a question stumps you on first reading, put an "X" next to it if you think you might be able to answer it if you came back to it. Put a check mark through a question if you think it's just too hard to bother with.

ACT ASSESSMENT STRATEGY 5: ELIMINATE FIRST, AND GUESS SECOND.

Only correct answers count on the ACT Assessment. Unlike the SAT I, there is no penalty for wrong answers, so there's no penalty for guessing. However, you don't want to guess randomly, because a point here and a point there can add up to a better score. You want to make an educated guess.

If you read a question, and you think you know the answer but aren't sure, try to eliminate at least one of the answer choices. If you can eliminate two, even better. Then choose the answer that seems most likely to fit, make sense in the context, or be appropriate. Chances are the answer will be correct—and even if it's not, you won't be out any points.

In the worst case, just guess. Listen to your intuition and go with it.

> As you eliminate answers, be sure to draw a line through them. If after eliminating one or two choices, you feel you can't answer a question and you move on, when you come back to it, you won't waste your time eliminating answer choices that you've already discarded.

ACT ASSESSMENT STRATEGY 6: FOCUS ON THE WORDING—IN THE QUESTIONS AND IN THE ANSWERS.

Find the "basic" question—what is being asked—and disregard anything else in the prompt. Underline, circle, or bracket this basic information and re-read just this information in the prompt.

For example, a question might read as follows:

The accountant trying to convince the young man of the suitability of her profession compared it to all of the following EXCEPT

You would want to underline *compared* and *EXCEPT*. If you were in a hurry and ignored *EXCEPT*, more than likely you would answer the question incorrectly. Similarly,

The main idea of the second paragraph in relation to the current crisis is

has some extraneous information in it. If you are looking for the main idea of the paragraph, that's what you're looking for. *In relation to the current crisis is filler.*

ACT ASSESSMENT STRATEGY 7: ANSWER THE RIGHT QUESTION.

One of the great things about a multiple-choice test is that the answer is always there in front of you. *But* test writers can use this fact to confuse and mislead you. Some of the questions, especially in the Math Test, may require a couple of steps to get to the final answer. Some of those intermediate steps might appear as answer choices. This is true in the Science Reasoning Test as well. An intermediate result in a science experiment might be listed to distract you from the final result, which is what the question asked for.

This strategy complements ACT Assessment Strategy 6, underlining, circling, or bracketing important words in the question. If you hone in on the key words in the question, you will be more likely to understand what the question is asking and then be able to find the correct answer choice.

Besides nouns and verbs, key words could be *except, least,* and *not; true* and *correct;* and *because, primarily, best describes, best states, most likely,* and *significance.*

Look also for qualifying words such as *seldom, always, usually, sometimes, never, often,* and *occasionally.* Qualifying words can substantially change the meaning of a sentence.

Deb seldom walks the dog in the morning.

Deb always walks the dog in the morning.

Deb usually walks the dog in the morning.

Deb never walks the dog in the morning.

Beware of qualifying words that are absolutes, such as *always* and *never*. Ask yourself if the idea makes sense with the qualifier. Does the qualifier make the idea too broad or too narrow?

The home team always wins the first game of the World Series.

While home-field advantage is important, to say that the home team *always* wins doesn't seem logical. A better opponent could overcome the home-field advantage to win.

ACT ASSESSMENT STRATEGY 8: REFER TO THE PASSAGE OR PROBLEM.

This strategy complements both ACT Assessment Strategies 7 and 8. Don't rely on your memory for what the passage says or the question asks. Don't just read the passage, the question, and the answer choices and then pick an answer—especially if the question asks about the meaning of a specific word or phrase. Go back to the passage, find the reference, and read a couple of lines above and below it.

For a math problem, read the problem and the answers. Then check the problem again to be sure you know what you're being asked to find or do.

ACT ASSESSMENT STRATEGY 9: BE EFFICIENT IN HOW YOU FILL IN YOUR ANSWERS.

Unlike other standardized tests with which you may be familiar, the ACT Assessment uses (A), (B), (C), and (D) for odd-numbered questions and (F), (G), (H), and (J) for even-numbered questions for the English, Reading, and Science Reasoning Tests. These three tests have only four item choices for the answers.

The Math Test has five item choices for the answers—(A), (B), (C), (D), and (E) for odd-numbered questions and (F), (G), (H), (J), and (K) for even-numbered questions.

This odd assortment of answer letters actually makes it easier for you to fill in the correct answer oval when you are skipping around answering questions. If you are trying to answer question 33 with a "B" and the answer row you are looking at has F, G, H, and J, you know you're in the wrong row.

There are two ways to deal with filling in the answers. Fill in as you go, checking after two or three questions to make sure that you are working in the right row. Or circle your answer choices in the test booklet and then transfer those answers to the answer sheet at the end of each page or passage.

The second strategy will save you time, because for each question you answer, you won't spend time checking to be sure you are answering on the right line. It does mean that you will have to pace yourself so that you will have time to fill in your last answers.

ACT ASSESSMENT STRATEGY 10: FINISH EARLY AND CHECK.

This is part of pacing. Be sure to leave enough time to go back to check your answers. This is time to try to answer some of the questions you put an "X" next to.

Instant Replay

Ten General Strategies for the ACT Assessment
1. KNOW the directions.
2. SKIM the passages and PLAN the order in which to answer them.
3. PACE yourself.
4. Answer the EASY ITEMS first.
5. ELIMINATE first, and GUESS second.
6. FOCUS on the wording—in the questions and in the answers.
7. Answer the RIGHT QUESTION.
8. REFER to the passage or problem.
9. Be EFFICIENT in how you FILL IN your answers.
10. FINISH EARLY AND CHECK.

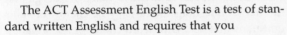

Day 3

About the English Test

Assignments for Today:

- Learn the structure of the English Test.
- Learn some strategies to help you do well on the test.

The ACT Assessment English Test is a test of standard written English and requires that you

- know, understand, and can apply certain rules of usage and mechanics, and
- can identify writing strategies, organization, and style.

Standard written English is the writing style that your teachers expect to see in your essays and reports. Newspaper articles, television news reports, and nonfiction books are typically written in standard English. Slang, colloquialisms, jargon, technical terms, and ethnic and regional dialects are inappropriate in standard English.

CONTENT OF THE ACT ASSESSMENT ENGLISH TEST

The ACT Assessment English Test asks questions related to usage and mechanics and rhetorical skills. The usage and mechanics questions focus on parts of sentences and test such topics as

- subject/verb agreement and noun/pronoun agreement,
- correct verb tenses,
- parallelism, and
- proper use of punctuation.

The questions about rhetorical skills refer to the strategy, or choices, a writer makes in crafting a piece of writing; the organization of a paragraph or of an entire passage; and the style of the piece. Topics such as the following are tested:

- the appropriateness of a particular sentence in a paragraph,
- the order of sentences in a paragraph,
- the use of transitions, and
- avoidance of problems of style such as redundancy and vagueness.

Let's take another look at the division of items between usage and mechanics and rhetorical skills on the English Test. But this time, let's look at a further breakdown of topics:

- Usage and mechanics (40 of the 75 items)
  - Punctuation, 10 items
    - Commas; apostrophes; colons and semico-lons; parentheses and dashes; periods, question marks, and exclamation points
  - Basic grammar and usage, 12 items
    - Agreement; verb forms; pronoun forms and cases; comparative and superlative forms of adjectives and adverbs; idioms
  - Sentence structure, 18 items
    - Clauses; run-on sentences; comma splices; sentence fragments; misplaced modifiers; shifts in construction
- Rhetorical skills (35 of the 75 items)
  - Strategy, 12 items
    - Appropriateness; effectiveness
  - Organization, 11 items
    - Order, or sequence; unity; coherence, or clarity
  - Style, 12 items
- Word choice; vagueness and awkwardness of expression; redundancy, or repetitiveness; and wordiness

Does it all look like Greek to you? Remember that you only need to get about half right to get the average score of 21 for the test. There are 33 topics listed here and only 75 questions, so the chances are you won't find 2 or more questions about each topic. Decide which topics you are strongest in and answer those first on the test. Mark the others as you learned in Day 2 and come back to them at the end. You'll find a quick review of some of these topics in Day 4.

By the way, "it all looks like Greek to me" is an idiom—that is, a phrase that is recognized as an expression with a particular meaning. This idiom means that something seems or looks incomprehensible. It is an unusual idiom.

On the test, you're more likely to find an ordinary phrase you use all the time without thinking about it, such as "write down" or "work on (as in, the project)." These are phrases you use

so often that you don't think about the individual words in them. On the test, rely on your "ear"—how a phrase sounds to you—in answering a question about an idiom. You probably won't even notice that you're looking for an idiom. It'll just be a question that you answer quickly and move on without giving much thought to it.

QUESTION FORMATS

As noted in Day 1, the questions on the English Test are embedded in reading passages, and the test is set up in two columns. The left column contains the passage, and directly across from it in the right column are the answer choices. Sometimes there are questions with the answer choices, and sometimes there are not. In the latter instance, all you will find are four answer choices. The presence of a stated question signals that the test item is about a rhetorical skill. *But* not all underlined items are usage and mechanics questions. Some may be rhetorical skills questions that deal with word choice or redundancy.

But there is another difference besides the two-column format between the English Test and other tests with passages to read. The format for the questions on the English Test is set up in one of three ways.

- A portion of the passage may be underlined and a numeral placed under it.

resulted from the lack of a traffic signal. The parents
<u>*make sure that they went*</u> *to the next town*
                          2
council meeting to lobby for a light.

- A numeral in a box may appear at the beginning, in the middle, or at the end of paragraph and may refer either to the entire paragraph or to a sentence, depending on where the boxed numeral is placed.

. . . Parking had become such a problem that students were being ticketed for parking on the street for more than the allotted two hours. [3]

- Occasionally, you may find a boxed notice above the final one or two questions for a passage. The wording will be similar to the following:

Item 30 poses a question about the essay as a whole.

There is no text in the left-hand column in this case, because you must refer to the entire passage to answer the question.

A WORD ABOUT THE ANSWER CHOICES

The multiple-choice questions have four responses. The first answer response may be "NO CHANGE." If you read the underlined portion and feel that it is correct or most appropriately stated as it is, then choose "NO CHANGE." About 25 percent of the time, "NO CHANGE" is the answer, so don't "overcorrect" your test.

Very rarely you may find the wording "OMIT the underlined portion" as your last answer choice. This often signals a question about wordiness or redundancy. Read the underlined portion and a line or two above and below it very carefully to determine if the underlined portion can be omitted without taking any meaning away from the sentence. Often in this case, "OMIT the underlined portion" is the correct answer. This is related to ACT Assessment English Strategy 8 below, "Shorter is better."

> Remember that "NO CHANGE" will always be either A or F on the answer sheet.

DIRECTIONS FOR THE ENGLISH TEST

The directions for the English Test are similar to the following:

DIRECTIONS: This test consists of five passages in which particular words or phrases are underlined and numbered. In the right-hand column, you will see alternative words and

phrases that could be substituted for the underlined part. You must select the alternative that expresses the idea most clearly and correctly in terms of standard written English or that best fits the style and tone of the entire passage. If the original version is best, select "NO CHANGE."

The test also includes questions about entire paragraphs and the passage as a whole. These questions are identified by a numeral in a box.

After you select the correct answer for each question, mark the oval representing the correct answer on your answer sheet.

Note that the directions explain

- how the test is set up—in two columns with test items either underlined or identified by a numeral in a box.

- what you are to do—choose the answer that expresses the idea *most clearly*, is *correct*, or *best fits* the style and tone.

> Remember to read and reread these directions until you are familiar with them. Knowing ahead of time what the test asks you to do will save you time on test day.

SOME STRATEGIES TO HELP YOU DO WELL ON THE TEST

On Day 2, you learned some overall strategies for answering questions on the ACT Assessment. Today, you'll learn eight strategies to help you specifically with the English Test.

ACT Assessment English Strategy 1: Figure out the ERROR ON YOUR OWN.

Read the whole sentence that includes the underlined words. Try to figure out what's wrong with the underlined portion before you read the answer choices. In this way, a wrong answer choice won't influence your judgment.

> Don't bother to read answer choices A and F for test items that are underlined. Very rarely will they be something other than "NO CHANGE."

ACT Assessment English Strategy 2: Look for COMMON ERRORS.

Most of the usage and mechanics errors are the ones that people make all the time—lack of agreement between noun and pronoun, incorrect verb tense, or incorrect placement of an apostrophe. You'll review these in Day 4, but for now the following is a list of questions that you should ask yourself when you come across an error that you can't quickly identify.

- Do the subject and verb agree?
- Does the sentence have a subject and a verb?
- Is the verb tense correct?
- Does the pronoun agree in person and number with its antecedent noun?
- Are similar ideas expressed in parallel construction?
- Are modifiers attached to what they're meant to modify?
- Is the apostrophe in the right place?

ACT Assessment English Strategy 3: LISTEN for the error.

Sometimes when you hear someone speaking, you'll recognize that the person made a grammatical error. You don't necessarily have that conscious thought, but you notice that what the person said sounded "funny"—that is, strange or wrong—to you. "I don't need no help" sounds wrong, because you've both learned informally and been taught formally that using two negative words (*don't* and *no*) is incorrect.

Use this "listening" skill to your advantage when you take the test. If you're having trouble figuring out the error, read the sentence silently to yourself. Listen for what sounds "funny" to you. Check the answer choices and go with what sounds right to you.

ACT Assessment English Strategy 4: Don't create a NEW ERROR.

The ACT Assessment test writers can be tricky. Some answer choices may introduce a new error into the sentence while correcting the original one. Always be careful in choosing an answer that any new words that are added to the underlined portion aren't adding an error.

ACT Assessment English Strategy 5: SUBSTITUTE your answer into the passage.

Once you've made your choice, check your answer by substituting it into the passage. This is a check to make sure that it is indeed grammatically correct, appropriate, and/or fits the tone and style. If not, go back to the answers, cross this one out, and try again. Remember to pace yourself, though. If you can't make a quick decision, move on.

ACT Assessment English Strategy 6: ADD ONLY relevant details.

For questions where you are asked to add a sentence to a paragraph, identify the main idea of the paragraph first. Then read the answer choices, looking only for ideas that will develop or build on that idea. Like a good writer, you don't want to add extraneous details to the passage.

ACT Assessment English Strategy 7: ORDER sentences or paragraphs based on the MAIN IDEA.

When you are asked to consider the order, or sequence, of a paragraph, find the main idea of the paragraph first. The sentence that contains this overall topic will most likely become the first sentence in the paragraph. If you have to reorder an entire passage, the paragraph that introduces the overall topic, or main idea, of the passage will most likely become your first paragraph. If you are correct, the other sentences in the paragraph or the other paragraphs in the passage should fall into logical order easily.

ACT Assessment English Strategy 8: SHORTER is better.

For questions of style, the shortest answer—if it is grammatically correct—is often the right choice. Remember that style questions deal with wordiness, awkwardness, redundancy, and vagueness. When extraneous words are removed and convoluted constructions are unraveled, what's left is often brief and to the point. Note, however, that the shortest answer choice also has to be grammatically correct.

Instant Replay

ACT Assessment English Test Strategies

1. Figure out the ERROR ON YOUR OWN.

2. Look for COMMON ERRORS.

3. LISTEN for the error.

4. Don't create a NEW ERROR.

5. SUBSTITUTE your answer into the passage.

6. ADD ONLY relevant details.

7. ORDER sentences or paragraphs based on the MAIN IDEA.

8. SHORTER is better.

DON'T FORGET TO USE THE OVERALL STRATEGIES.

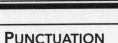

Day 4

Quick Review of Some Basic Usage and Mechanics Rules

Assignment for Today:

- Review some basic usage and mechanics rules.

One of the strategies for the English Test is to spot common errors and correct them. Today, you're going to take a quick look at some errors that people commonly make—and that may show up on the English Test. This brief review gives you an example of a common error and then how to fix it. For a more complete review of usage and mechanics, check your English/language arts textbook. It's always a good idea to brush up on the basics of usage and mechanics before you take the test.

The usage and mechanics questions on the English Test assess your knowledge of punctuation, basic grammar, and sentence structure. This review is divided into the same three categories. The example sentences are very brief, so you can spot the errors easily. Sentences on the English Test will be longer with more phrases and modifiers to make spotting errors more difficult.

> Remember to read the entire sentence when you are answering a question that is an underlined portion of a sentence. Reading just the underlined portion won't necessarily tell you enough to select the correct answer choice.

PUNCTUATION

Comma

Common error: Using commas to set off a restrictive clause or phrase (one that is needed for the sense of the sentence; it limits, or restricts, the meaning of the sentence)

The old cat, sunning itself on the windowsill, looked content.
Correct:
The old cat _ sunning itself on the windowsill _ looked content.

Common error: Omitting commas to set off a nonrestrictive clause or phrase (one that is not needed for the sense of the sentence; also called a parenthetical)

The science class visited the Franklin Institute which has a new exhibit on space.
Correct:
The science class visited the Franklin Institute, which has a new exhibit on space.

Common error: Omitting the second comma in a parenthetical (nonrestrictive) phrase or clause

The Franklin Institute, which has a new exhibit on space is open until 6 p.m. on Sundays.
Correct:

The Franklin Institute, which has a new exhibit on space, is open until 6 p.m. on Sundays.

Apostrophe

Common error: Incorrect form of possessive pronouns
The book was hers' (yours').
Correct: Omitting apostrophe with possessive pronouns

The book was **hers (yours).**

Common error: Incorrect form of a possessive noun
One schools' team was late for the tournament.
Both school's teams were late for the tournament.
Correct: Using 's for singular and s' for plural possessives

One school's team was late for the tournament.
Both schools' teams were late for the tournament.

Colon and Semicolon

Common error: Using a colon to separate independent clauses

He was the school's all-around athlete: he was the valedictorian of his class, also.
Correct: Using a semicolon to separate independent clauses

He was the school's all-around athlete; he was the valedictorian of his class, also.

Period and Question Mark

Common error: Mistaking a sentence for a question
She asked what is the right thing to do in this situation?
Correct:

She asked what is the right thing to do in this situation.

BASIC GRAMMAR

Agreement

Subject and Verb

Common error: Plural subject and singular verb
Tara and Keishawn, who is the better athlete, always makes time for sports.
Correct: Plural subject and plural verb
Tara and Keishawn, who is the better athlete, always **make** time for sports.

Common error: Singular subject and plural verb
Everyone on the three teams know the time of the games.
Correct: Singular subject and singular verb
Everyone on the three teams **knows** the time of the games.

Focus on the subject and verb and eliminate all extraneous words and phrases. *Knows* in this example may sound strange to your ear, but it is correct because the pronoun *everyone* is singular and requires a singular verb.

Pronoun and Antecedent

Common error: Singular antecedent and plural pronoun
Everyone in the school should know their course schedule by now.
The basketball team won all their games this year.
Correct: Singular antecedent and singular pronoun
Everyone in the school should know **his or her** course schedule by now.
The basketball team won all **its** games this year.

Team is a collective noun in this sentence—the players are talked about as a unit—and so *team* takes a singular pronoun and a singular verb.
Correct:
The basketball team walks to its bus after the game.
But
The members of the basketball team walk to their bus after the game.

Remember the following rules:

- Pronouns ending in *-one*, *-body*, and *-thing* always take a singular verb.

- The pronouns *some*, *any*, *none*, *all*, and *most* may be singular or plural, depending on their use in the sentence.

Verb Forms

Common error: Using the wrong principle part for a verb

The sparrow had flew out of the reach of the cat.

Correct:

The sparrow had **flown** out of the reach of the cat.

Most verbs form their past and past participle by adding *-ed* and *-ing*. For the verbs that form them in other ways, you will need to memorize the verbs and their parts. The following tables show some of the more common irregular verbs.

Same present, past, and past participle

Present	Present Participle	Past	Past Participle
bid	bidding	bid	(have) bid
burst	bursting	burst	(have) burst
cost	costing	cost	(have) cost
cut	cutting	cut	(have) cut
hurt	hurting	hurt	(have) hurt
let	letting	let	(have) let
put	putting	put	(have) put
split	splitting	split	(have) split
spread	spreading	spread	(have) spread

Same past and past participle

Present	Present Participle	Past	Past Participle
bind	binding	bound	(have) bound
build	building	built	(have) built
catch	catching	caught	(have) caught
find	finding	found	(have) found
get	getting	got	(have) got, gotten
hang	hanging	hung	(have) hung
keep	keeping	kept	(have) kept
lead	leading	led	(have) led
lend	lending	lent	(have) lent
pay	paying	paid	(have) paid
shine	shining	shone	(have) shone, shined
spin	spinning	spun	(have) spun
wring	wringing	wrung	(have) wrung

Change in various ways

Present	Present Participle	Past	Past Participle
arise	arising	arose	(have) arisen
become	becoming	became	(have) become
break	breaking	broke	(have) broken
draw	drawing	drew	(have) drawn
eat	eating	ate	(have) eaten
freeze	freezing	froze	(have) froze
go	going	went	(have) gone
know	knowing	knew	(have) known
shrink	shrinking	shrank	(have) shrunk
spring	springing	sprang, sprung	(have) sprung
steal	stealing	stole	(have) stolen

Verb Tense

Common error: Mixing tenses for simultaneous actions

On Tuesday, the soccer team will play an away game and the basketball team is playing at home.
Correct:

On Tuesday, the soccer team will play an away game and the basketball team **will play** at home.

Common error: Mixing tenses for consecutive actions

After the guest spoke, the principal had given the award.
Correct:

After the guest had spoken, the principal **gave** the award.

> The past perfect tense (*had spoken*) is farther back in time then simple past (*gave*); that is, something in the past perfect tense (*had* form of the auxiliary verb *to have*) occurred before the past tense. The present perfect tense (*has* or *have* form of the auxiliary verb *to have*) means that something began in the past and continues to happen.
>
> The Senator **had spoken** about the proposed bill *yesterday*.
>
> The Senator **has spoken** about the issue *often and as recently as today*.
>
> Watch out for verb tense questions involving sequence on the ACT Assessment English Test.

Pronouns and Cases

Common error: Using the incorrect pronoun as subject

Him and I will make the posters.
Correct:

He and I will make the posters.

Common error: Using the incorrect pronoun as object

Mary and Sam will go with he and I to the game.
Correct:

Mary and Sam will go **with him and me** to the game.

Adjectives versus Adverbs

Common error: Using an adjective in place of an adverb to modify a verb

The team captain ran triumphant around the basketball court.
Correct:

The team captain ran **triumphantly** around the basketball court.

Common error: Using an adjective in place of an adverb to modify an adjective

The audience was most quiet during the speech.
Correct:

The audience was **mostly quiet** during the speech.

> This example uses the verb *to be*. Remember that all forms of the verb *to be* along with the linking verbs *appear, become, continue, feel, grow, look, remain, seem, smell,* and *taste* take the same case after them as before. They do not have objects, but rather have subject complements. The proper pronoun form is *I* or *we*. The proper modifier is an adjective.
>
> The team leader is **I**. (**I** am the team leader.)
>
> The boy felt **bad** about the ruined experiment.

Comparative and Superlative Modifiers

Common error: Using the incorrect form

The day was more clearer than usual for July.
Correct:

The day was **clearer** than usual for July.

Common error: Using the superlative form to compare two things

Of the two race cars, hers was fastest.
Correct: Using the comparative form to compare two things

Of the two race cars, hers was **faster.**

Common error: Using the comparative form to compare three or more things

Of the five actors in the play, his role was the more difficult.

Correct: Using the superlative form to compare three or more things

Of the five actors in the play, his role was the **most difficult.**

Idioms

Idioms are, for the most part, learned by hearing other people use them. They become so ingrained in our speech that we don't really notice their use. Would you say "children tend to *look down* to athletes" or "children tend to *look up* to athletes"? Some words and prepositions just "seem to go together." Review the following list of idiomatic expressions.

according to the law
accuse of treason
agree about the number to invite
agree on the terms of the treaty
agree to invite the twins
agree with the policy
bored by the argument
comply with the rules
conform to the rule
die of boredom
different from what the mayor said
different than the mayor's message
encroach on the other's territory
feel well (healthy)
in accordance with the rules
independent of his actions
intention of doing the work
known by his nickname
known for her team spirit
look at the picture
look in the book
look into the complaint
look through the names on the list
look up to the athlete
look up the word in the dictionary

SENTENCE STRUCTURE

Dependent Clause

Common error: Using the incorrect coordinating conjunction

Jake looked in every room for the dog, and it was outside.
Correct:
Jake looked in every room for the dog, **but** it was outside.

Run-on Sentence

Common error: Joining two or more independent clauses without the use of a coordinating conjunction or a semicolon

The coach canceled practice on Thursday many of the team members were taking midterms.
Correct:
Many of the team members were taking midterms, **so** the coach canceled practice on Thursday.

Comma Splice

Common error: Using only a comma to join two independent clauses

The coach canceled practice on Thursday, many of the team members were taking midterms.
Correct:
The coach canceled practice on Thursday, **because** many of the team members were taking midterms.

Sentence Fragment

Common error: Omitting a subject or a verb
Rain clouds daily for a month but no rain.
Correct:
There were rain clouds daily for a month but no rain.

Misplaced Modifier

Common error: Lack of the word or phrase being modified; that is, a dangling modifier

Concerned about the effects of the cold weather on an old battery, the car was run for awhile every day.
Correct:
Concerned about the effects of the cold weather on an old battery, **the owner** of the car ran it for awhile every day.

Shifts in Construction

Common error: Inconsistent verb tense
See verb tense above.

Common error: Inconsistent person
One must understand the rules or you will never succeed.
Correct:
One must understand the rules or **one** will never succeed.
OR
You must understand the rules or **you** will never succeed.

Parallelism

Common error: Lack of parallel form in a list
Participating in track meets, reading books, and golf are his favorite activities.
Correct:
Participating in track meets, reading books, and **golfing** are his favorite activities.

Common error: Lack of parallel form in comparing two things
To work efficiently is more important than working quickly.
Correct:
To work efficiently is more important than to work quickly.
OR
Working efficiently is more important than working quickly.

SOME MISCELLANEOUS COMMON USAGE PROBLEMS

1. *accept,* to receive
   except, other than

2. *among,* for three or more items
   between, for two

3. Use *about* rather than *as to.*

4. Eliminate *at* or *about* in the construction *at about.*

5. Use *since* or *because* in place of *being as, being that.*

6. Use *since* or *because* in place of *due to the fact that.*

7. Use *fewer* with things that are counted.
   Use *less* with qualities or quantities that are not counted.

8. Eliminate *a* in *kind of* and *sort of.*

9. Use *only* immediately before the word it logically modifies.

10. Do not use *says* in place of *said.*

11. Use *since* when time is involved.
    Use *because* when a reason is involved.

12. *Then* refers to time.
    Than is used in a comparative construction, such as *better than.*

13. *That* refers to people and things.
    Which refers to things.
    Who refers to people.

14. *Their* is a possessive pronoun.
    There is an adverb or used in place of a noun: *There are four people there.*
    They're is the contraction for *they are.*

15. *Its* is a possessive pronoun.
    It's is the contraction meaning *it is.*

There is an easy way to check whether the word you want is *they're* or *their* or *its* or *it's.* Restate the sentence using the full phrase rather than the contraction.

_____ dog is a black Labrador.

Their dog or *They are dog?*

_____ bone is under the couch.

Its bone or *It is bone?*

Instant Replay

Study these common errors and how to correct them.

Check your English/language arts textbook for additional help.

Day 5

About the Math Test

Assignment for Today:

- Learn the structure of the Math Test.

The ACT Assessment Math Test assesses how well you understand and can manipulate a range of mathematical subject matter from pre-algebra to trigonometry. As noted on Day 1, only four of the test items are based on trigonometry, so if you haven't taken trig, you won't blow your score.

CONTENT OF THE ACT ASSESSMENT MATH TEST

As you read on Day 1, the Math Test has 60 test items that are taken from the following six categories:

- Pre-Algebra, 14 items
- Elementary algebra, 10 items
- Intermediate algebra, 9 items
- Coordinate geometry, 9 items
- Plane geometry, 14 items
- Trigonometry, 4 items

As you can see, most of the test items focus on algebra I and geometry topics. Slightly more than half

the test items require knowledge of pre-algebra and algebra. One ACT Assessment publication lists close to sixty possible topics that might appear in some way on the Math Test. Since the ACT Assessment takes into consideration a broad range of high school math curricula, assume that the more arcane topics won't be included in any depth on any single test.

However, it's a given that you'll need to know the basic operations—addition, subtraction, multiplication, and division—and the order of operations. Figure, too, since most math courses across the country are similar that you might find questions that involve the following:

- Fractions and decimals
- Ratio, proportion, and percent
- Mean, median, and mode
- Simple probability
- Quadratic equations
- Negative numbers
- Square roots and the roots of polynomials
- Factoring

- Real number lines
- Slope
- Distance
- Parallel and perpendicular lines
- Properties and relations of triangles, circles, and quadrilaterals
- Perimeter, area, and volume
- Trigonometric equations
- Values and properties of functions

QUESTIONS FORMAT AND TYPES

All 60 test items are multiple choice, and each has five possible answers. The answer choices are lettered (A), (B), (C), (D), and (E) for odd-numbered questions and (F), (G), (H), (J), and (K) for even-numbered questions.

There are seven question types that you will undoubtedly find on the test:

- Straightforward equations
- Word problems
- Problems involving graphs and charts
- Algebra problems
- Geometry problems with and without diagrams
- Trigonometry problems
- Multiple problems that use the same graph or chart

Because you are going to remember to skim the 60 test items before you begin, you will have a good idea of which ones are the kind you are most comfortable answering and which ones you'll put off until your second pass through the test.

Remember that the questions in the first third of the Math Test are easier than the questions in the middle third, which are easier than the ones in the last third. But unlike the SAT I that has tricky questions, the ACT Assessment Math Test items are fairly straightforward. It doesn't mean that there are no complicated questions that require careful reading, but don't expect to find one early in the test.

Remember that what may seem easy to the test writers may not be to you and what they think is difficult may be fun for you. Some people really like solving trig equations and some people find word problems difficult no matter how easy a particular problem is supposed to be. Skim the Math Test and decide for yourself what are the easiest, next easiest, and hardest questions to answer and follow your plan.

DIRECTIONS FOR THE MATH TEST

The directions for the Math Test are similar to the following.

DIRECTIONS: Solve each problem below and choose the correct answer. Mark the oval on the answer sheet that corresponds to that answer.

Be careful not to spend too much time on any one question. Instead, solve as many questions as possible, and then use any remaining time to return to those questions that you were unable to answer at first.

You may use a calculator on any problem; however, not every problem requires the use of a calculator.

Note: Unless otherwise indicated, assume all of the following to be true:

- Diagrams that accompany problems are not necessarily drawn to scale.
- All figures lie in a plane.
- A line indicates a straight line.
- *Average* refers to arithmetic mean.

The directions are straightforward. Read the question, solve it, and fill in the answer sheet. Don't spend too much time on any one answer.

Of the items in the "Note," the one to remember is the last: *Average* refers to arithmetic mean. This is the number obtained by dividing a sum by the number of its addends (numbers added together; 3, 4, 5 = 12 ÷ 3 = 4 as average).

> Remember to read and reread these directions until you are familiar with them. Knowing ahead of time what the test asks you to do will save you time on test day.

SOME STRATEGIES TO HELP YOU DO WELL ON THE TEST

Days 6 through 9 provide strategies that show you how to work through test items. The following are some general do's and don'ts about the Math Test.

About Calculators

You may use a calculator on the Math Test, but it cannot be part of a pocket organizer, pen input device, electronic writing pad, or a computer keyboard pad; have a paper tape; or beep as you work on it. A four-function scientific calculator is probably best. If you have any questions, see the guidelines for calculators that ACT, Inc., publishes in its bulletin and on its Web site.

Also, don't go out and buy a new calculator just to take the test. If you decide you need a new calculator, be sure that you use it enough before test day to be thoroughly familiar with it.

> Be sure that you put fresh batteries in your calculator and try it out to be sure it works.

But as important as the type of calculator you bring to the test is how you use it. The math items are designed so that you don't need a calculator to answer them. The test writers specifically design questions that rely on reasoning abilities and knowledge of the correct procedures to follow in order to arrive at the answer. If you feel more secure using a calculator, then the following types of questions are the ones for which using your calculator could be most beneficial:

- Arithmetic calculations
- Square roots
- Percentages

About Checking Your Answers

One of the problems about using calculators is that you have no paper trail if your answer and none of the five answer choices match. Always check your answer before you move on to the next question.

That means checking more than the calculations. That means checking to make sure that your answer solves the problem. For example, if you are trying to find the number of pizza slices that students sold if they sold 80 percent of 12 pizzas cut into 6 slices and your answer is 72, you didn't answer the right question. You answered how many pieces the students had to sell, not how many they sold. See Day 6 for more about answering the right question.

To check answers, you also have to be sure that they make sense in the context of the problem. Given the information, should your answer be greater or lesser?

About Showing Your Work

The test makers leave a whole column for you in the test booklet to do your figuring in, so use it. Even if you use a calculator, make some notes in the right-hand column about what you are doing. Then, if you decide that you just can't figure out how to solve the problem and move on, you will have some information about what you were trying to do, if you have time to come back to the problem.

About Graphs and Diagrams

You may find line, bar, and circle graphs as well as diagrams on the Math Test. These offer great clues to help you figure out answers. Read the graphs and diagrams very carefully—even before you read the question. Reading them first gives you the context for the question.

> If a geometry question doesn't have a diagram, draw one based on the information in the question. You'll be surprised how often drawing a diagram can show you the answer.

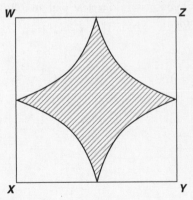

Day 6

Math Strategies

Assignments for Today:

- Learn to use the answer choices.
- Identify the right question to answer.

ACT ASSESSMENT MATH STRATEGY 1: READ THE **ANSWER CHOICES** BEFORE SOLVING THE PROBLEM.

As noted in Day 5, all the math questions on the ACT Assessment are multiple-choice questions. In general, answering a math question—or any question—that is accompanied by five choices is easier than answering the same question with no answer choices available. The main advantage, of course, is that the correct answer is staring you right in the face. There are four incorrect answers also staring you in the face, but knowing that one of the five answer choices must be correct offers you major help in deciding how to attack the problem.

Even if you think you know how to approach the solution to a problem, it is still a good idea to look at the options before you begin to solve the problem. Reading the choices will give you an idea of what sort of answer you are supposed to find. If you are not certain about how to solve a problem, the possible answers may give you enough of a hint to get you started. Consider the geometry problem below:

In the figure below, *WXYZ* is a square, and the four unshaded pieces inside the square are quarter circles, each having the same radius. If the length of a side of *WXYZ* is 6, what is the area of the shaded part of the figure?

(A) 9π

(B) $36 - 6\pi$

(C) $36 - 18\pi$

(D) $36 - 9\pi$

(E) 18π

One of the first things that you probably noticed as you read the answers is that they all involve π. Now, π turns up in geometric formulas involving the circumference and the area of circles. Since this problem asks about areas, it is likely that the geometric formula for the area of a circle, which is $A = \pi r^2$, will be involved somehow in finding the answer.

The answer choices also give you another hint. Note that three of the five answer choices involve subtraction. In fact, in each of these three choices, a quantity involving π is subtracted from 36. If you note that the area of the square is 6^2 (36), then these answer choices give you an idea of how to proceed. You need to subtract the areas of the four quarter circles from the area of the square; what remains will be the area of the shaded portion.

After realizing this, solving the problem is straightforward. Each of the quarter circles has a radius of 3, which is half the length of the side of the square. You might also realize that the sum of the areas of four quarter circles is equal to the area of *one* entire circle. Therefore, you need to subtract the area of a circle of radius 3 from the area of the square, which is 36. The answer is $36 - \pi (3)^2 = 36 - 9\pi$, or answer choice (D).

Not all problems will be this easy to decipher from the answer choices, but try the answer choices first and you may find a clear path to follow to solve the problem.

ACT ASSESSMENT MATH STRATEGY 2: ANSWER THE RIGHT QUESTION.

This strategy isn't so much a problem-solving technique as it is something to always bear in mind when solving ACT Assessment problems. Always be certain that, when you pick your answer choice, you answer the question that is being asked. You learned this on Day 2 as an overall strategy for answering questions on ACT Assessment tests, but it bears repeating specifically for the Math Test.

When the test writers create their multiple-choice answers, they try to select answers that represent the most common mistakes that a student, under the pressure of taking a test, would make.

If $x + 5 = 41$, and $x + y = 12$, what is the value of $x - y$?

(A) –60

(B) –24

(C) 12

(D) 36

(E) 60

This is a very easy question, as long as you don't rush. Begin by solving the first equation for x:

$x + 5 = 41$

Subtract 41 from both sides:

$x = 36$

Be careful at this point not to jump to the wrong answer and select answer choice (D). The problem is not asking for the value of x, which you just found. It is asking for $x - y$.

If $x + y = 12$, you can find the value of y:

$x + y = 12$

Substitute $x = 36$:

$36 + y = 12$

Subtract 36 from both sides:

$y = -24$

Be careful not to jump and select answer choice (B) either. The problem is not asking for the value of y, but $x - y$.

$x - y = 36 - (-24) = 36 + 24 = 60$

The correct answer is choice (E).

Many of the problems you will encounter on the ACT Assessment Math Test will involve multiple steps, and many of the answer choices will be the results you will get if you correctly solve for the intermediate steps. Don't be fooled by these answer choices. If you have carefully read the problem, underlined what you are solving for, and keep your focus on that, you won't be distracted by partially correct answers.

Instant Replay

1. Read the ANSWER CHOICES before solving the problem.
2. Answer the RIGHT QUESTION.

Day 7

Math Strategies

Assignments for Today:

- Estimate the answer.
- Translate word problems into mathematical operations.

ACT ASSESSMENT MATH STRATEGY 3: ESTIMATE THE ANSWER.

Because you know that one of the five answer choices must be correct, estimation becomes a very useful problem-solving technique. Consider, for example, the following problem:

Rosemary Miller buys sweaters from a wholesaler for $8 each and sells them at her store for $20 each. Her selling price is what percent of her purchase price?

(F) 40%

(G) 60%

(H) 66.7%

(J) 150%

(K) 250%

Let's say that you weren't exactly sure how to solve this percent problem. As a way of getting started, you could try to make some estimates to determine about what number the answer should be. To begin, if Rosemary bought sweaters for $8 and

sold them for $8 (not a very savvy marketing decision), her selling price would have been 100% of her purchase price. Since she marked the sweaters up, her selling price is greater than 100% of her purchase price, and answer choices (F), (G), and (H) can, therefore, be eliminated.

> Notice that so far, you haven't done any computation. You've just thought about the content of the problem. Remember that the Math Test assesses mathematical skills, knowledge, and reasoning abilities. As one ACT, Inc., publication states: " . . . [T]he questions on the test are designed to emphasize your ability to reason mathematically, not to test your computation ability or your ability to recall definitions, theorems, or formulas."

You can go even a bit further with this line of thinking. If Rosemary doubled the price, selling the sweaters for $16, her selling price would be 200% of her purchase price. Since $20 is actually *greater than double* the price, answer choice (J) cannot be correct either. The only possible correct answer must be answer choice (K).

Don't get the wrong idea. It certainly is not true that you can always use estimation to cut the five answer choices down to one. In fact, as you will see later in this book, test writers sometimes cluster answer choices around the correct answer to make it more difficult for you to estimate. However, estimating almost always will help you eliminate some of the answer choices, setting you up for an educated guess with a good chance of being correct.

> Also remember that after you select your answer to a question, it is a good idea to make a quick estimate to see if your answer seems realistic. You will catch many mistakes this way.

ACT ASSESSMENT MATH STRATEGY 4: FIND THE MATHEMATICAL OPERATION IN WORD PROBLEMS.

Figuring out what a word problem is asking you to do can be the hardest part of answering a word problem. You may be perfectly comfortable with a, b, and c, but gallons of paint, prices of sweaters, and distance driven between point A and point B in 2 hours leave you dumbfounded. The mathematical operation, once you figure it out, is usually simple; it's getting to the computation that is difficult. To help, follow these steps:

1. Break the problem into its smallest pieces of information.

2. Use the numbers given or assign letters and make numerical expressions of these small pieces of information.

3. Use the numbers and/or letters to write your own formula/equation to describe the relationships of the parts.

4. Solve the equation that results.

Suppose you were given the following problem:

Jack is 4 years older than Sophia. Four years ago, Sophia was half the age Jack is now. How old is Sophia now?

What are you looking for? You're looking for Sophia's age now.

Make S represent Sophia's age.

Make J stand for Jack's age.

Now write two simple equations to stand for what the problem states in words.

"Jack is 4 years older than Sophia" becomes $J - 4 = S$.

"Four years ago, Sophia was half the age Jack is now" becomes $S - 4 = \dfrac{J}{2}$.

Multiply both sides of the equation by 2 and the result is $2S - 8 = J$, which is Jack's age.

Now you can solve for the S in the equation $J - 4 = S$.

$$(2S - 8) - 4 = S$$
$$2S - 12 = S$$
$$- 12 = -S$$
$$S = 12$$

Sophia is 12 today (and Jack is 16).

The most difficult thing about word problems can be figuring out what the words are telling you to do—that is, translating the words into mathematical relationships and then into mathematical operations. The following list of signal, or key, words will help you take some of the problem out of word problems.

Word-Problem Term	Operation
amounts to	equals
by	multiplication
difference	subtraction
each	multiplication
fewer than	subtraction
fraction	division
greater than	addition
is, is the same as	equals
larger than	addition
less than	subtraction
more than	addition
of	multiplication
part of	division
per	multiplication
piece	division
portion of	division
product	multiplication
reduced by	subtraction
smaller than	subtraction
take away	subtraction
with	addition
without	subtraction

Instant Replay

1. Read the ANSWER CHOICES before solving the problem.

2. Answer the RIGHT QUESTION.

3. ESTIMATE the answer.

4. Find the mathematical operation in WORD PROBLEMS.

Day 8

Math Strategies

Assignment for Today:

- Substitute answer choices into the question.

ACT ASSESSMENT MATH STRATEGY 5: SUBSTITUTE ANSWER CHOICES INTO THE QUESTION.

The fact that you are solving multiple-choice problems sets up another useful problem-solving strategy. Many problems can be solved by trial and error. Instead of working the problem forward, work it backward. Take the answer choices one at a time and substitute them into the problem itself. As the example below illustrates, this technique is particularly useful in problems involving algebraic equations.

If $\sqrt{x^2 + 11} = x + 1$, then what is the value of x?

(A) –5

(B) 3

(C) 4

(D) 5

(E) 6

This equation certainly can be solved directly using algebraic techniques. It also can be solved by taking the answer choices one at a time and substituting them for the value of x until you find the one that works. This is an especially good strategy to use in cases where you are not certain how to solve the problem.

Test choice (A) $x = -5$:

$$\sqrt{(-5)^2 + 11} = \sqrt{25 + 11} = \sqrt{36} = 6.$$

$x + 1 = -5 + 1 = -4$ No!!

By the way, if you had noticed that the left-hand side of this equation is always going to be positive and that $x = -5$ makes the right-hand side negative, you wouldn't have had to bother testing this answer choice.

Test choice (B) $x = 3$:

$$\sqrt{(3)^2 + 11} = \sqrt{9 + 11} = \sqrt{20}.$$

$x + 1 = 3 + 1 = 4$ No!

Test choice (C) $x = 4$:

$$\sqrt{(4)^2 + 11} = \sqrt{16 + 11} = \sqrt{27}.$$

$x + 1 = 4 + 1 = 5$ No!

Test choice (D) $x = 5$:

$$\sqrt{(5)^2 + 11} = \sqrt{25 + 11} = \sqrt{36} = 6.$$

$x + 1 = 5 + 1 = 6$ Yes!

Using the technique of substitution, you have identified the correct answer as choice (D).

This technique can also be used to solve certain word problems. Consider the following investment problem:

> Dan Preston has $10,000 to invest. He invests some of this money in an account that pays 5% annual interest and the rest in an account that pays 6% annual interest. If, at the end of one year, he has earned $560 in interest, how much money did he invest at 5%?
>
> (F) $3,000
>
> (G) $4,000
>
> (H) $5,000
>
> (J) $6,000
>
> (K) $7,000

This problem can be solved using the standard algebra method—that is, writing and solving a system of equations. However, you can also substitute in the answers and see which one "works."

Test choice (F) $3,000:

If Dan invested $3,000 at 5%, then he invested $7,000 at 6%. In this case, the amount of interest he earned will be

$3,000 \times 0.05 + $7,000 \times .06 =
$150 + $420 = $570. No!

Test choice (G) $4,000:

If Dan invested $4,000 at 5%, then he invested $6,000 at 6%. In this case, the amount of interest he earned will be

$4,000 \times 0.05 + $6,000 \times .06 =

$200 + $360 = $560. Yes!

Substitution is always a strategy to consider when you are not certain how to solve the problem directly.

This problem is a good one to use as a reminder to you about answering the right question—the question that is the one being asked, ACT Assessment Math Strategy 2. In working through to the answer, you determined that $4,000 was the amount to be invested at 5%. However, note that if $4,000 were invested at 5%, then $6,000 were invested at 6%. The test writers have inserted $6,000 as one of the answer choices. In a rush, if you haven't read the problem carefully, you might be tempted to pick answer choice (J), since it is a part of the answer to the problem. It just isn't the part that you are asked to find. Before you select your final answer choice, go back to the problem and be certain that you are answering the question that is being asked.

Instant Replay

1. Read the ANSWER CHOICES before solving the problem.

2. Answer the RIGHT QUESTION.

3. ESTIMATE the answer.

4. Find the mathematical operation in WORD PROBLEMS.

5. SUBSTITUTE answer choices into the question.

Day 9

Math Strategies

Assignment for Today:

- Use numerical values for variables.

ACT ASSESSMENT MATH STRATEGY 6: USE NUMERICAL VALUES FOR VARIABLES.

Consider the following algebra problem:

Which of the following expressions is equivalent to $\dfrac{2x^2+11x-21}{2x^2-5x+3}$?

(F) $\dfrac{2x+3}{2x-3}$

(G) $\dfrac{x+7}{x+1}$

(H) $\dfrac{2x-3}{2x+3}$

(J) $\dfrac{2x-3}{x-1}$

(K) $\dfrac{x+7}{x-1}$

This problem can be solved by factoring, and dividing, the algebraic fraction in the problem statement. If you are uncertain how to do this, however, there is another strategy that you can use that typically will enable you to determine the answer: simply pick a value for x. Perhaps the easiest value to work with is $x = 0$. Substitute this value into the algebraic fraction in the problem statement, and compute its resulting value:

$$\frac{2x^2+11x-21}{2x^2-5x+3} = \frac{2(0)^2+11(0)-21}{2(0)^2-5(0)+3} =$$
$$\frac{-21}{3} = -7$$

Therefore, when $x = 0$, the fraction in the problem statement is equal to −7. Whichever of the answer choices is equivalent to the original fraction must also have a value of −7 when $x = 0$ is substituted. It is easy to test and find out which one satisfies this property:

(F) $\dfrac{2x+3}{2x-3} = \dfrac{2(0)+3}{2(0)-3} = \dfrac{3}{-3} = -1$ No!

(G) $\dfrac{x+7}{x+1} = \dfrac{0+7}{0+1} = \dfrac{7}{1} = 7$ No!

(H) $\dfrac{2x-3}{2x+3} = \dfrac{2(0)-3}{2(0)+3} = \dfrac{-3}{+3} = -1$ No!

(J) $\dfrac{2x-3}{x-1} = \dfrac{2(0)-3}{0-1} = \dfrac{-3}{-1} = 3$ No!

(K) $\dfrac{x+7}{x-1} = \dfrac{0+7}{0-1} = \dfrac{7}{-1} = -7$ Yes!

By using this strategy, you can determine the correct answer without going through the algebraic manipulations needed to determine the answer directly.

Note that if you use this strategy, it is possible that two different answer choices might give you the correct value. If this is the case, then the answer must be one of those two choices. Simply pick a different value for x, and substitute it into the two possible answers. Chances are that only one of them will give you the correct value this time!

Let's take a look at one more example of numerical substitution with variables, this time with a proportion problem.

A recipe calls for F cups of flour for every W cups of water. How many cups of water would be needed if G cups of flour were used?

(A) $\dfrac{F}{GW}$

(B) $\dfrac{GF}{W}$

(C) $\dfrac{W}{GF}$

(D) GWF

(E) $\dfrac{GW}{F}$

Of course, this problem can be solved by using the technique of solving proportions. But you can also solve it by using variable substitutions.

Suppose that $F = 1$ and $W = 3$. Then you need 1 cup of flour for every 3 cups of water.

Suppose G, the unknown, is 2. Then you need 2 cups of flour and 6 cups of water.

Now you would need to check to see which of the answer choices gives a value of 6 when $F = 1$, $W = 3$, and $G = 2$. If you check, you will see that only choice (E) works:

$$\frac{GW}{F} = \frac{(2)(3)}{1} = \frac{6}{1} = 1$$

Instant Replay

1. Read the ANSWER CHOICES before solving the problem.

2. Answer the RIGHT QUESTION.

3. ESTIMATE the answer.

4. Find the mathematical operation in WORD PROBLEMS.

5. SUBSTITUTE answer choices into the question.

6. Use NUMERICAL VALUES for variables.

Day 10

About the Reading Test

Assignments for Today:

- Learn the structure of the Reading Test.
- Learn some strategies to help you do well on the test.

As its name states, the ACT Assessment is an assessment test, and the purpose of the Reading Test is to assess how well you understand what you read. The ability to read and understand material comparable to what you will be reading in college is an important indicator of future college success.

CONTENT OF THE ACT ASSESSMENT READING TEST

As noted on Day 1, the content on the Reading Test is taken from four areas:

- Prose fiction, 10 items
- Humanities, 10 items
- Social studies, 10 items
- Natural science, 10 items

The prose reading will be either a complete short story or an excerpt from a larger short story, a novella, or a novel. The other three readings will be nonfiction and will be pieces from actual books, journals, and magazines. The humanities category refers to the visual arts, music, philosophy, dance, literary criticism, film, and theater. The reading may be a factual account or a personal essay. The natural sciences may be about any of the physical sciences, biology, chemistry, and physics.

The purpose of the natural science passage is to test how well you read and understand a passage about a topic in science, not what you already know about that topic. Remember that everything you need to know to answer a question about any of these passages is on the page in front of you. You don't need to know the content of the subject matter to read a passage closely, think critically about what the question is asking you, and then choose the correct answer.

TYPES OF SKILLS ASSESSED

According to the developers of the ACT Assessment, there are eight skills that form the basis of most questions on the Reading Test:

- Main idea of a paragraph or passage
- Important details
- Comparison

- Cause and effect
- Generalization
- Using context clues to determine word meaning
- Inference
- Author point of view

As you can probably infer from this list, the Reading Test asks both straightforward recall questions and more complex critical-thinking questions. A straightforward question would be one that asks you what a paragraph or passage is mainly about. A more sophisticated question would ask you to infer a character's personality based on his or her behavior in a particular situation.

The approach of the questions will differ from passage to passage based on the kind of passage you are reading. For example, questions that relate to a

- prose passage may ask about plot, setting, characters, and mood;
- humanities reading may ask you to compare ideas or infer author point of view, especially if the piece is a personal essay;
- social studies reading may ask you typical social studies questions, such as to compare events and to identify cause-and-effect relationships; and
- natural science selections may ask about steps in a process or cause-and-effect relationships.

QUESTION FORMAT

The Reading Test is made up of four passages followed by 10 questions each. All 40 questions are multiple choice, and each has four possible answers. All the answer choices are different; there are no "NO CHANGE" or "OMIT the underlined portion" answers.

Note that the answer choices are (A), (B), (C), and (D) for odd-numbered questions or (F), (G), (H), and (J) for even-numbered questions. Your answer sheet will list only those four choices per line. You don't have to worry about accidentally marking an (E) or a (K).

There are a few two-part or tiered questions. The question itself will have three options, and you have to decide which option(s) is (are) true and then select the multiple-choice response that lists the correct answer. Here is an example.

The main character's view of his family is that it is

   I. charmingly dysfunctional.

  II. made up of eccentrics.

 III. hopelessly out of touch with the lower classes.

(F) I only

(G) I and II only

(H) III only

(J) I and III only

First, you would need to check the passage to decide whether I, II, and/or III are true. Say you decide that I and III are true. Find the multiple-choice response that corresponds to those two options, answer choice (J), and that is your answer.

DIRECTIONS FOR THE READING TEST

The directions for the Reading Test are similar to the following:

DIRECTIONS: This test consists of four passages, each followed by several questions. Read each passage, select the correct answer for each question, and mark the oval representing the correct answer on your answer sheet. Refer to the passages as needed.

There are just these easy steps to remember: read, select, and fill in. Note the last sentence in the directions. It encourages you to refer to the passage as you answer the questions. This is good advice from the test developers and an important test-taking strategy to follow.

Remember to read and reread these directions until you are familiar with them. Knowing ahead of time what the test asks you to do will save you time on test day.

SOME STRATEGIES TO HELP YOU DO WELL ON THE TEST

Before you take a look at the specific strategies for the Reading Test, go back to Day 2 and reread ACT Assessment Strategies 2, 3, 6, 7, and 8. They are especially important for the Reading Test.

- ACT Assessment Strategy 2: SKIM the passages and PLAN the order in which to answer them.

It's not just the category—social studies, humanities— that matters but the subject matter of the passage as well. You may find that while you thought you'd probably read the fiction piece first, the social studies passage is about a topic you just studied or really like.

- ACT Assessment Strategy 3: PACE yourself.

It's really important not to get bogged down reading the passages. ACT Assessment Reading Strategy 1 below will help you avoid this pitfall.

- ACT Assessment Strategy 6: FOCUS on the wording—in the questions and in the answers. For the Reading Test, add "and in the passage."

ACT Assessment Reading Strategy 1 below will explain why paying attention to the phrasing in the passage is important.

- ACT Assessment Strategy 7: Answer the RIGHT QUESTION.

This goes along with ACT Assessment Strategy 6: focus on the wording so you are sure what you are being asked. One of the answer choices may be a true statement, but that doesn't mean it answers the question you are being asked.

- ACT Assessment Strategy 8: REFER to the passage or problem.

As ACT Assessment Reading Strategy 1 will explain, you can't rely on your memory of what these passages say. You need to go back to the passage, scan to find the relevant portion, reread it, and choose your answer.

There's a difference between skimming and scanning.

- *Skimming* is a quick read to get a general idea. You don't read every word, but rather only words here and there to give you a sense of the piece.

- *Scanning* is reading quickly to look for specific information.

Will knowing the difference between the two make a difference for the test? Only in the sense that when the two terms are used in this discussion of strategies, you'll know what you're supposed to do.

ACT Assessment Reading Strategy 1: SKIM, READ, REVIEW.

After you've chosen the order in which you are going to answer the passages, go to the first passage.

- SKIM the passage to get a general overview of its content.

- SKIM the questions to find out in general what they are asking. Don't take time to read the answer choices.

- READ the passage. Read it thoughtfully—that is, read it with the questions in mind and a pencil in hand. As noted in ACT Assessment Strategy 6, underline, circle, or bracket the important information that relates to the questions you just read. You might be looking for the main idea of the passage, the meaning of a word or phrase, or a cause-and-effect relationship. As you will see in ACT Assessment Reading Strategies 2 and 3, the main idea and the organization of the passage are two things to always look for as you read.

Read thoughtfully, but don't get bogged down in details. Skimming the questions before you begin your reading step will help you avoid this time-killing pitfall.

- REVIEW the passage. Before you return to the questions, skim the passage again. Try to lock in where the important information is in the passage. But DON'T answer questions from memory. Remember ACT Assessment Strategy 8: Refer to the passage. If you did a good job marking important information as you read, finding it again will be quick.

ACT Assessment Reading Strategy 2: Read for the BIG picture.

Finding details is not so difficult as discerning the big picture. When you read, be sure to look for the main idea of the passage and of each paragraph. The main idea, or theme, of the passage will usually be in the first paragraph. Look for the main idea of individual paragraphs in the first sentence or two as an introduction or at the end as a summary statement.

ACT Assessment Reading Strategy 3: Read for the ORGANIZATION.

Determining the way the passage is organized can help you answer questions. Look for the following types of organization:

- One idea and several examples to illustrate it
- One idea and several theories to explain it
- Comparison between two ideas, events, or people
- Pro-and-con arguments about one idea
- Cause-and-effect relationship
- Sequence of events

ACT Assessment Reading Strategy 4: Read ALL the answer choices.

As noted in ACT Assessment Reading Strategy 1, when you skim the passage on your first read-through, don't take the time to look at the answer choices; but when you're ready to answer the questions, read all the answer choices. Even though you think answer choice (A) is correct, read all four answers. You might find that one answer is more correct—that is, fits the question better than another.

ACT Assessment Reading Strategy 5: SUBSTITUTE vocabulary answers.

You may be asked for the meaning of a word or phrase used in the reading. To answer this type of question, refer to the line in the passage with the word and read several lines above and below the cited word in order to understand the context in which the word is used. Then read the answers, make your choice, and substitute your answer into the cited line in order to make sure it makes sense.

Instant Replay

ACT Assessment Reading Strategies

1. SKIM, READ, REVIEW.

2. Read for the BIG picture.

3. Read for the ORGANIZATION.

4. Read ALL the answer choices.

5. SUBSTITUTE vocabulary answers.

Day 11

About the Science Reasoning Test

Assignments for Today:

- Learn the structure of the Science Reasoning Test.
- Learn some strategies to help you do well on the test.

The Science Reasoning Test assesses your critical thinking abilities rather than your knowledge of scientific topics. The test questions will ask you to understand, analyze, interpret, compare, evaluate, and predict using various kinds of scientific information. You will be asked to read tables and graphs as well as summaries of experiments and statements of theories. All the information that you will need to answer a question is within the passage—in the text or on the tables, diagrams, charts, and graphs.

CONTENT OF THE SCIENCE REASONING TEST

The subject matter of the Science Reasoning Test is drawn from the following subject areas:

- Biology
- Earth and space science
- Chemistry
- Physics

The test items are divided into three types of passages, as follows:

- Conflicting viewpoints, 7 items
- Research summaries, 18 items
- Data representation, 15 items

The data representation questions use graphics and tables as the basis for questions. Typically, there are one or two short paragraphs followed by one to five graphs, tables, charts, diagrams, or pictures.

The research summaries questions ask about the designs and results of experiments. These passages contain one or two paragraphs to introduce the material followed by two or three descriptions of experiments.

The conflicting viewpoints questions ask you to understand and compare different hypotheses about scientific subject matter. You will see one or two introductory paragraphs followed by descriptions of typically two or three differing theories or ideas about a scientific question.

Again, the purpose of these questions is to test your ability to interpret and analyze problems, not to test your prior knowledge of the subject matter.

You may need to do some math computation to answer a question, but any calculations will be very simple. You are *not* allowed to use a calculator for the Science Reasoning Test.

> If you are trying to do some long, involved calculation to arrive at an answer, you're going in the wrong direction. Back up, because any math you need for an answer is simple.

WHAT TO LOOK FOR AS YOU READ

The focus of the three types of information on the test is different, and you should be aware of different things as you read each type of passage.

In data representation, look for
- what is being measured,
- relationships among the variables, and
- trends, or patterns, in the data.

In research summaries, look for
- the hypothesis, or theory, being tested,
- the variables being tested, and
- the differences in the results of the experiments.

In conflicting viewpoints, look for
- the scientific question being explained,
- similarities and differences, especially differences, and
- hidden assumptions, those unstated ideas that if false make the argument false.

If this were the Reading Test, we'd be talking about these pieces of information as main ideas and details. You are indeed reading these passages and the graphics for their main ideas and details. Especially in the data representation questions, you'll need to read the axes of the graphs and all the labels in order to find the information to answer the questions.

> Ignore the pros and cons of the arguments in the conflicting viewpoints passage. That is, don't get caught up trying to decide if you agree with theory A or theory B. All that's important is answering the questions correctly. But *do* pay attention to whether there are any faulty assumptions underlying the arguments.

QUESTION FORMAT

The Science Reasoning Test typically has seven passages and 40 questions. All 40 questions are multiple choice and are based on text and graphics. Each question is followed by four multiple-choice answers, labeled either (A), (B), (C), or (D) for odd-numbered questions or (F), (G), (H), or (J) for even-numbered questions.

DIRECTIONS FOR THE SCIENCE REASONING TEST

You will find directions similar to the following for the Science Reasoning Test:

> **DIRECTIONS:** This test consists of seven passages, each followed by several questions. Read each passage, select the correct answer for each question, and mark the oval representing the correct answer on your answer sheet. Refer to the passages as needed.
>
> You may NOT use a calculator on this test.

The directions are very clear: read, answer, and fill in. As in the directions for the Reading Test, the test developers are encouraging you to refer to the passages as you answer the questions.

> Remember to read and reread these directions until you are familiar with them. Knowing ahead of time what the test asks you to do will save you time on test day.

SOME STRATEGIES TO HELP YOU DO WELL ON THE TEST

Before you take a look at the specific strategies for the Science Reasoning Test, go back to Day 2 and re-read ACT Assessment Strategies 2, 3, 6, 7, and 8.
- ACT Assessment Strategy 2: SKIM the passages and PLAN the order in which to answer them.

Here are some clues to help you determine the type of passage:

- Data representation (there will be several charts or graphs)

- Research summaries (paragraphs may be labeled *Study* or *Experiment*)

- Conflicting viewpoints (paragraphs may be labeled *Theory* or *Hypothesis*)

In choosing your order, don't just look at the type of passage—data representation, research summaries, or conflicting viewpoints—but at the topics of the passage as well. You may find the topic in a conflicting viewpoints passage about a biological theory easier than a research summary passage about geology.

- ACT Assessment Strategy 3: PACE yourself.

It's really important not to get bogged down reading the passages, which are filled with details and some jargon. ACT Assessment Science Reasoning Strategy 1 below will help you avoid this pitfall.

- ACT Strategy 6: FOCUS on the wording—in the questions and in the answers. For the Science Reasoning Test, add "and in the passage."

Because there are so many details, be sure you know what's a variable, what's a result, what's supporting information, and so on. ACT Assessment Science Reasoning Strategy 1 will help you focus on the information.

- ACT Assessment Strategy 7: Answer the RIGHT QUESTION.

This goes along with ACT Assessment Strategy 6: focus on the wording in the question, too, so you are sure what you are being asked. One of the answer choices may be a true statement about an experimental result, but that doesn't mean it answers the question you are being asked. Or the question may ask you about Figure 1 and you confuse it with Table 1.

- ACT Assessment Strategy 8: REFER to the passage or problem.

As we've said over and over, don't rely on your memory of what these passages say. You need to go back to the passage, scan to find the relevant portion, reread it, and choose your answer.

> If you don't remember what it means to skim versus scan, read page 41.

ACT Assessment Science Reasoning Strategy 1: SKIM, READ, REVIEW.

This is the same as ACT Assessment Reading Strategy 1. After you've chosen the order in which you are going to answer the passages, go to the first passage.

- SKIM the passage to get a general overview of its content.

- SKIM the questions to find out in general what they are asking. Don't take time to read the answer choices.

- READ the passage and the graphics. Read them thoughtfully—that is, read them "with the questions in mind and a pencil in hand." As noted in ACT Assessment Strategy 6, underline, circle, or bracket the important information that relates to the questions you just read. You might be looking for the result of an experiment, for a variable that changes a result, or for differences between two hypotheses.

> The Science Reasoning passages are filled with numbers and detail and some jargon. Read thoughtfully, but don't get bogged down in the details and numbers. Skimming the questions before you begin your reading step will help you avoid this time-killing pitfall.

- REVIEW the passage and graphics. Before you return to the questions, skim the passage and look at the labels and axes on the graphics again. Try to lock in where the important information is on the graphics and in the passage. But *don't* answer questions from memory. Remember ACT Assessment Strategy 8: REFER to the passage. If you did a good job marking important information as you read, finding it again will be quick.

ACT Assessment Science Reasoning Strategy 2: Read for the BIG picture.

You learned this as a strategy for the Reading Test, but it's important for the Science Reasoning Test as well. It always helps to know what the overall theme of the passage is. To find it, check the last sentence of the introductory paragraphs and you'll usually see

- the relationship between and among the variables for data representation passages,
- the purpose of the experiments for research summaries, and
- the hypothesis under study for conflicting viewpoints passages.

ACT Assessment Science Reasoning Strategy 3: Find the DIFFERENCES.

The differences between results and theories are often the subject of questions, so be sure to locate differences as you read.

ACT Assessment Science Reasoning Strategy 4: Find CHANGES.

Cause-and-effect relationships and sequence are important aspects of scientific investigations: Change X, then Y happens, which results in Q. Look for what changes and then how that change results in other changes.

ACT Assessment Reasoning Strategy 5: Read ALL the answer choices.

It is important to read all the answer choices, even if you think you've found the correct answer in choice (E). The wording may be close enough to the right answer that it may seem right, but checking all the answers can show you the error.

Instant Replay

1. SKIM, READ, REVIEW.

2. Read for the BIG picture.

3. Find DIFFERENCES.

4. Find CHANGES.

5. Read ALL the answer choices.

Day 12 to Day 29

Practice Questions, Answers, and Explanations

Practice English Test: Passages I and II

Assignment for Today:

- Take a sample of the ACT Assessment English Test under actual test conditions. For the real test, you will have 45 minutes to answer 75 questions. For this practice, set your timer for 18 minutes. Remember to skim to decide which passage to answer first. Then use the ACT Assessment English Strategies to answer the questions.

DIRECTIONS: *This test consists of two passages in which particular words or phrases are underlined and numbered. In the right-hand column, you will see alternative words and phrases that could be substituted for the underlined part. You must select the alternative that expresses the idea most clearly and correctly in terms of standard written English or that best fits the style and tone of the entire passage. If the original version is best, select "NO CHANGE."*

The test also includes questions about entire paragraphs and the passage as a whole. These questions are identified by a numeral in a box.

After you select the correct answer for each question, mark the oval representing the correct answer on your answer sheet.

Passage I

Monet's House and Garden at Giverny

One of the most memorable trips that I
<u>have taken has been</u> to Claude Monet's garden at
1
Giverny about an hour and a half from Paris.
Although it was a <u>chilly, late autumn day,</u> the garden
2
was still in bloom. Gardeners rotate flower plantings
by season from spring through the end of fall. **[3]**

On the day my companion and I
<u>were there, there were dahlias</u> everywhere, in a
4
multitude of colors and shades—red, pink, yellow,
orange, purple, lavender. The last roses of the season
were so massive they could hardly hold their heads
up. Leggy pink and magenta cosmos waved in the
cool breeze.

Monet's house is a <u>marvel—inside and out.</u>
5
<u>Painted pink ivy covers large swaths of the facade.</u>
6
A trellis <u>rises up</u> from the railing around the front
7
porch and frames the house in greenery. The day I
visited, there were no flowers, but in summer little
red blooms peak from the green leaves.

The house itself is filled with light and
color. [1] Every room has several large windows. [2]
Walls are painted light blue, sea green, tan, and
pale yellow. [3] A collector of Japanese prints,
<u>they are displayed</u> throughout the house. [4] The
8
kitchen walls are covered with blue and white
tiles. [5] Monet's interest in Japanese art is reflected
in the sparseness of the furnishings and the use of
wicker for some of the chairs. [6] **[9]**

But the most amazing element is the Japanese
water garden. Long a lover of Monet's series of
water lily paintings, I had expected to see a huge
pond. Well, first I had expected that Monet's house
was set on a large estate, but it's right in the village

of Giverny. [10] The water garden is across the
street from Monet's <u>house. It's</u> about the size of an
11
Olympic swimming pool.

Even on a cloudy day in autumn, the garden
was beautiful. Willows hung over the water and
were reflected in its stillness. Gray vines,
<u>all that were left</u> of the wisteria at this time
12
<u>of year entwined the railings</u> of the Japanese
13
footbridge. In summer the sight of the bridge
draped with long purple clusters of wisteria blooms
must be dazzling. [14] <u>Above all, a quietness.</u>
15

1. (A) NO CHANGE
    (B) have taken had been
    (C) have taken was
    (D) took has been

2. (F) NO CHANGE
    (G) chilly and late autumn day.
    (H) chilly, late, autumn day.
    (J) chilly late autumn day

3. (A) NO CHANGE
    (B) Enclose the sentence in parentheses.
    (C) Move the sentence to the end of the
         paragraph.
    (D) Omit the sentence.

4. (F) NO CHANGE
    (G) were there dahlias were
    (H) were there; dahlias were
    (J) were there, dahlias were

5. (A) NO CHANGE
    (B) marvel, inside and out.
    (C) marvel.
    (D) marvel: inside and out.

6. (F) NO CHANGE
   (G) Painted pink, ivy covers large swaths of the facade.
   (H) Large swaths of the facade, which is painted pink, are covered with ivy.
   (J) Painted pink, large swaths of the facade are covered with ivy.

7. (A) NO CHANGE
   (B) rose up
   (C) raised up
   (D) was raised up

8. (F) NO CHANGE
   (G) he displayed them
   (H) he is displayed
   (J) A collection of Japanese prints, they are displayed

9. To better organize the description of the house, the writer wants to reorder the sentences in this paragraph. Which of the following would be the most logical order of the sentences?
   (A) 1, 4, 2, 3, 5, 6
   (B) 1, 2, 3, 5, 4, 6
   (C) 1, 2, 3, 5, 6, 4
   (D) 4, 6, 1, 2, 3, 5

10. On rereading the passage, the writer realizes that the tone of this sentence is not appropriate for the rest of the passage and so revises it. Now, the writer is not sure where the revision best fits. What should the writer do?

    I had originally expected to find Monet's house and garden on a large estate in the country. Instead, it is right in the village of Giverny.

    (F) Delete the original and revised sentences completely.
    (G) Leave the revised sentences in the current position.
    (H) Move the two revised sentences to paragraph 1 and place them after sentence 1.
    (J) Move the two revised sentences to the end of their current paragraph.

11. (A) NO CHANGE
    (B) and is about
    (C) and its about
    (D) house, which is about

12. (F) NO CHANGE
    (G) was left
    (H) was remaining
    (J) had been left

13. (A) NO CHANGE
    (B) of year, entwined the railings,
    (C) of year, entwined the railings
    (D) of year. Entwined the railings

14. The writer wants to add more description about the water garden. Which of the following additions would best fit?
    (F) Water lily pads, adorned with a fading bloom or two, dotted the pond's surface. Feathery dried grasses lined the shore.
    (G) But now, only a few fading blooms dotted the scattered water lily pads, and feathery dried grasses lined the shore.
    (H) However, only a few fading blooms dotted the scattered water lily pads, and feathery dried grasses lined the shore.
    (J) In their own way on this gray day, the few fading blooms that dotted the scattered water lily pads and the feathery dried grasses that lined the shore lent their own beauty to the scene.

15. (A) NO CHANGE
    (B) Above all, there is a quietness.
    (C) dazzling; above all, a quietness.
    (D) dazzling—above all, a quietness.

Passage II

Hurricane Watch

The following paragraphs may or may not be organized in the most logical order. The numerals in brackets indicate paragraph order. Question 29 will ask you to choose the most logical order.

[1]

The National Oceanic and Atmospheric Administration (NOAA) is a branch of the federal government. Two of its agencies, the National Hurricane Center (NHC) and the National Weather Service (NWS), are on the front line of monitoring potential weather hazards.

[2]

One of the greatest dangers that the U.S. agencies track is hurricanes, which begin
    16
as tropical storms in the Atlantic Ocean, Gulf of Mexico, or Caribbean Sea. About six of these giant storms each year gather force and become hurricanes. On average, about five hurricanes every three years move inland over the United States, they bring with them violent
    17
winds, torrential downpours, coastal flooding, and even, sometimes, tornadoes.
    18

[3]

The NOAA has three major ways that it keeps track of hurricanes, namely, satellites, reconnaissance aircraft, and radar. The satellites are called Geostationary Operational Environmental Satellites. They are positioned above the equator. **[19]** Orbiting the earth at an altitude of about 22,000 miles, images from the satellites enable meteorologists
    20
to estimate the location and size of hurricanes. By analyzing the satellite's images, meteorologists are
    21
also able to estimate the intensity of a storm.

[4]

If reconnaissance aircraft sounds like a spy plane, in a way, they are. However, the targets are
    22
hurricanes. Both the U.S. Air Force Reserve and NOAA have airplanes equipped to monitor storms. Air Force Reserve pilots fly special aircraft equipped to take storm readings into the center of hurricanes to collect data. The wind speed and force, the
    23
amount of air pressure, the temperature, and the humidity within the storm are measured. NOAA also sends its own aircraft into the center of hurricanes to monitor their intensity and movement.

[5]

Together, the NOAA and the Air Force Reserve continually provide information to help scientists better understand hurricanes and how to make better predictions about their flow. The sooner this
    24
information is available, the sooner people can be warned. Little can be done to avert property damage along coastal areas, but people can be evacuated earlier and loss of life averted.

[6]

The NWS monitors hurricanes as they approach land using weather radar. The service is
    25
currently updating their radar technology. The new
    26
Doppler radar will enable the NWS to make more accurate forecasts, not only about hurricanes, but also about tornadoes, coastal floods, and high winds inland. **[28] [29] [30]**
    27

16. (F) NO CHANGE
    (G) that the agencies track are
    (H) that the agencies track has been
    (J) that the agencies track, is

17. (A) NO CHANGE
    (B) over the United States to bring
    (C) over the United States, bringing
    (D) over the United States: they bring

18. (F) NO CHANGE
    (G) even tornadoes.
    (H) sometimes even tornadoes.
    (J) tornadoes.

19. (A) NO CHANGE
    (B) The satellites, called Geostationary Operational Environmental Satellites, are positioned above the equator.
    (C) The satellites are positioned above the equator.
    (D) The satellites called Geostationary Operational Environmental Satellites are positioned above the equator.

20. (F) NO CHANGE
    (G) Orbiting the earth at an altitude of about 22,000 miles, meteorologists use satellite images
    (H) Orbiting the earth at an altitude of about 22,000 miles, the satellites send back images that enable meteorologists
    (J) Orbiting the earth at an altitude of about 22,000 miles, satellite images enable meteorologists

21. (A) NO CHANGE
    (B) the satellite images
    (C) the satellites' images,
    (D) the satellites images,

22. (F) NO CHANGE
    (G) sound like a spy plane and, in a way, it is.
    (H) sounds like spy planes, and in a way, they are.
    (J) sound like spy planes and, in a way, they are.

23. (A) NO CHANGE
    (B) special aircraft, which are equipped to take storm readings, into the center of the hurricanes to collect data.
    (C) these special aircraft into the center of the hurricanes to collect data.
    (D) these special aircraft, equipped to take storm readings, to collect data.

24. (F) NO CHANGE
    (G) how better to understand and make predictions about their flow.
    (H) better understand hurricanes and better predict their flow.
    (J) better understand hurricanes and, therefore, make better predictions about their flow.

25. (A) NO CHANGE
    (B) land, using weather radar.
    (C) hurricanes, using weather radar,
    (D) Using weather radar, the NWS

26. (F) NO CHANGE
    (G) its
    (H) they're
    (J) its'

27. (A) NO CHANGE
    (B) high winds' inland.
    (C) high wind inland.
    (D) high wind's inland.

Questions 28, 29, and 30 relate to the passage as a whole.

28. The writer is considering adding the following sentence to the passage:

    Hurricane Andrew in 1992 caused 26 deaths and an estimated $25 billion in damage.

    Would it be a logical and relevant addition to the passage?
    (F) Yes, because the new sentence adds some human interest to the passage, which is otherwise dry.
    (G) Yes, because the new sentence provides examples to illustrate the destructiveness of hurricanes and why it is important to warn people in advance.
    (H) No, because the new sentence contains extraneous details.
    (J) No, because the passage is about the ways the government monitors hurricanes.

29. For the sake of unity and coherence, what would be the best reorganization of paragraphs?

    (A) 2, 1, 3, 4, 6, 5

    (B) 1, 5, 2, 3, 4, 6

    (C) 1, 2, 3, 4, 6, 5

    (D) 1, 2, 5, 3, 4, 6

30. To dramatize the potential danger from hurricanes, the writer would like to add the following sentence to the passage:

    The storm tide generated by a hurricane can be as high as 20 feet above normal, and a storm surge can push a wall of water 50 to 100 miles wide over a coastline.

    The sentence would fit most logically into Paragraph

    (F) 2, after the second sentence.

    (G) 2, as the last sentence.

    (H) 5, after the first sentence.

    (J) 5, as the last sentence.

QUICK ANSWER GUIDE:
PASSAGES I AND II

Passage I		Passage II	
1.	C	16.	F
2.	J	17.	C
3.	D	18.	G
4.	J	19.	D
5.	A	20.	H
6.	J	21.	C
7.	A	22.	J
8.	G	23.	C
9.	B	24.	H
10.	H	25.	D
11.	B	26.	G
12.	F	27.	A
13.	C	28.	J
14.	G	29.	C
15.	B	30.	G

For explanations to these questions, see Day 13.

English Test: Passages I and II
Explanations and Answers

Assignment for Today:

• Review the explanations for the test you just took.

Passage I

1. **The correct answer is (C).** This is a verb tense question. Because the writer mentions the phrase "one of the most memorable trips," you know that the writer has taken several trips and you can conjecture that the writer probably will take more; therefore, the present perfect tense "have taken" is correct. Present perfect tense indicates action that began in the past and continues. There is no reason for the second verb to be in any tense other than simple past tense.

(A) This choice uses present perfect tense for both verbs. No time sequence is indicated.

(B) *Have taken* is correct, but the past perfect tense *had been* for the form of the verb *to be* is not. The trip to Giverny could not have happened before the writer took any trips, which is what the use of past perfect tense implies.

(D) In this choice, the correct verb tenses are reversed.

2. **The correct answer is (J).** Don't use a comma to separate adjectives that are not coordinate. One way to check if adjectives are coordinate is to interchange them; in this case, the phrase would read *Although it was a late and chilly autumn day*. The reader could be confused and think the writer visited late on a chilly day in autumn. In addition, the usual way to refer to timing with seasons is to place the word indicating time immediately before the season; for example, *late autumn, early spring,* or *mid winter.*

(F) The construction indicates that the two adjectives are coordinate, which they are not.

(G) There is no reason to change the construction and substitute this slightly awkward one.

(H) This choice separates the final adjective *autumn* from the noun *day* that it modifies.

3. **The correct answer is (D).** The sentence provides interesting information but is intrusive as written. That the gardeners change seasonal plantings doesn't relate to why the garden is still in bloom

in late fall. The author of the piece could have chosen to provide a transition that explained the relationship, but since the writer did not, omit the sentence.

(A) The sentence as written is intrusive.

(B) The information in the sentence is interesting, but enclosing the sentence in parentheses would not correct the main problem, its lack of relevance.

(C) If the sentence were moved to the end of the paragraph, its intrusiveness would be even more noticeable. In its current position, a reader giving the piece a casual reading might think that information relates to the fact that flowers are still in bloom. Any connection to that idea would be so far removed as to make the irrelevance of the sentence very clear.

4. **The correct answer is (J).** Rewrite the sentence to remove any possibility of misreading it. An introductory clause is set off by a comma.

(F) The sentence is awkward as written.

(G) While this choice corrects the possible misreading, it is incorrect because an introductory clause should be separated from the main clause by a comma.

(H) The use of a semicolon to set off a dependent clause is incorrect. Semicolons are used to separate two or more independent clauses.

5. **The correct answer is (A).** A dash is used to set off a parenthetical element for emphasis. The sentence could stand without the phrase *inside and out,* but the writer has chosen to emphasize how unusual the house is. It fits the admiring and enthusiastic tone the writer has adopted for this personal essay.

(B) While grammatically this choice is not incorrect, it does not fit the tone as well as choice (A).

(C) There is no grammatical reason to omit the phrase *inside and out,* and it adds to the tone of the piece.

(D) The use of a colon to set off a parenthetical element is incorrect, and this construction cannot be considered a summary or a series.

6. **The correct answer is (J).** This construction is an example of a misplaced modifier. The ivy isn't painted pink; the facade is. Choice (J) corrects the error through the use of a dependent clause.

(F) The ivy is not painted pink.

(G) A comma may be used to set off a short introductory phrase or clause, but in this instance, this is not the error.

(H) Large swaths are not painted pink; they are covered by ivy. It is the entire facade that is painted pink.

7. **The correct answer is (A).** *Rises* is one of the two verbs in the compound predicate in the sentence and parallels the tense used in the second verb. The present tense is the correct tense to use in describing the characteristics of an existing building.

(B) *Rose* is past tense and does not parallel the other verb in the compound predicate.

(C) *Raised* is past tense and is, therefore, incorrect. Also, *raised* is the past tense of the verb *to raise,* not *to rise.*

(D) *Was raised up* is passive voice and is not parallel in voice to the other part of the compound predicate. Also, *raised* is the past participle of the verb *to raise,* not *to rise.*

8. **The correct answer is (G).** This is another misplaced modifier question. The prints were not a collector of themselves; Monet collected them. Choice (G) rewrites the construction to introduce "he," meaning Monet, as the collector.

(F) The prints were not a collector of themselves; Monet collected them.

(H) While it is true that paintings by Monet are displayed in the house, the sentence is discussing Monet's collection of others' work.

(J) There is no antecedent for *they* except the phrase *collection of Japanese prints,* which makes *they* redundant. The corrected sentence would then read "A collection of Japanese prints is displayed throughout the house."

9. **The correct answer is (B).** Sentence 5, which discusses the kitchen, intrudes on the connection between the Japanese prints and their influence on Monet's work. Sentence 5 fits better with the discussion of the wall colors in various rooms.

(A) This places sentence 5 about Monet's print collection right after the topic sentence noting the use of light and color in the house. Sentence 5 interrupts the development of the idea of light.

(C) This sequence places sentence 5 more appropriately, but sentence 6 precedes sentence 4. The connection between Monet's print collection and its influence on his work is not developed.

(D) Placing sentence 4, a detail, at the beginning of the paragraph takes the sentence out of context and makes no logical sense.

10. **The correct answer is (H).** This is a strategy question: What should the writer do with these two sentences? The original sentence is intrusive not only in tone, but also in its placement. However, it does add information about both the writer and the house and garden. This is a personal essay, so the information about the writer's idea is important. The best placement is in paragraph 1 to reinforce the genre as personal essay and to set the house and garden in its context.

(F) The revision provides relevant information about both the writer and the house and garden, so they should not be deleted.

(G) Even as revised, the sentences intrude on the development of the main idea of the paragraph, the Japanese garden.

(J) While placing the revision at the end of the paragraph eliminates the problem of interrupting the logical development of the paragraph, it does not particularly add to it. The better placement is in paragraph 1 to set the scene and reinforce the personal essay format.

11. **The correct answer is (B).** Turn these two independent clauses into one sentence with a compound predicate and eliminate potential confusion over the antecedent of *it.*

(A) As written, the reader might think the house, which is the closest noun to the pronoun *it,* is the size of an Olympic swimming pool.

(C) This choice confuses the verb contraction *it is* with the possessive pronoun, *its.*

(D) This choice confuses the pronoun *it* with the house. *It* refers to the water garden.

12. **The correct answer is (F).** This is a pronoun agreement question, and the answer depends on the number of the pronoun *all.* Is it singular or plural in this sentence? The antecedent of *all* is the noun *vines,* which is plural, so *all* is plural and the predicate must be plural.

(G) *All* is plural, so the predicate must be plural. *Was* is the singular form of the verb *to be* and is, therefore, incorrect.

(H) The error is not with the participle but rather with the auxiliary verb form. Changing the participle does not correct the error.

(J) There is no reason to change the tense from simple past to past perfect. All the other tenses in the paragraph are in simple past. This fact should be a clue to help you choose the correct answer. Remember to read more than just the underlined portion of the sentence.

13. **The correct answer is (C).** The answer choices for this question are a good example of why it is important to read all the possible answers. You might have read choice (B), seen the comma in the correct position after *year,* and jumped to that answer—without realizing that the comma after *railings* introduced an error. The correct answer is choice (C), which completes the commas around a nonrestrictive clause.

(A) As written, the second comma for the nonrestrictive clause is omitted incorrectly.

(B) The comma after *railings* incorrectly sets off the prepositional phrase *of the Japanese bridge* from the noun it modifies, *railings*.

(D) This choice incorrectly ends the sentence before the object of the predicate and creates a sentence fragment of "the railings of the Japanese bridge."

14. **The correct answer is (G).** The strongest addition provides a transition from the current last sentence to whatever details the writer wishes to add. Choice (G) provides this transition. It begins with the word *but* to set up the opposition to the summer scene and continues with the word *now* to bring the reader back to the autumn scene that the writer is describing.

(F) While the information is interesting, there is no transition and there is no opposition. The reader is left to assume that the scene that is described in these two sentences relates to the autumn and not the summer.

(H) The writer uses the transitional word *however* but does not include any reference to time. Choice (G) is stronger.

(J) While the transition is strong, setting up the opposition, the answer choice is overwritten and does not match the style of the essay, which while descriptive is not ornate. The sentences tend to be short, many of them simple sentences.

15. **The correct answer is (B).** To answer this question, you must decide how best to correct a sentence fragment. Both choices (C) and (D) attach the fragment to a sentence where it does not logically belong. The quietness is not related to the dazzling wisteria in summer, but rather to the current autumn garden in its entirety. Therefore, creating a new sentence is the best solution.

(A) The underlined portion is a sentence fragment.

(C) In addition to attaching the fragment to a sentence to which it does not belong, choice (C) uses

the semicolon incorrectly. Semicolons are used to separate two independent clauses. The phrase *above all, a quietness* is not an independent clause.

(D) A dash to set off the parenthetical expression might be acceptable except that the parenthetical is not related to the sentence to which it would be attached.

Passage II

16. **The correct answer is (F).** The subject of the main clause is *one*; therefore, the verb must be singular to agree in number with its subject. *Is* is singular, so the correct answer is choice (F), NO CHANGE. Look for questions like this in which there are one or two constructions between the subject and verb. What might also confuse you here is the use of a plural subject predicate, *hurricanes*. The linking verb *to be* takes the same case after it as before it (that is, *hurricanes* is not the object of *is*), but the rule says nothing about having the same number before and after the verb *to be*.

(G) This is incorrect because it uses a plural form of *to be* when the subject is singular.

(H) The passage is describing what these agencies do now. Present perfect tense indicates past activity continuing into the present, and while these agencies had the same duties in the past, the passage is concerned with what they are doing currently.

(J) While it is true that a long dependent clause that begins a sentence may be set off by a comma, even if it is the subject of the main clause, this is not the case here. The dependent clause "that they track" is relatively short and modifies the subject of the sentence, "one."

17. **The correct answer is (C).** As presently written, the sentence is an example of a comma splice. The writer attempts to join two independent clauses with only a comma. The best solution offered is choice (C), which turns the second clause into a participial phrase.

(A) The current sentence has a comma splice.

(B) This is an example of an answer choice that is not technically incorrect, but it is awkward and the sense is not quite right. The hurricanes move inland, and as result of that, winds, downpours, flooding, and tornadoes occur over land. It is not the purpose of the hurricanes to bring them; they come with and are a part of hurricanes. The implication of the phrase *to bring* in this sentence is to state the purpose of the hurricane.

(D) This choice attempts to correct the comma splice but in its place introduces a new error, the use of a colon to separate two independent clauses.

18. **The correct answer is (G).** The construction *even, sometimes,* is an example both of wordiness and of a superfluous comma. The writer is attempting to indicate that tornadoes are not a usual occurrence with hurricanes. While it is true that the connotations of the two words are slightly different, both words are not needed in the construction. In addition, a comma is used incorrectly to set off two noncoordinate adjectives, *even* and *sometimes*. One is assuming that the comma before *tornadoes* is meant for emphasis. If not, it is incorrect. Choice (G) is the best answer; it reduces the wordiness and retains the idea that tornadoes are somewhat unusual.

(F) As written, the construction is wordy and at least one comma is incorrectly positioned.

(H) This choice is still wordy.

(J) The dash provides too much emphasis to the occurrence of tornadoes.

19. **The correct answer is (D).** While an occasional simple sentence adds interest to writing, these two sentences are very short and describe the same thing, the satellites. Combining them in some way would improve the style of the paragraph. This eliminates choice (C). "Called Geostationary Operational Environmental Satellites" is a restrictive phrase and, therefore, should not be set off by commas. Only choice (D) includes this correct construction.

(A) Combining these two sentences would improve the flow and style of the paragraph, so choice (A) is incorrect.

(B) This sentence uses commas to set off a restrictive phrase, which is incorrect.

(C) This answer choice combines only part of the information given in the two sentences.

20. **The correct answer is (H).** This is another example of a misplaced modifier. It is not the images that orbit the earth, but rather the satellites. Only choice (H) corrects this sentence structure error. When you see an underlined portion that begins with a participial phrase (*-ing* ending), look first for a misplaced modifier error.

(F) The participial phrase is modifying the subject of the sentence, which makes no sense. The images are not orbiting the earth.

(G) This choice substitutes *meteorologists* for *images*, but the participial phrase is still misplaced.

(J) This choice is tricky because it uses *satellite* to identify the images, but they still do not orbit the earth. On a quick reading though, you might have overlooked the word *images*. Read quickly but attentively the questions and the answer choices.

21. **The correct answer is (C).** If you read more than just the underlined portion, you would have known that there was more than one satellite and that, therefore, choice (C) is correct.

(A) There is more than one satellite, so this construction, which indicates only one satellite, is incorrect.

(B) Using the word *satellite* to identify the images is correct. However, in this sentence, the use of the word *the* limits the number of satellites to one, *the satellite*. Because there are several satellites in orbit sending back these images, the construction would have to be "analyzing satellite images."

(D) This choice is incorrect because *satellites* in this construction as a plural is a noun and should have *s'* at the end.

22. **The correct answer is (J).** The word *aircraft* can be either singular or plural, so the way to approach this question is to look for consistency in the answers. Which one has either all relevant words—verbs and pronouns—in the singular or plural? Only choice (J) has both verbs in the plural, and in that case, the correct pronoun is also plural. The simile *like spy planes* is an added clue to help you choose the plural form of the verbs and pronoun.

    (F) The verb in the dependent clause is singular (*sounds*), but the verb and pronoun in the independent clause are plural, so this answer choice can't be correct.

    (G) The verb in the dependent clause is plural (*sounds*), but the verb and pronoun in the independent clause are singular, so this answer choice can't be correct.

    (H) The verb in the dependent clause is singular, but the verb and the pronoun in the independent clause are plural, so this can't be the correct choice.

23. **The correct answer is (C).** This is an instance when "shorter is better" is the answer. The sentence before the underlined portion notes that the planes are "equipped to monitor storms." The underlined portion says that the aircraft are "equipped to take storm readings." Choice (C), the deletion of this phrase, will shorten the sentence and remove a potentially confusing construction. Note that choice (C) includes a word to help the reader understand that the planes in the underlined sentence are the same as in the preceding sentence.

    (A) The phrase is redundant and unnecessary.

    (B) Turning the underlined portion into a dependent clause removes the potential for misreading but does not remove the redundancy.

    (D) This choice encloses the potentially confusing section of the sentence in commas and sets it off as nonrestrictive, but in that case, the information is not needed and omitting it is the better answer.

24. **The correct answer is (H).** The placement of the adverbs (*better*), the verbs (*understand, predict*), and the objects (*hurricanes, flow*) are completely parallel. While not all constructions will be so neatly parallel, because this one does so and is the only one among the answer choices that accomplishes parallelism, this is the correct answer.

    (F) This is an example of inconsistent sentence structure. The two clauses are not parallel.

    (G) This answer choice omits what the scientists are trying to understand and make predictions about (*hurricanes*). It is also awkward.

    (J) You might be thrown off by the use of the word *therefore*, which adds emphasis to the sentence, and think that this is the best choice. However, the second part of the construction uses *better* as an adjective to modify *predictions* and has the prepositional phrase *about their flow*. Note also that this answer is longer than choice (H), which is often the signal that a choice is not the best.

25. **The correct answer is (D).** This is an example of confusing placement of a modifier. Even the use of a comma before the participial phrase *using weather radar* is not so good a solution as moving the phrase to the beginning of the sentence. It then introduces the sentence and is beside the noun it modifies, in this case the abbreviation for the National Weather Service (*NWS*).

    (A) The phrase appears to be modifying the word *land*. It is actually modifying *NWS* at the beginning of the sentence.

    (B) Addition of the comma to set off the phrase helps the sense, but the better solution is to move the phrase closer to the word it modifies.

    (C) This answer choice moves the phrase next to what the weather radar monitors (*hurricanes*), which makes the sentence more awkward. The phrase now separates the parts of the single thought about monitoring "hurricanes as they approach land."

26. **The correct answer is (G).** The NWS is a single agency, so the third-person singular possessive pronoun is correct (*its*).

    (F) The sentence as written uses the third-person plural possessive pronoun and is, therefore, incorrect.

    (H) *They're* is the contraction for "they are" and makes no sense in the sentence.

    (J) *Its'* is an incorrect form of the possessive pronoun. *S'* is not added to the possessive pronoun *its*.

27. **The correct answer is (A).** *Winds* is a noun, and both *high* and *inland* are adjectives modifying the noun. Therefore, the phrase as written is correct.

    (B) *Inland* is an adjective modifying *winds*. Adding an *s* to *winds* would turn it into the possessive form and by extension make *inland* a noun, which it isn't in this construction.

    (C) The clue here is that the other words in the series, *tornadoes* and *floods,* are plural. In that case, the most logical choice would be one that uses the plural of *winds.* Choice (C) uses the singular, so it's not the correct answer.

    (D) This choice is incorrect for the same reason that choice (B) is. Also, this choice makes *winds* singular, whereas the other two words in the series are plural.

28. **The correct answer is (J).** The topic of the passage is the ways that the government monitors hurricanes, and while the new sentence is interesting, it does not help to explain the topic.

    (F) Don't be fooled because this answer choice uses the term *human interest.* The new sentence provides statistical information, not an anecdote involving a person and a storm. The statistics are in keeping with the straightforward tone of this nonfiction article.

    (G) The first part of this answer choice may tempt you to choose it, but there is nothing in the new sentence that indicates that early warning saved

property or lives. To do that, the sentence would have to compare the destructiveness of Hurricane Andrew with an earlier or later hurricane in order to show that advance warning makes a difference.

    (H) This answer choice says the details are extraneous but doesn't say why. Answer choice (J) is better because it states why the new sentence doesn't fit within the context of the passage. It gives a more concrete answer. Remember to read all choices before selecting your answer.

29. **The correct answer is (C).** Paragraph 5 is a summary of the passage, whereas paragraph 6 is the third way that the NOAA and the Air Force Reserve monitor hurricanes. As currently organized, the summary paragraph interrupts the discussion of monitoring.

    (A) This choice orders paragraphs 5 and 6 correctly but transposes paragraphs 1 and 2. While the information about hurricanes in paragraph 2 might come before a discussion of ways to monitor them, as written, there would be no transition between the two paragraphs if they were reversed. Paragraph 1 would appear to be unconnected to paragraph 2.

    (B) This choice places the summary immediately after the opening paragraph and summarizes information that has not been introduced. It is an illogical organization.

    (D) This choice places paragraph 5, the closing paragraph, in the middle of the discussion of ways to monitor hurricanes. The order makes no sense.

30. **The correct answer is (G).** The new sentence provides specific information about hurricanes and, therefore, belongs with the discussion of hurricanes, paragraph 2. Inserting it as the last sentence in paragraph 2 is better than as the second sentence, because if inserted after the second sentence, the new statement would interrupt the discussion of the way a hurricane develops and moves. The storm tide and storm surge relate to the hurricane once it makes landfall, which is the topic of the current last sentence in paragraph 2.

(F) Inserting the new sentence after sentence 2 would interrupt the discussion of the development and movement of hurricanes.

(H) This is an illogical placement of the new sentence because it doesn't relate to a better understanding of hurricanes or a greater ability to predict them. The new sentence states facts about two effects of hurricanes.

(J) This placement is also illogical, because the new sentence doesn't relate to warning people.

Day 14

Practice English Test: Passages III, IV, and V

Assignment for Today:

- Take a sample of the ACT Assessment English Test under actual test conditions. For the real test, you will have 45 minutes to answer 75 questions. For this practice, set your timer for 27 minutes. Remember to skim to decide which passage to answer first. Then use the ACT Assessment English Strategies to answer the questions.

DIRECTIONS: This test consists of three passages in which particular words or phrases are underlined and numbered. In the right-hand column, you will see alternative words and phrases that could be substituted for the underlined part. You must select the alternative that expresses the idea most clearly and correctly in terms of standard written English or that best fits the style and tone of the entire passage. If the original version is best, select "NO CHANGE."

The test also includes questions about entire paragraphs and the passage as a whole. These questions are identified by a numeral in a box.

After you select the correct answer for each question, mark the oval representing the correct answer on your answer sheet.

Passage III
Benjamin Franklin: Unsung Hero

That may seem like a strange title for a biographical sketch of Benjamin Franklin, but few people realize the important role he played in the American Revolution. Most people think of Franklin— when they think of him— as the inventor of the
31
lightning rod and perhaps the Franklin stove. Overshadowed in history books by Washington, Jefferson, and even the Marquis de Lafayette.
32
However, had it not been for Franklin's letter of
33
introduction to Washington on Lafayette's behalf, the Marquis would never have served in the war.

[34] Franklin had spent almost eighteen years in London as an agent for Pennsylvania and several other colonies. His reputation as a serious scientist and philosopher as well as his wit and charm had
35
gained him entrance to the drawing rooms and studies of many important and influential men and women in England and on the continent. When war broke out in 1776, the Continental Congress sent Franklin, then seventy to France to lead a commission
36
to gain France's support. [37]

It was through Franklin's efforts that France and the United States signed a treaty in 1778 pledging its support for American independence.
38
[1] Once diplomatic relations were established, Franklin was named United States minister to France. [2] One of his earliest requests was for French troops to be sent to the United States to fight alongside Washington's forces. [3] The offer was denied, but France did provide money. [4] The
39
American army was badly in need of uniforms,
40
food, weapons, and ammunition. [5] In 1781, the French finally dispatched troops and a contingent of the French navy. [6] It was these ships that blockaded the British at Yorktown, which forced Great Britain to surrender their claim to the former
41
colonies. [7] Lord Cornwallis and his soldiers marched out of Yorktown between two rows of French and American soldiers. [8] [42]

When the war ended, Franklin stayed on in France and negotiated the final peace treaty between the United States and Great Britain. When it was signed, he returned to Pennsylvania where he was elected President of the Pennsylvania Executive Council. When the Constitutional Convention was convened in 1787, among its many illustrious members were Benjamin Franklin. At the time of his latest role,
43   44
he was 81. Franklin died three years later.
45

31. (A) NO CHANGE
    (B) (when they think of him)
    (C) when they think of him,
    (D) OMIT the underlined portion.

32. (F) NO CHANGE
    (G) stove, overshadowed in history books by Washington, Jefferson, and even the Marquis de Lafayette.
    (H) Franklin overshadowed in history books by Washington, Jefferson, and even the Marquis de Lafayette.
    (J) Franklin has been overshadowed in history books by Washington, Jefferson, and even the Marquis de Lafayette.

33. (A) NO CHANGE
    (B) without Franklin's letter,
    (C) accept for Franklin's letter
    (D) were it not for Franklin's letter

34. The writer has decided that a transition is needed between paragraphs 1 and 2. Which of the following provides the best transition?
    (F) Franklin seemed a good choice.
    (G) In 1776, the Continental Congress was looking for someone to approach France.
    (H) Franklin's role in the American Revolution came about in an interesting way.
    (J) No one would be more surprised than Franklin at how his role has been overlooked.

35. (A) NO CHANGE
    (B) His reputation as a serious scientist and philosopher as well as, his wit and charm,
    (C) His reputation for serious science, philosophy, wit and charm
    (D) His reputation for serious science and philosophy and his reputation for wit and charm

36. (F) NO CHANGE
    (G) Franklin, then seventy, to France
    (H) Franklin then seventy to France
    (J) Franklin then seventy, to France

37. The writer would like to add an explanation of why the Continental Congress thought Franklin would be successful. Assuming each sentence to be true, which alternative does that best?
    (A) For many years, Franklin had spent several weeks each summer in France.
    (B) France and Great Britain were centuries-old rivals for territory and power, first in Europe and later around the world.
    (C) France was still smarting from British gains at its expense in Asia.
    (D) The new nation hoped to take advantage of the rivalry between France and Great Britain.

38. (F) NO CHANGE
    (G) to pledge its support
    (H) pledging France's support
    (J) pledging their support

39. (A) NO CHANGE
    (B) denied and France
    (C) denied but France
    (D) denied; but France

40. (F) NO CHANGE
    (G) badly in need of:
    (H) bad in need of, namely,
    (J) bad in need of

41. (A) NO CHANGE
    (B) its claim to
    (C) there claim to
    (D) their claiming of

42. Which of the following sentences could be deleted from the paragraph without altering the essential flow and information in the paragraph?
    (F) Sentence 3. The request was denied and, therefore, has no impact on what happened.
    (G) Sentence 5. While interesting, the information is not essential to Franklin's role.
    (H) Sentence 7. While essential to understanding the defeat of the British, the information is not essential in describing Franklin's role.
    (J) Sentence 8. While an interesting detail, the information is not essential to understanding Franklin's role.

43. (A) NO CHANGE
    (B) were none other than
    (C) had been
    (D) was

44. (F) NO CHANGE
    (G) his last
    (H) the latter
    (J) his late

45. To provide closure to the passage, the writer wishes to link the ideas in the first and last sentences of the essay. Which of the following would be the best alternative to achieve this aim?

(A) NO CHANGE

(B) Franklin died three years later and was soon forgotten.

(C) Franklin died three years later and his quiet diplomacy abroad was soon overshadowed by the exploits of military men and younger politicians.

(D) Franklin died three years later and his role in bringing France into the war was soon forgotten.

Passage IV
The Globe Theater

The original Globe Theater was built on the south bank of the Thames River in London in 1598. Home to the plays of Shakespeare and other Elizabethan playwrights, the Globe burned down in 1613, was rebuilt the following year, and was a victim of the Puritan purges of the 1640s. The 1613
46
blaze was caused by a cannon that caught fire during a performance of Shakespeare's *Henry VIII.*

[47] In 1949, American actor, director, and producer Sam Wanamaker determined to reconstruct the theater. It took forty-seven years to realize his dream, but the new Globe Theater opened in 1996.

[48] Little but the approximate site of the original building was known when Wanamaker began his campaign to reconstruct it. The size and shape of the Globe and even the design of the stage
49
had to be gleaned from drawings and archaeological excavations of the original Globe as well as other Elizabethan theaters. Letters and diaries of theatergoers also provided clues. Even Shakespeare's plays were a source of information where a reference here and there to the theater can be found.
50

The Globe was not a perfect circle, but actually a polygon of twenty small sides. The stage jutted out into the center and three tiers with multiple rows of seats ringed the other three-quarters of the
51
polygon. Between the stage and the first tier of seats was a large open area. This was the pit where groundlings stood to watch the performance.

The new Globe is as true to what an Elizabethan theater can be given what scholars
52
have been able to learn and what modern craftworkers
53
could construct. They used building techniques from the
54
sixteenth century and building materials that sixteenth-century workers would have been familiar with. The
55
roof is thatch as was the original. All the wood supports are oak, and the walls over them are made of a lime plaster mix.

The desire to make the Globe as authentic as possible extends to its performances. The audience may sit on hard benches (cushions can be rented for two British pounds, roughly $3) that ring the
56
theater in three tiers or stand in the pit. Groundlings may find themselves in the way of King Lear's soldiers if you aren't careful. Actors'
57
entrances and exits often take place through the pit. Swordplay, however, is usually confined to the stage.

In the beginning, performances were going to be held in the new Globe only during the day as was true with the original Globe. However, summer days in London are light late and theaters
58
typically attract larger audiences in the evening. As a result, performances at the Globe are now given in the evening. [59] Rain, however, will cancel a performance, for like the original Globe, the new one has no roof over most of the stage and the groundlings' pit. For the same reason, there are no winter performances. [60]

46. (F) NO CHANGE
    (G) the Globe burned down in 1613; was rebuilt the following year; and was a victim of the Puritan purges of the 1640s.
    (H) the Globe burned down in 1613, and was rebuilt the following year and a victim of the Puritan purges of the 1640s.
    (J) burned down in 1613, the Globe was rebuilt the following year and was a victim of the Puritan purges of the 1640s.

47. The writer wishes to add a transitional sentence between this paragraph and the preceding one. Which of the following would best fit the context?
    (A) An unlikely candidate would be responsible for rebuilding the Globe.
    (B) It would be more than 300 years before the Globe would reopen.
    (C) Almost 300 years later, a young man enchanted with the theater, London, and Shakespeare dreamed of rebuilding the Globe.
    (D) While many over the centuries may have thought about reconstructing the Globe, one man turned the idea into reality.

48. (F) NO CHANGE
    (G) Combine this paragraph with the previous paragraph.
    (H) Begin the sentence with the dependent clause, "When Wanamaker began his campaign to reconstruct it, . . ." and combine this paragraph with the previous paragraph.
    (J) Begin the sentence with the dependent clause, "When Wanamaker began his campaign to reconstruct it, . . ." and transfer this sentence only to the previous paragraph as the last sentence.

49. (A) NO CHANGE
    (B) The size, shape, and design of the stage of the Globe
    (C) The size, shape of the Globe, and design of the stage
    (D) The size and shape of the Globe and even the stage's design

50. (F) NO CHANGE
    (G) information, where a reference here and there to the theater could be found.
    (H) information, here and there a reference to the theater can be found.
    (J) information with a reference here and there to the theater.

51. (A) NO CHANGE
    (B) seats, ringed
    (C) seats ring
    (D) seats ringing

52. (F) NO CHANGE
    (G) can be.　　Given what
    (H) can be, given what
    (J) can be dependent

53. (A) NO CHANGE
    (B) had been able to learn
    (C) were able to learn
    (D) are able to learn

54. (F) NO CHANGE
    (G) Scholars and craftworkers
    (H) The workers
    (J) Scholars

55. (A) NO CHANGE
    (B) building materials with which sixteenth-century workers would have been familiar.
    (C) building materials, which sixteenth-century workers would have been familiar.
    (D) building materials that sixteenth-century workers would have been familiar.

56. (F) NO CHANGE
    (G) benches—cushions can be rented for two British pounds, roughly $3—that
    (H) benches, cushions can be rented for two British pounds, roughly $3, that
    (J) OMIT underlined portion.

57. (A) NO CHANGE

(B) As a groundling, you could find yourself in the way of King Lear's soldiers if you aren't careful.

(C) Groundlings may find one's self in the way of King Lear's solders if one isn't careful.

(D) Groundlings may find themselves in the way of King Lear's soldiers if they aren't careful.

58. (F) NO CHANGE

(G) there are many hours of sunlight during a typical summer day in London

(H) sunlight lingers late into the evening in London during the summer

(J) summer days in London have many hours of sunlight

59. The writer wishes to add more information about the evening performances at the Globe. Which of the following sentences would add relevant information and best fit within the paragraph?

(A) Also, since the 1600s, candles have been replaced by electricity, making evening performances safer.

(B) The fact that electrical lighting has replaced candles since the 1600s makes evening performances safer.

(C) This is made possible because electrical lighting has replaced candles since the 1600s.

(D) Since the 1600s, the introduction of electricity has made evening performances safer.

Question 60 refers to the essay as a whole.

60. The writer has realized that the passage needs a closing statement. Which of the following would be most appropriate?

(F) Unfortunately, Sam Wanamaker died before he could see his dream realized, but those who share that dream continue in his lead.

(G) Unfortunately, Sam Wanamaker died before he could see his dream realized, but the new Globe Theater stands as a testimony to his determination.

(H) The new Globe rises from the ashes of the original Globe.

(J) The new Globe Theater recreates as closely as possible for modern audiences the experience of Elizabethan theatergoers.

Passage V
Globalization

[1]

The 1990s saw the rise of the concept of <u>globalization, the idea</u> that the economies of the world are
      61
becoming ever more interrelated. In reality, the process has been at work for several decades. A number of factors account for this interconnectedness, namely, the reduction, or elimination of tariffs; the rise of multinationals; and the free flow of capital and workers.

[2]

[62]A major cause of globalization has been the reduction, or elimination of <u>trade barriers in the form of tariffs.</u> Tariffs are taxes added to the cost of imports,
      63
which <u>raises their</u> price to consumers. By decreasing
      64
or eliminating tariffs, the price of imported goods is allowed to seek its own level, which may be lower than a <u>similarly domestically produced</u> good.
      65

[3]

Another factor that has impacted how and where companies do business is the growth of multinationals.
66
Thousands of U.S. companies have offices in other nations as do thousands of other nation's companies
67   68
have presences in the United States. In fact, companies that many Americans think of as United States in origin are owned by corporations in other nations. This is true from publishing companies to food manufacturers to music producers.

[4]

The free flow of money and workers from nation to nation is another aspect of globalization. The European Union has eliminated the need for passports and visas between member nations. The Japanese before their nation's own economic problems were heavy investors in foreign businesses; for example, in real estate and
69
entertainment companies in the United States. Multinationals based in the United States are now pouring large amounts of capital into China, hoping to reap huge profits from China's market of 6 billion people. **[70]**

[5]

The question is whether all this globalization is a good thing or a bad thing for the world's people?
71
As the recession in the United States in 2001 and 2002 showed, the interconnectedness of economies can depress activity across many nations when a high-flying economy begins to lose economic steam.
72
Often, it's the low-level factory worker who is hurt. As economies slow, the demand for goods decline, and people lose their jobs. Economists note that
73
international trade theory is based on the ideal rather than on reality. In the ideal world, any worker who loses a job because low-priced imports force his or her company to lay off employees will immediately find a new job in an industry that competes better in the marketplace. **[74] [75]**

61. (A) NO CHANGE
    (B) globalization. The idea
    (C) globalization; the idea
    (D) globalization: the idea

62. The writer is trying to decide whether to add a transition between the first and second paragraphs. Which of the following is the most appropriate solution?
    (F) NO CHANGE
    (G) So a major cause
    (H) Perhaps the most important cause
    (J) Of these factors, a major cause

63. (A) NO CHANGE
    (B) tariffs, which act as barriers to trade across nations.
    (C) trade barriers, in the form of tariffs.
    (D) tariffs, in the form of trade barriers.

64. (F) NO CHANGE
    (G) raised their
    (H) raised the
    (J) raises its

65. (A) NO CHANGE
    (B) similar domestically-produced
    (C) similar good that is produced domestically.
    (D) similar good, which is produced domestically.

66. (F) NO CHANGE
    (G) has been
    (H) was
    (J) had been

67. (A) NO CHANGE
    (B) just as
    (C) while
    (D) as

68. (F) NO CHANGE
    (G) thousands of other nations' companies
    (H) thousands of other companies of nations
    (J) thousands of companies of other nations

69. (A) NO CHANGE
    (B) businesses, for example,
    (C) businesses. For example,
    (D) businesses, for example

70. The writer wishes to add some details to paragraph 4. Does the following sentence fit the context of the paragraph?

    An item such as a camera, a computer, or a vacuum cleaner may have its components manufactured in three or four countries and assembled in still another.

    (F) Yes, because paragraph 4 discusses how workers travel across national borders, and this provides an example.
    (G) Yes, because paragraph 4 uses an example to illustrate each idea.
    (H) No, because this sentence does not provide a concrete example.
    (J) No, because paragraph 4 discusses money and workers, not goods.

71. (A) NO CHANGE
    (B) world's people.
    (C) world's peoples?
    (D) people of the world?

72. (F) NO CHANGE
    (G) the interconnectedness of economies can depress activity across many nations when one economic powerhouse begins to lose steam.
    (H) it only takes a misstep by one economically powerful nation to cause a chain reaction across other economies.
    (J) when one economic powerhouse begins to lose steam, many nations begin to slow down.

73. (A) NO CHANGE
    (B) As economies slow the demand for goods decline, and people
    (C) As economies slow the demand for goods, declines, and people
    (D) As economies slow, the demand for goods declines, and people

74. Is the final sentence an appropriate closing statement for paragraph 5?
    (F) Yes, because it provides an example to answer the question posed in the first sentence of the paragraph.
    (G) Yes, because it discusses tariffs and workers, aspects of globalization.
    (H) No, because it discusses only one aspect of globalization, the elimination, or reduction, of tariffs.
    (J) No, because the topic sentence of the paragraph doesn't discuss an ideal world.

75. The writer wishes to add the following sentence to flesh out the discussion of tariffs.

    A number of economists believe that free trade forces industries to modernize, thereby becoming more efficient and producing goods at less cost to the consumer.

    Where would be the best place to add it?
    (A) Paragraph 1, as the final sentence
    (B) Paragraph 2, as the final sentence
    (C) Paragraph 4, as the final sentence
    (D) Paragraph 5, as the sixth sentence

QUICK ANSWER GUIDE: PASSAGES III, IV, AND V

Passage III

31. D
32. J
33. A
34. J
35. A
36. G
37. D
38. H
39. A
40. F
41. B
42. J
43. D
44. F
45. C

Passage IV

46. F
47. D
48. F
49. A
50. J
51. A
52. H
53. B
54. H
55. B
56. F
57. D
58. H
59. A
60. G

Passage V

61. A
62. J
63. A
64. F
65. C
66. G
67. D
68. J
69. B
70. J
71. B
72. J
73. D
74. H
75. B

For explanations to these questions, see Day 15.

English Test: Passages III, IV, and V Explanations and Answers

Assignment for Today:

- Review the explanations for the test you just took.

Passage III

31. **The correct answer is (D).** This slightly flippant clause does not match the tone of the autobiographical sketch, which is a straightforward discussion of Franklin. Even if you did not recognize the disparity in tone, you could still discern the correct answer. The clause contradicts the idea of the first sentence, which implies that Franklin is well known but for reasons other than his role in the American Revolution.

(A) The clause contradicts the implication of the first sentence of the passage, which implies that Franklin is well known and, therefore, should be omitted.

(B) Parentheses are used to set off supplementary, or illustrative, material. This clause neither adds to the information about Franklin nor illustrates anything about him. In addition, it contradicts the implication that Franklin is well known.

(C) This choice omits the parentheses and replaces the second one with a comma. If the writer was intending to convert this clause into a nonrestrictive clause, it should be set off with a comma before and after it.

32. **The correct answer is (J).** This question presents you with a sentence fragment to correct. Only answer choice (J) correctly adds a subject (*Franklin*) and verb (*has been overshadowed*) to the construction.

(F) As written, this construction is a sentence fragment.

(G) This choice attaches the participial phrase to the previous sentence and makes no sense, either grammatically or as a sentence.

(H) Franklin is the one being overshadowed, not the one overshadowing others. (*Washington, Jefferson, and even the Marquis de Lafayette overshadow Franklin . . .*) In this case, the verb *to overshadow* is in the passive voice and needs some form of the verb *to be*. Therefore, this choice is incorrect.

33. **The correct answer is (A).** While this construction may strike you as overly formal, it is correct. It also sets up a parallel with the independent clause.

(B) You need to read answer choices carefully, because this answer choice might look correct on first reading, but it introduces an error. The comma after *letter* is incorrect and separates the noun from the prepositional phrase *of introduction* that modifies it.

(C) This answer choice confuses the words *accept*, meaning to receive, and *except*, meaning to leave out or to exclude. "To receive Franklin's letter of introduction . . . Marquis would never . . ." makes no sense and is, therefore, incorrect.

(D) This answer choice hinges on verb tense. Franklin wrote his letter before the Marquis served; therefore, past perfect tense is correct, and the simple past used in this answer choice is incorrect.

34. **The correct answer is (J).** The transition needs to create a bridge that will connect the two paragraphs, but it also has to fit naturally within the context of the paragraph to which it's being added. Only choice (J) matches both criteria. The sentence both plays on the idea that Franklin had an important role, which has been overlooked, and sets up the idea that Franklin thought he was doing something important.

(F) This choice does not explain what Franklin would be a good choice for or to do.

(G) While this choice might be a good topic sentence for paragraph 2, it does not relate the information in paragraph 1 to the content in paragraph 2.

(H) While this sentence may pique a reader's interest, it does not create a link between paragraphs 1 and 2 as well as choice (J) does. Choice (J) refers to the fact that Franklin's role has been overlooked, an idea in paragraph 1, and sets up paragraph 2 by indicating that Franklin thought he was doing something important. It's Franklin who is interesting, not the way he became involved in the war. There is nothing in the paragraph that supports the idea that Franklin became involved in an interesting way.

35. **The correct answer is (A).** As written, the punctuation is correct, and the sentence displays a well-balanced set of parallel constructions. The phrase *as well as* introduces a comparison, meaning in addition to, and requires no punctuation before or after the phrase.

(B) Placing a comma after the phrase *as well as* separates the comparison incorrectly.

(C) This answer choice unnecessarily eliminates the parallel construction and introduces a potential error. A comma is used to set off words in a series, but some grammarians do not require the use of one before the coordinating conjunction *and*. Be safe in the ACT Assessment and choose the answer that does use a comma in this position. The ACT Assessment test writers tend to use rules of formal grammar, punctuation, and usage. This answer choice does not have a comma before the *and*, so avoid this answer.

(D) The original sentence notes that Franklin had a reputation as a scientist and philosopher; it does not say that he has a reputation for wit and charm, but rather that he is witty and charming. Note the use of the phrase *his wit and charm*. If the sentence meant that he had a reputation for wit and charm, the second use of the word *his* would be omitted (*his reputation as a serious scientist and philosopher as well as for wit and charm*).

36. **The correct answer is (G).** The second comma to enclose the parenthetical expression *then seventy* is missing. Choice (G) corrects this error.

(F) The second comma to set off the parenthetical phrase is missing, so the answer is incorrect.

(H) This choice removes the existing comma from the phrase *then seventy*. The phrase is parenthetical and needs to be set off with commas. It is an interesting fact but is not essential to understanding Franklin's role.

(J) This answer choice eliminates the comma before the phrase *then seventy,* which is needed, and inserts one after the phrase for no reason that is grammatically defensible.

37. **The correct answer is (D).** This sentence uses the phrase *new nation,* restating who sent Franklin, as a transition between old information and new information. Then the writer gives the reason why the new nation thought Franklin might be successful.

(A) This sentence provides information about Franklin's acquaintance with France but does not explain why or how this might lead to his success.

(B) This answer provides information about the relationship between France and Great Britain but does not explain how or why this might help the United States.

(C) This answer choice is incorrect for the same reason that choice (B) is. The sentence is not tied directly to the interests of the United States.

38. **The correct answer is (H).** This question deals with vagueness in the use of pronouns and antecedents. The antecedent is France, so the singular pronoun *its* is correct, but the sentence construction is such that there is a potential for confusion on the part of the reader. The clearest solution is to substitute the possessive form of *France,* *France's.*

(F) As written, the sentence may be confusing to readers, so it should be revised.

(G) Changing the participle to an infinitive does not solve the confusion problem. Eliminate this answer choice.

(J) This answer choice substitutes the correct pronoun form *its* for the incorrect *their,* so this answer choice is incorrect.

39. **The correct answer is (A).** Use of the comma to separate two independent clauses is correct, as is the choice of the coordinating conjunction *but.* The conjunction *and* is used to connect additions. The

conjunction *but* is used to indicate opposition. "France didn't do one thing, but it did something else" versus "France did this and it did this."

(B) The use of the coordinating conjunction *and* is incorrect because the activity in the second independent clause is in opposition to the activity in the first.

(C) A comma is used to separate independent clauses connected by a coordinating conjunction, so this answer choice is incorrect.

(D) There is no reason to use a semicolon to separate independent clauses joined by a coordinating conjunction. A semicolon is used in place of a coordinating conjunction to connect independent clauses.

40. **The correct answer is (F).** As written, the punctuation is correct. The adverb *badly* modifies *in need of.* It is not the predicate adjective modifying the American army. If it were, it would be *bad American army.*

(G) The use of a colon before a long list is correct, but this is not a long list of items and the colon is, therefore, superfluous.

(H) *Badly* is an adverb modifying the phrase *in need of.* It is not a predicate adjective modifying *American army.* If it were, it would be a *bad American army.* Therefore, this answer choice is incorrect. In addition, the word *namely* has been added. While using *namely* to introduce lists is correct, its placement here between the preposition and its list is awkward and unnecessary.

(J) The adverb *badly* modifies *in need of.* It is not the predicate adjective modifying the *American army.* If it were, it would be *bad American army.* This choice is, therefore, incorrect.

41. **The correct answer is (B).** On a quick reading, if you see *British* and not *Great Britain* in the dependent clause, you might think that the plural possessive is correct. However, the antecedent of the possessive adjective modifying *claim* is *Great Britain;* therefore, the correct possessive is *its,* choice (B).

(A) The antecedent is the singular noun *Great Britain,* so the correct possessive is *its*, not *their*.

(C) This answer choice confuses *there,* the indefinite pronoun or the adverb, with the possessive adjective *their.* Neither is correct.

(D) There is no reason to change the noun *claim* to the gerund *claiming* and, in addition, the incorrect possessive *their* is used.

42. **The correct answer is (J).** Sentence 7 is an interesting detail and illustrates a concrete way in which French soldiers aided the American Revolution, but it does not add anything directly related to Franklin's role in the war and could be deleted.

    (F) This reason is incorrect. The request for troops was denied, but the French provided money, so it did have an impact on the war.

    (G) The reason is incorrect. Sentence 5 explains why Franklin was asking France for aid and is essential to an understanding of what Franklin was doing.

    (H) The reason is incorrect. Sentence 7 indicates the pivotal role that Franklin's efforts had in securing American independence. It was the French navy that blockaded the British and cut them off.

43. **The correct answer is (D).** To help you answer this question, invert it to read "Benjamin Franklin _____ among its many illustrious members." Now it's easy to choose a singular verb form. Check the sentences around the one with the question, and you will see that the tense should be simple past. The only answer that satisfies both criteria is choice (D).

    (A) The subject of the sentence *Benjamin Franklin* is singular number, so the plural predicate is incorrect.

    (B) Not only does this answer add unnecessary words to the sentence and is out of character with the tone of the passage, but this answer choice also uses the incorrect number for the predicate. It should be *was.*

(C) There is no reason to use past perfect tense. The dependent clause is in simple past, and Franklin's presence at the convention occurred at the time it was convened; therefore, simple past is the correct tense. Remember that simultaneous actions in a sentence occur at the same time and take the same tense.

44. **The correct answer is (F).** You might assume that Franklin's role at the Constitutional Convention was his last, choice (G), but the text does not say that. (It wasn't; he served another term as President of the Pennsylvania Executive Council before retiring from politics.) You have to answer the question based on the passage, and in this case, *latest* is the correct word. The passage lists many things that Franklin had done, and his service at the Constitutional Convention was the latest—that is, most recent.

    (G) You can't say this was Franklin's last role, since the text does not indicate that.

    (H) *Latter* is used in a comparison of two things, events, or people to distinguish between them. (Franklin held two roles in state government, head of the militia and president of the council, and the latter was his favorite.) The only role listed in this sentence is that of member of the Constitutional Convention, so choice (H) is incorrect.

    (J) *Late* makes no sense in this context. *Late* can be used to mean deceased, but Franklin was very much alive at the time, and the man who wrote "early to bed, early to rise, makes a man healthy, wealthy, and wise" surely wasn't late for his daily attendance at the convention.

45. **The correct answer is (C).** Choice (C) pulls together ideas from the opening paragraph (overshadowed, military men [Washington and Lafayette] and younger politicians [Jefferson]), the middle paragraphs (service in France during the war), and the last paragraph (age and death) and incorporates them into a single statement.

    (A) The current sentence ends the story of Franklin's life but does not connect back to the beginning paragraph or summarize the passage in any way. It is not an effective closing statement.

(B) The opening paragraph does not say that Franklin was forgotten. It says that few people realize the important role that he had in the war.

(D) The opening paragraph does not say that Franklin's role was forgotten. It says that few people realize the important role that he had in the war.

Passage IV

46. **The correct answer is (F).** The construction as written is a correctly punctuated example of a compound predicate. Compound predicates have one subject (*Globe*) and are separated by commas.

(G) The use of semicolons to separate compound predicates is incorrect, making this choice incorrect. There is an exception to this rule. A semicolon could be used with compound predicates if there are phrases or clauses separated by commas within the word groups associated with the predicates. ("The Globe, which was built on the banks of the Thames, burned down in 1613; was rebuilt the following year, which was considered a waste of money; and was a victim . . .) In this case, the semicolon is used to help the reader make sense of the sentence.

(H) This choice confuses the use of *was*, thus eliminating the third compound predicate and leaving a predicate subject without a verb. In the construction *was rebuilt*, the word *was* is an auxiliary word with the past participle *rebuilt*. It is not a stand-alone verb, so it cannot function as the verb for the third part of the sentence *a victim of the Puritan purges of the 1640s.*

(J) This choice ignores the first part of the sentence. Although it is not underlined, it does exist, and any changes have to work in the context of it. Therefore, this answer cannot be correct, because it makes no sense. ("Home to the plays of Shakespeare and other Elizabethan playwrights, burned down in 1613, the Globe . . .")

47. **The correct answer is (D).** This sentence provides a transition from the demise of the Globe in the 1600s (*over the centuries*) to Sam Wanamaker in 1949 (*one man*). This is the only choice that connects the Globe, the time frame, and Sam Wanamaker.

(A) All the passage says about Wanamaker is that he was an American actor, director, and producer. There is nothing to indicate that he was unlikely to be interested in reconstructing the Globe, unless one assumes that an American wanting to rebuild an English theater is unlikely. Before you make that value judgment, look at the other answer choices.

(B) This is a matter-of-fact choice. Keep reading.

(C) The tone of this choice does not fit the straightforward expository style of the passage. While it is probable that Wanamaker was a young man in 1949, there is nothing in the passage to indicate that Wanamaker was "enchanted with the theater, London, and Shakespeare." He might have been interested in rebuilding the Globe for potential revenue.

48. **The correct answer is (F).** The information in the two paragraphs is very different. The second paragraph describes how the reconstruction came about, and the third paragraph discusses the actual reconstruction. There is no logical reason to combine the two.

(G) As written, there is no transition between the two paragraphs, so combining them would not enhance the development of the passage.

(H) While this answer choice provides a transition by using Wanamaker's name, it is not effective enough to bridge the difference in main ideas in the two paragraphs.

(J) This choice makes no sense. The current sentence discusses the aspect of missing information about the Globe. The second sentence in the third paragraph adds another element that was unknown. There is no logical reason for dividing these two sentences between two paragraphs.

49. **The correct answer is (A).** The sentence as written is correct in terms of punctuation and grammar and is an example of consistent parallelism in a compound subject.

    (B) This choice states that it was the size, shape, and design of the stage that had to be gleaned from other sources. The revision doesn't mention the theater building itself (the Globe).

    (C) This choice omits the conjunction *and* between *size* and *shape*, making it unclear whether it is the size and shape of the Globe, or only the shape of the Globe that had to be found in sources.

    (D) This choice destroys the parallel construction of the compound subject by revising the prepositional phrase and turning the word *stage* into a possessive.

50. **The correct answer is (J).** This choice condenses the information into a prepositional phrase and eliminates the awkward expression. Remember that shorter answers are often the right answer because they avoid possible errors in grammar and punctuation and tend to eliminate wordiness and redundancy.

    (F) As written, the clause is awkward.

    (G) The only change in this answer choice is the addition of a comma before the dependent clause, which makes it incorrect. The clause is restrictive; that is, it is essential to the sentence, because it explains how the plays provided information about the Globe. With or without the comma, the construction is still awkward.

    (H) This choice is less awkward but introduces an error. The use of a comma to separate two independent clauses is incorrect. Either a semicolon is needed or the two clauses have to be separated into two sentences.

51. **The correct answer is (A).** The sentence as written is correct. *Ringed* is the predicate of the independent clause and is simple past tense. The noun *seats* is the object of the preposition *of;* the noun is not related to the verb.

    (B) There is no reason to separate the object of the preposition from the predicate of the independent clause.

    (C) *Ringed* is the predicate of the second independent clause in this compound sentence. The first predicate is in simple past, and, therefore, the second predicate should be in simple past tense as well. The sense of the sentence and the paragraph is also a clue. The paragraph is talking about what the original was like; therefore, it makes sense that the verb tense is past rather than present.

    (D) The cited words are part of the second half of a compound sentence. If *ringed* was changed to the participial form *ringing,* the second clause would lose its predicate, and the meaning of the sentence would change. The revised sentence would state that the stage jutted out into the center and into three tiers of seats.

52. **The correct answer is (H).** This question is an example of how lack of punctuation can make it difficult for the reader to get the sense of a sentence. Reading this quickly, the reader would naturally read *can be given* as one unit and think it is the predicate. In reality, *given* in this construction is a participle introducing a dependent clause. The correct answer, choice (H), recognizes this and inserts a comma between *be* and *given.*

    (F) This phrase is incorrect because a comma should be used to clarify meaning.

    (G) This answer choice correctly recognizes that *given* is not part of the predicate but incorrectly makes it part of a separate independent sentence, thus creating a sentence fragment.

    (J) Changing *given* to *dependent* doesn't help the clarity issue. A comma is still needed.

53. **The correct answer is (B).** This question is an example of actions occurring consecutively. The scholars had to learn the information before the craftworkers could put it to use. Therefore, the correct tense is past perfect, choice (B).

    (A) The past perfect tense is required because the workers needed the information from the scholars before the workers could begin. As currently written, the verb tense is present perfect, which means that the scholars are still learning information, which is illogical in the context.

(C) Past tense is incorrect in this construction, which indicates time sequence.

(D) The use of present tense in a discussion of past events is illogical, so reject this answer choice.

54. **The correct answer is (H).** This question points out the vague use of a pronoun. Are the "they" scholars, workers, or both? When you stop and think about the sense of the sentence, only the workers would be using building techniques and building materials. The workers must be the "they." Clear writing would make this evident without your having to stop and think about the relationship.

(F) The antecedent for *they* is unclear and needs to be made clear.

(G) Scholars might be instructing the craftworkers about the building techniques, but the scholars wouldn't be using them, so choice (G) is invalidated. Remember that all parts of an answer choice must be correct in order for it to be the right answer.

(J) Scholars might be instructing the craftworkers about the building techniques, but the scholars wouldn't be using them, so this choice isn't correct.

55. **The correct answer is (B).** *With which* may sound strange to you, but it's correct. In this meaning, the idiom is *familiar with,* so any answer that doesn't include the complete idiom is incorrect. The test writers use formal English, so keep that in mind as you answer questions.

(A) The placement of *with* is incorrect.

(C) The idiom is correct, but a second error is introduced. The clause *sixteenth-century workers would have been familiar* is essential to the sense of the sentence. It should not be separated from the main clause by a comma.

(D) The idiom is incorrect.

56. **The correct answer is (F).** Parentheses are used to set off parenthetical—that is, nonessential—information as well as supplementary or illustrative material. In this case, the information is supplementary; it tells you something more about the seats. Therefore, the use of parentheses rather than any other punctuation is correct.

(G) Dashes are used to set off parenthetical elements if the writer wishes to emphasize the information or to clarify information. Neither criterion applies to this case, so eliminate choice (G).

(H) Enclosing the parenthetical information in commas intrudes on the sense of the sentence and creates confusion for the reader, so reject this choice.

(J) The information is interesting, is in keeping with the tone of the piece, and notes a difference between the original Globe and the new one, a topic the writer will develop further in the next paragraph. There is more reason to keep the underlined portion than to omit it.

57. **The correct answer is (D).** This question assesses your knowledge of the consistent use of person. The sentence begins with the third person and then shifts to second person in the dependent clause. Correct the shift in person by substituting *they* for *you.*

(A) As written, the sentence shifts from third to second person.

(B) This answer choice uses second person consistently in the sentence, but the revised sentence then doesn't fit the tone or sense of the paragraph. The rest of the paragraph is in third person, making this answer choice incorrect. Remember to read around the cited sentence to be sure that your correction makes sense in the paragraph.

(C) The third person is used consistently in this answer choice, but the use of *one* makes the sentence very stilted. It may be grammatically correct, but the tone doesn't match the passage, so reject it.

58. **The correct answer is (H).** Choice (H) not only untangles the writer's idea about the length of sunlight during summer in London, but it also uses the word *evening* to echo the idea developed in the second half of the sentence (evening performances attract larger audiences to the Globe).

    (F) The sentence is unclear and needs to be re-worked for clarity.

    (G) This statement is true but does not help the reader make a connection to the idea in the second half of the sentence. The two halves seem to be unrelated ideas connected by *and*.

    (J) This answer choice is incorrect for the same reason that choice (G) is incorrect.

59. **The correct answer is (A).** Choice (A) is the best answer because it sets up safety as an issue with evening performances in the 1600s, and then it explains why evening performances have become safer since then.

    (B) The use of the phrase the *fact that* is one of those constructions that writers should avoid. It makes writing stilted, so eliminate this choice.

    (C) The reason why the replacement of candles is important is missing from this sentence. Keep reading.

    (D) The reason that electricity has made evening performances safer is missing from this choice. Sometimes, when you're not sure about an answer dealing with style or strategy, eliminate answers and see what's left.

60. **The correct answer is (G).** Only choice (G) ties together Sam Wanamaker's dream and the recon-structed Globe.

    (F) Wanamaker is mentioned, but the sentence is vague. Who shares his dream? Where are they going with it? It does not sum up the passage.

    (H) This answer may tempt you, because it seems poetic, but what is it really saying? It doesn't mention Wanamaker, and it doesn't sum up the passage.

(J) This answer choice restates only part of what the passage is about. It doesn't mention Wanamaker or imply anything about how diffi-cult it was to build the new Globe.

Passage V

61. **The correct answer is (A).** A comma is used to set off a nonrestrictive appositive. An appositive re-names a noun; in this case, the appositive *idea that the economies . . .* renames, or explains, globaliza-tion. While useful, the definition is not essential to the main idea of the sentence (the concept of globalization developed in the 1990s). Therefore, a comma is the appropriate mark of punctuation, and the construction is correct as written.

    (B) This answer choice creates a sentence fragment by separating the appositive from the rest of the sentence.

    (C) Semicolons are used to separate independent clauses. In this answer choice, the semicolon is dividing a single sentence.

    (D) Colons may be used to call attention to what follows, but the definition of globalization is not so startling that it needs special emphasis. Reject this answer choice as overkill.

62. **The correct answer is (J).** Choice (J) uses a very simple strategy to develop a transition. It simply restates that there are factors to be discussed. In analyzing answers, the shorter and the simpler may be the best.

    (F) The second paragraph begins abruptly with one of the factors of globalization. A transition would smooth the beginning.

    (G) The conjunction *so* is used to introduce results. (X happened, so Y occurred.) There is no logical reason to use *so* in this context. Paragraph 2 is not discussing the result of some cause described in paragraph 1. In fact, paragraph 2 discusses a cause of globalization, not a result.

    (H) Paragraph 1 doesn't assign priorities to the causes, so you can't accept the value judgment in choice (H). There is nothing to indicate that the reduction, or elimination, of tariffs is the most important cause of globalization.

63. **The correct answer is (A).** As written, the underlined portion is logical and succinct.

    (B) That tariffs are barriers to trade is an essential piece of information in the sentence. Relegating this information to a nonrestrictive clause is incorrect. Note also that this is the longest of the answer choices.

    (C) Again, by separating the information about tariffs from the rest of the sentence, this answer choice relegates tariffs to the position of a nonrestrictive phrase.

    (D) This answer choice reverses the sense of the sentence, making tariffs the only trade barriers. This cannot be assumed from the passage, so avoid this answer.

64. **The correct answer is (F).** Present tense and plural number for the pronoun are correct. The main predicate in the sentence (*are*) is plural, and the pronoun refers to *imports*.

    (G) The main predicate is in the present tense, so the predicate in the clause should be in the present tense. The actions in the two clauses involve a cause-and-effect relationship. Don't be fooled because part of the answer, the plural pronoun, is correct; all parts of an answer choice have to be correct.

    (H) The predicate for the dependent clause has to be in the present tense, and there is no reason to substitute the definite article *the* for the pronoun.

    (J) Only half of this answer choice is correct. The verb is singular, but the pronoun should be plural, so eliminate this choice.

65. **The correct answer is (C).** As written, the underlined portion is grammatically correct. *Similarly* is modifying the adjectival phrase *domestically produced* and must be an adverb. For the same reason, *domestically* is modifying *produced* and must be an adverb. Adjectives modify nouns, but

adverbs modify verbs and adjectives. This may be correct, but it's very awkward. Look for a correct version that avoids this awkwardness. Choice (C) eliminates the awkward phrasing and correctly indicates that *is produced domestically* is essential to the meaning of the sentence.

(A) Avoid the awkward construction.

(B) Inserting a hyphen between a modifier ending in *-ly* and the word it modifies is incorrect. Choice (B), then, is incorrect.

(D) This answer choice incorrectly indicates that *is produced domestically* is not essential to the meaning of the sentence.

66. **The correct answer is (G).** The verb in the dependent clause is in the present perfect tense because the impact began in the past and is continuing into the present. The only answer choice that continues this relationship is answer choice (G). The growth of multinational corporations began in the past and continues to be a factor today. The actions are simultaneous.

    (F) The actions are simultaneous, so the verb tenses should be the same. Both actions began in the past and continue into the present. Present tense for the verb in the main clause is incorrect, so this answer is incorrect.

    (H) Past tense for the main clause is incorrect, because the dependent clause is in the present perfect tense. That the impact continues into the present, whereas the growth as a factor ended, which past tense signifies, makes no sense.

    (J) Use of the past perfect tense indicating that the action is over is incorrect for the same reason that simple past tense is incorrect.

67. **The correct answer is (D).** The use of the verb *do* in the construction *as do* is redundant. The predicate in the second clause is *have*. Pull the clause apart and it says *thousands do have*. All that is needed is the conjunction *as*, choice (D), which indicates two parallel thoughts.

    (A) The use of the verb *do* is redundant and needs to be eliminated.

(B) *Just* is a qualifier that is also redundant, making this answer incorrect.

(C) The conjunction *while* is generally used to indicate time frame, which is not an element of this construction, so it is not the appropriate conjunction for this construction.

68. **The correct answer is (J).** This is an example of awkward phrasing and a punctuation error. To answer a question involving possessives, you may find it helpful to pull the expression apart. As written, the phrase says "thousands of companies of other nation." Immediately, you can see that *nation* should be plural, and plural possessives are formed by adding *s'*. The correct answer is choice (J).

(F) As written, the phrase is both awkward to say and incorrectly punctuated.

(G) This revision makes no sense, because it's not thousands of other nations but thousands of companies.

(H) It's not other companies but other nations.

69. **The correct answer is (B).** This question involves the proper use of commas with nonessential phrases. The rule is that nonessential, or nonrestrictive, phrases are set off from the rest of the sentence by commas, choice (B). This is true even when the phrase is introduced by the expression *for example.*

(A) Using a semicolon in front of the expression *for example* is a common error that people make. Semicolons are used to separate two independent clauses. Illustrative material that is not an independent clause and that is introduced by the expression *for example* should be set off by commas.

(C) This answer creates a sentence fragment by separating the examples from the main clause that the examples illustrate.

(D) This answer is half right. It uses a comma before the expression *for example* but omits it after the phrase. Nonrestrictive phrases are enclosed in commas.

70. **The correct answer is (J).** This is a two-part question; both the yes/no response and the reason underlying the response have to be correct. In this case, only choice (J) meets these criteria. The proposed additional sentence does not fit, because the paragraph discusses the free flow of money and workers, not goods or components of goods.

(F) This choice is incorrect, whereas paragraph 4 does talk about the free flow of workers; the proposed addition is an example of how the components of goods move from country to country. It doesn't provide an example of workers moving between borders.

(G) Whereas it is true that paragraph 4 uses examples to illustrate ideas, the examples are all based on specific nations. The proposed addition is general and not specific in identifying countries.

(H) The answer is too vague in stating that the proposed addition doesn't provide a concrete example. Ask yourself, "Example of what?" No answer? Move on.

71. **The correct answer is (B).** You may think this is another question about possessives, but it's a question about end marks. Unlike the direct question in the explanation of choice (H) above, the question in the sentence in which the underlined portion appears is an indirect question. Therefore, the end mark should be a period and not a question mark.

(A) The question in the sentence is an indirect question and requires a period, not a question mark.

(C) This answer choice continues the incorrect end mark.

(D) This answer choice continues the incorrect end mark.

72. **The correct answer is (J).** This is a style question. The metaphor at the end of the sentence (*high-flying* and *lose steam*) is mixed. You don't need to know that this is a mixed metaphor, but you do need to recognize that airplanes and steam don't

go together. Choice (J) corrects this error, shortens the sentence, and is clearer than the original.

(F) *High-flying* and *steam* aren't comparable, and the underlined portion is made complex and stilted by the use of jargon.

(G) This choice corrects the mixed metaphor by substituting *powerful* and *steam* but retains the jargon of the original, which makes the sentence seem very dense and complex.

(H) This answer substitutes *powerful* and *chain reaction*, which is an improvement over the existing metaphor but still not quite right (chain reaction goes with nuclear power). But the sentence begins with the indefinite pronoun *It*, which is inconsistent with the style of the piece, which is concrete.

73. **The correct answer is (D).** Look out for a phrase with a plural noun between a singular subject and its predicate. The plural noun is meant to confuse you into thinking the verb should be plural. This is the trick in this question. The subject of the verb *decline* is *demand*, not *goods*.

    (A) The verb should be singular to match the singular subject.

    (B) The verb should be singular, not plural. In addition, the omission of the comma between *slow* and *the demand* creates a potential for misreading the sentence. Short introductory phrases and clauses may be set off by a comma, which in this case would eliminate any misunderstanding.

    (C) The verb *declines* is singular, but the underlined portion no longer reflects the meaning of the sentence. The comma between *slow* and *the demand* has been omitted, and a comma has been placed after *goods*. The clause makes sense, but the word *declines* doesn't. To avoid errors like this, remember to read around the underlined portion so you know the context of the cited section.

74. **The correct answer is (H).** In two-part questions like this one, both the yes/no answer and the reason have to be correct. The final sentence in paragraph 5 gives an example that illustrates how the reduction of tariffs by lowering prices on imports may affect workers. The sentence doesn't relate this example to either multinationals or the free flow of money or workers, both aspects of globalization. The sentence also doesn't summarize the information in the paragraph.

    (F) The final sentence does provide an example, but the example illustrates theory, not practice, so it doesn't answer the question in the opening sentence.

    (G) The final sentence discusses workers in the context of a single industry within a nation. It's the flow of workers between nations that is an aspect of globalization, so this reason is not correct.

    (J) Whereas it is true that the topic sentence doesn't discuss an ideal world, that's not the reason the final sentence isn't an effective closing statement for the paragraph. It's not effective because it doesn't summarize the paragraph.

75. **The correct answer is (B).** Paragraph 2 discusses the reduction, or elimination, of tariffs. The proposed addition explains how this tactic can affect domestic industries when they are faced with lower-priced imports. The current final sentence is a natural bridge to this addition.

    (A) The proposed addition deals with a theory about free trade. The first paragraph introduces the three factors in list form that contribute to globalization. The paragraph sets up the theme of globalization for the rest of the passage. Adding information on free trade would interrupt and dilute that purpose. In other words, the addition would add irrelevant details.

    (C) Paragraph 4 is about the free flow of workers and capital. An addition dealing with the effect of free trade on industries doesn't relate to the topics of the paragraph. Again, it would add irrelevant details.

    (D) This answer choice may tempt you because the addition talks about what economists believe about free trade, and paragraph 5 discusses what economists theorize about international trade. However, the addition is a very specific aspect of trade theory and relates better to paragraph 2, which discusses the effect of tariffs on domestic goods.

Day 16

Practice Math Test: Questions 1 through 30

Assignment for Today:

- Take a sample of the ACT Assessment Math Test under actual test conditions. For the real test, you will have 60 minutes to complete 60 items. The questions progress in difficulty, so for these 30 questions, set your timer for 30 minutes, but see if you can finish them in a little less than 30 minutes.

DIRECTIONS: *Solve each problem below and choose the correct answer.*

Be careful not to spend too much time on any one question. Instead, solve as many questions as possible, and then use any remaining time to return to those questions you were unable to answer at first.

You may use a calculator on any problem; however, not every problem requires the use of a calculator.

Note: Unless otherwise indicated, assume all of the following to be true:

- *Diagrams that accompany problems are not necessarily drawn to scale.*

- *All figures lie in a plane.*

- *A line indicates a straight line.*

- *Average refers to arithmetic mean.*

1. A roller hockey team played 40 games. If the team won 21 games and tied 4 games, what fractional part of its games did the team lose?

   (A) $\dfrac{5}{8}$

   (B) $\dfrac{3}{8}$

   (C) $\dfrac{21}{40}$

   (D) $\dfrac{19}{40}$

   (E) $\dfrac{5}{7}$

2. If $a = 4$, $b = -2$, and $c = -3$, what is the value of $-ab^2c$?

   (F) −48

   (G) −192

   (H) 192

   (J) 48

   (K) −19

3. The value of a particular car decreases by 15% of its purchase price each year. If the purchase price of the car is $20,000, what is its value after three years?

   (A) $7,717.50

   (B) $11,000

   (C) $9,000

   (D) $12,282.50

   (E) $14,450

4. How many different three-digit numbers can be made from the digits 5, 6, 7, 8, and 9 if none of the numbers contain any repeated digits?

   (F) 24

   (G) 60

   (H) 64

   (J) 120

   (K) 125

USE THIS SPACE FOR YOUR FIGURING.

5. In the figure below, if ∠ABC is a right angle, then
    $x - 20 =$ _____.

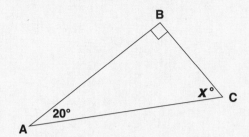

(A) 50

(B) 60

(C) 70

(D) 140

(E) 160

6. Which of the following is NOT equal to 6.52×10^{-3}?

    (F) 652.1×10^{-5}

    (G) 0.06521×10^{-1}

    (H) 0.00006521×10^{2}

    (J) $0.0000006521 \times 10^{4}$

    (K) 6521×10^{-7}

7. At the Martin Luther King Jr. High School, 62.5%
    of the students who took Algebra I went on to
    take Algebra II, and 60% of those who took Alge-
    bra II went on to take Algebra III. If 15 students
    took Algebra III, how many took Algebra I?

    (A) 39

    (B) 40

    (C) 42

    (D) 96

    (E) 104

8. All of the CDs in a bargain bin are discounted by 20% to 30%. Brian wishes to buy a CD whose regular price is $16. What is the difference between the least possible discount price of the CD and the greatest possible discount price of the CD?

    (F) $1.60

    (G) $3.20

    (H) $4.80

    (J) $11.20

    (K) $12.80

9. Solve the equation $cx = 5a - 2bx$ for x in terms of a, b, and c.

    (A) $x = \dfrac{5c}{c - 2b}$

    (B) $x = \dfrac{5c}{c + 2b}$

    (C) $x = \dfrac{5a - c}{2b}$

    (D) $x = \dfrac{5a - 2b}{c}$

    (E) $x = \dfrac{c + 2b}{5a}$

10. If the expression $9x - 1$ represents an even integer, which of the following expressions represents the next least even integer?

    (F) $9x$

    (G) $8x - 2$

    (H) $7x - 1$

    (J) $8x - 1$

    (K) $9x - 3$

11. Find all of the values of a for which $-4a - 3 > -11$.

    (A) $a > 2$

    (B) $a > -2$

    (C) $a < 2$

    (D) $a < -2$

    (E) $a < \dfrac{7}{2}$

12. What percent of 75 is 15?

    (F) 5%

    (G) 20%

    (H) 25%

    (J) 80%

    (K) 500%

13. If $7a = 5b = 45$, then what is the value of $14ab$?

    (A) 90

    (B) $\dfrac{405}{7}$

    (C) 405

    (D) 810

    (E) 11,340

14. The rectangle in the figure below has been partitioned into six congruent squares. If the longer side of the rectangle is 9, what is the perimeter of one of the squares?

    (F) 6

    (G) 9

    (H) 12

    (J) 18

    (K) 30

USE THIS SPACE FOR YOUR FIGURING.

15. $\dfrac{\dfrac{3}{8}+\dfrac{3}{4}}{\dfrac{1}{8}+\dfrac{1}{4}} =$

    (A) 6

    (B) 9

    (C) $\dfrac{27}{64}$

    (D) 3

    (E) $\dfrac{9}{512}$

16. In the diagram below, line segments AD and BC intersect at point H. If line segments FH and GH trisect ∠AHB, what is the measure of ∠CHD?

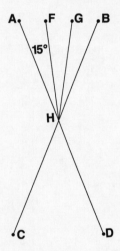

    (F) 15°
    (G) 30°
    (H) 45°
    (J) 50°
    (K) 135°

17. If x is the number that is obtained by rounding 3.2782 to the nearest hundredth, and y is the number obtained by rounding 7.8452 to the nearest tenth, then $x + y =$

    (A) 11.07

    (B) 11.08

    (C) 11.1

    (D) 11.13

    (E) 11.18

18. The figure below shows three intersecting lines. What is the value of $x + y$?

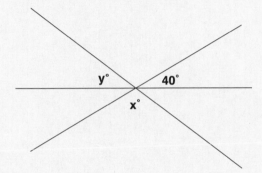

    (F) 50

    (G) 80

    (H) 130

    (J) 140

    (K) 150

19. If $y^2 + 3y - 5 = 5$, then one possible value for y is

    (A) −5

    (B) −2

    (C) 3

    (D) 5

    (E) $\dfrac{-3+\sqrt{29}}{2}$

20. The four triangles shown in the figure below share a common vertex. What is the value of $a + b + c + d$?

USE THIS SPACE FOR YOUR FIGURING.

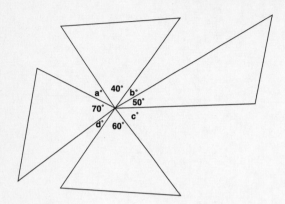

(F) 140°

(G) 160°

(H) 220°

(J) 320°

(K) 500°

21. Janet wishes to have $4,770 in a savings account at the end of one year. How much must she deposit in her account at the start of the year if her account pays her 6% interest a year?

(A) $286.20

(B) $4,483.80

(C) $4,490.00

(D) $4,500.00

(E) $4,520.00

22. Which of the following is equivalent to $8^{-1}(12x - 24)$?

(F) $96x - 192$

(G) $-96x + 192$

(H) $12x - 3$

(J) $\dfrac{3x - 6}{2}$

(K) $3x - 12$

23. If the average of seven numbers is equal to A, which of the following statements must be true about A?

    I.   At least one of the seven numbers must be greater than A.

    II. At least one of the seven numbers must be less than or equal to A.

    III. At least three of the seven numbers are greater than A.

    (A) I only

    (B) II only

    (C) I and II only

    (D) I, II, and III

    (E) None of the above

24. In the figure below, if ℓ_1 is parallel to ℓ_2, what is the value of x?

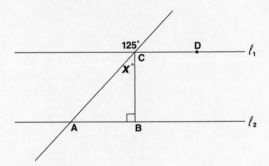

    (F) 30°

    (G) 35°

    (H) 40°

    (J) 55°

    (K) 70°

25. What is the slope of the line described by the equation $3x = -7$?

    (A) 0

    (B) $-\dfrac{7}{3}$

    (C) $-\dfrac{3}{7}$

    (D) $\dfrac{7}{3}$

    (E) The line has no slope.

26. What is the area of the rectangle shown in the figure below?

    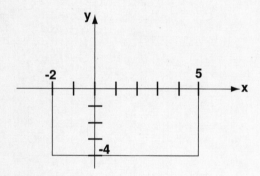

    (F) 11
    (G) 18
    (H) 20
    (J) 22
    (K) 28

27. What is the value of $9 + 3 \times 12 \div 6 - 2$?

    (A) 9
    (B) 13
    (C) 18
    (D) 22
    (E) 36

USE THIS SPACE FOR YOUR FIGURING.

28. If the length of a rectangle increases by 10% and the width decreases by 20%, by what percent does the area decrease?

    (F) 10%

    (G) 11%

    (H) 12%

    (J) 28%

    (K) 32%

29. If 20% of 50% of 30a is equal to 21, what is the value of a?

    (A) $\dfrac{203}{300}$

    (B) 1

    (C) 7

    (D) 10

    (E) 70

30. In the figure below, triangle XYZ is inside the circle with center Y. If the length of side XY is 8, what is the length of arc XZ?

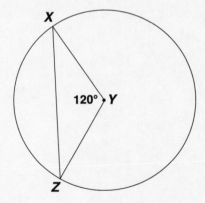

    (F) $8\sqrt{3}$

    (G) 16π

    (H) $\dfrac{64}{3}\pi$

    (J) $\dfrac{16}{3}\pi$

    (K) $\dfrac{8}{3}\pi$

USE THIS SPACE FOR YOUR FIGURING.

QUICK ANSWER GUIDE:
QUESTIONS 1 THROUGH 30

1. B
2. J
3. D
4. G
5. A
6. K
7. B
8. F
9. B
10. K
11. C
12. G
13. D
14. H
15. D
16. H
17. B
18. J
19. A
20. F
21. D
22. J
23. B
24. G
25. E
26. K
27. B
28. H
29. C
30. J

For explanations to these problems, see Day 17.

Math Test: Questions 1 through 30
Explanations and Answers

Assignment for Today:

- Review the explanations for the first 30 math problems that you solved. See which answer is correct and learn what makes the other choices incorrect.

---

1. **The correct answer is (B).** Of the 40 games played, the team won or tied $21 + 4 = 25$ games. This leaves $40 - 25 = 15$ games that the team lost. Thus, the team lost 15 games out of 40. The fractional representation of this is $\frac{15}{40}$. This fraction can be simplified by dividing the numerator and denominator by 5:

$$\frac{15}{40} = \frac{15 \div 5}{40 \div 5} = \frac{3}{8}$$

If you selected any of the wrong answers below, you were in too much of a rush. Slow down, read the problem more carefully, and make certain to answer the question that is being asked.

(A) If you chose this answer, you read the problem too quickly. The fraction $\frac{5}{8}$ represents the fractional part of the games that the team won or tied, not the fractional part of the games that the team lost.

(C) This is the answer that you will get if you find the fractional part of the games the team won. However, you are looking for the fractional part of the games the team lost.

(D) This is the fractional part of the games the team lost or tied. However, you want the fractional part the team lost. The number of ties should not be included.

(E) This is the ratio of losses to wins. However, you were asked to find the ratio of losses to total games played.

2. **The correct answer is (J).** This problem is asking you to substitute the values for a, b, and c into the algebraic expression $-ab^2c$ and to determine the resulting value. To avoid making an error, it is best to put all numbers in parentheses before substituting. Also, pay careful attention to the negative signs:

$$-ab^2c = -(4)(-2)^2(-3)$$

Now, according to the Order of Operations, you need to evaluate the factor with the exponent first:

$$-(4)(-2)^2(-3) = -(4)(4)(-3)$$

Next, perform the indicated multiplications:

$-(4)(4)(-3) = -(-48) = 48$

(F) This is the correct number but with the wrong sign. Somewhere along the line, you must have dropped one of the negative signs. Be certain to keep careful track of all negative signs when evaluating an algebraic expression.

(G) If you obtained this answer, you made two mistakes. First, you violated the Order of Operations by multiplying the 4 and the –2 before squaring. You also lost track of one of the negative signs.

(H) Here, you made the same Order of Operations error as in choice (G), but you handled the signs correctly.

(K) If you obtained this answer, you made the fundamental error of misinterpreting the final multiplication as a subtraction. That is, instead of computing $-(4)(4)(-3)$, you computed $-(4)(4) - 3 = -16 - 3$.

3. **The correct answer is (D).** In order to find the value of the car after three years, you need to decrease the purchase price by 15% three times. Perhaps the quickest way to do this is to realize that, if 15% of the price is removed, 85% of the price remains. Thus, if you determine 85% of $20,000, and then find 85% of the result, and 85% of that result, you will have the answer. This is a question where using your calculator would be a time saver.

$\$20,000 \times 85\% = \$20,000 \times 0.85 = \$17,000$

$\$17,000 \times 85\% = \$17,000 \times 0.85 = \$14,450$

$\$14,450 \times 85\% = \$14,450 \times 0.85 = \$12,282.50$

(A) This value is the amount that the price of the car has been decreased. You answered the wrong question. Be sure to answer the question that is asked.

(B) This choice would be the most common wrong answer. If you made the mistake of thinking that decreasing the price of the car by 15% three times is the same as decreasing it once by

45%, you would get this answer. Remember that once you decrease the price of the car, the second discount is on the resulting lesser price.

(C) This answer is the result of two errors. First is the mistake of thinking that three 15% discounts are equivalent to a 45% discount. Then, it's selecting the amount that the value of the car would be decreased instead of selecting the value of the car.

(E) This is the value of the car after two years. Read the problem carefully!

4. **The correct answer is (G).** This problem can be solved by using the Multiplication Principle. There are five possible choices for the first digit of the number. Since no digits can be repeated, there are only four possible choices for the second digit and then three possible choices for the final digit. The number of possible values, then, is $5 \times 4 \times 3 = 60$.

(F) If you read the problem too quickly and mistakenly thought that you were forming the number from a choice of four digits instead of five, you would obtain the answer $4 \times 3 \times 2 = 24$.

(H) This answer represents the number of four-digit numbers that can be formed if repeated digits are allowed, since $4 \times 4 \times 4 = 64$. The other mistake is that you were asked how many three-digit, not four-digit, numbers.

(J) This choice represents the number of four-digit numbers that could be formed, since $5 \times 4 \times 3 \times 2 = 120$. Again, this is a mistake that could be made by reading the problem too quickly. You want to form three-digit numbers.

(K) This common wrong answer represents the number of three-digit numbers that can be made if repeated digits are allowed. Note that $5 \times 5 \times 5 = 125$. Read the questions carefully.

5. **The correct answer is (A).** There are two basic facts about triangles that you need to know in order to find the correct solution to this problem. First, remember that the sum of the measures of the angles of every triangle is 180°. Second, know that a right angle measures 90°.

Knowing this, you can add up the degree measures of the three angles and set the sum equal to 180:

$20 + 90 + x = 180$

Combine like terms:

$70 + x = 180$

Subtract 70 from both sides:

$x = 70$

Now, be very careful to answer the question that is being asked. This question does not ask you for the value of x, but for the value of $x - 20$, which is $70 - 20 = 50$.

(B) This answer choice is close to being the correct answer, but it is placed here to make it a bit harder for you to guess the answer by estimating sizes based on the diagram.

(C) It should be obvious why this answer is here. If you did not notice that you were being asked for $x - 20$ instead of x, you would have selected this answer.

(D) You would obtain this answer if you forget to include the right angle in your computation. There are 180° in a triangle, and taking away the 20° angle would leave you with 160 as the value of x. Then, $x - 20 = 140$.

(E) You would have to make two errors to get this answer. First, as in choice (D), if you forget to include the right angle in your computation, you would get 160°. Then, forgetting that you are being asked for $x - 20$, you would select 160 as the answer.

6. **The correct answer is (K).** One way to solve this question is to take all of the numbers that are currently written in exponential notation and write them as decimals. If you do this, they will be easier to compare.

The number given in the problem statement is 6.521×10^{-3}. The exponent of –3 tells you that the decimal point must be moved three places to the left. Therefore:

$6.521 \times 10^{-3} = 0.006521$

Now, consider the number 6521×10^{-7}. The exponent of –7 tells you to move the decimal point seven places to the left. If you do this, you get 0.0006521, which is not the same as 0.006521.

If you selected any one of the wrong answers, you most likely either counted incorrectly or moved the decimal point the wrong way.

(F) For 652.1×10^{-5}, the decimal point must be moved five places to the left, which gives you 0.006521.

(G) To write 0.06521×10^{-1} as a decimal, the decimal point must be moved one place to the left, which gives you 0.006521.

(H) This answer choice has a positive exponent. In this case, you must move the decimal point two places to the right, which gives you 0.006521.

(J) For this answer choice, you must move the decimal point four places to the right, which also gives you 0.006521.

7. **The correct answer is (B).** In order to find the answer to this question, you need to solve two percent problems. To begin, you know that 15 students took Algebra III and that this was 60% of those who took Algebra II. If you let x represent the number of students who took Algebra II, you can write:

$60\% \times x = 15,$ or $0.6x = 15$

Divide both sides by 15:

$x = \dfrac{15}{0.6} = 25$

Therefore, 25 students took Algebra II.

You need to do the same thing again to find the number who took Algebra I. You know that 25 students took Algebra II, and that this was 62.5% of the students who took Algebra I. If you let y represent the number of students who took Algebra I, you can write:

$62.5\% \times y = 0.625y = 25,$

or $y = \dfrac{25}{.625} = 40$

Therefore, 40 students took Algebra I.

(A) This is probably the most common wrong answer. If you start with the 15 students who took Algebra III and increase it by 60%, you will get 24 students. If this is then increased by 62.5%, you will get 39 students. Remember, however, that the figure 60% represents a percent of the number of Algebra II students and cannot be directly applied to the number of Algebra III students.

(C) This answer is very close to the actual answer and is placed here to make it more difficult for you to estimate the answer without doing all the work.

(D) This answer results from the incorrect computation of dividing 60% by 62.5%:

$$\frac{.60}{.625} = 96$$

(E) This answer results from the incorrect computation of dividing 62.5% by 60%:

$$\frac{.625}{.60} = 104$$

8. **The correct answer is (F).** There are several different ways to find the answer to this problem. The most straightforward way is to find the least possible discount price and the greatest possible discount price and subtract them.

Because the least possible discount is 20%, the least possible discount price is:

100% − 20% = 80% of $16

$16 × 80% = $16 × .80 = $12.80

In the same way, the greatest possible discount is 30%, so the greatest possible discount price is:

100% − 30% = 70% of $16

$16 × 70% = $11.20

The difference between the least possible discount price of the CD and the greatest possible discount price of the CD is:

$12.80 − $11.20 = $1.60

A quicker way to find the answer is to realize that the difference between the greatest possible dis-

count and the least possible discount is 30% − 20% = 10%. Then you can compute that 10% of the $16 CD price is $16 x 10% = $1.60.

(G) To choose this answer, you misread the question. $3.20 is the least possible discount that Brian could receive. The problem asks for the difference between this and the greatest possible discount.

(H) This is another misread. $4.80 is the greatest possible discount that Brian could receive. The problem asks for the difference between this and the least possible discount.

(J) As the solution above points out, $11.20 is the greatest possible discount price. This is not what the problem is asking for. Be sure to read each problem carefully.

(K) $12.80 is the least possible discount price. This is also not what the problem is asking for.

9. **The correct answer is (B).** In order to solve the equation for x, begin by moving all terms that contain x to the same side of the equation:

$cx = 5a - 2bx$

Add $2bx$ to both sides:

$cx + 2bx = 5a$

Factor x from both terms on the left side:

$x(c + 2b) = 5a$

Divide both sides by $c + 2b$:

$x = \dfrac{5c}{c+2b}$

(A) If you got this answer, you were very close to being correct. You did all the steps correctly and in the right order, but, at the beginning, when you moved the $2bx$ to the left side of the equation, you forgot to change the sign.

(C) This answer is the result of a careless error. Apparently, you began by rewriting the equation as $5a - cx = 2bx$ and then divided both sides by $2b$, losing the x next to the c in the process. In order to solve the equation, you must begin by putting all terms involving x on the same side of the equation.

(D) Another careless error. This is the result that would be obtained by taking the equation $cx = 5a - 2bx$, dividing by c, and "losing" the x next to the $2b$ along the way. Practice working quickly—and carefully.

(E) This is the reciprocal of the correct answer. This answer results from dividing both sides by the wrong quantity in the last step.

10. **The correct answer is (K).** If you have an even integer, the next least even integer is always two less than the given even integer. Therefore, to find the next least even integer to $9x - 1$, you simply need to subtract 2:

$9x - 1 - 2 = 9x - 3$

(F) This is the next greatest integer, but if $9x - 1$ is even, $9x$ would be odd.

(G) This answer results from a misconception about finding the next least even integer. If you decrease the coefficients of both of the terms of $9x - 1$ by 1, you get $8x - 1$. This number, however, is not the next least even integer.

(H) This answer results if you realize that one of the coefficients of one of the terms in $9x - 1$ needs to be decreased by 2, but you decreased the incorrect term.

(J) This answer results from decreasing the coefficient of the $9x$ by 1, which does not give you the next least even integer—or even the next least integer.

11. **The correct answer is (C).** The procedure for solving a linear inequality is the same as the procedure for solving a linear equation with one key difference: Whenever you multiply or divide by a negative number, the inequality sign must be reversed.

$-4a - 3 > -11$

Add 3 to both sides:

$-4a > -8$

Divide both sides by -4. Reverse the inequality sign.

$a < 2$

(A) This is probably the most common wrong answer. If you got this answer, you did everything correctly, except flip the inequality sign when you divided by -4.

(B) This answer choice results from two errors. First is forgetting to flip the inequality sign, and the second is making a sign error when dividing by -4.

(D) Here, the inequality sign was correctly reversed, but a sign error was made.

(E) This answer will result if you make a mistake early on: moving the -3 to the right side and forgetting to change its sign.

12. **The correct answer is (G).** In this problem, the number 75 represents the whole, and the number 15 represents the part. In order to find the percent, you need to divide the part by the whole and multiply by 100%. That is:

$$\frac{15}{75} \times 100 = 0.2 \times 100\% = 20\%$$

(F) This answer is the result of dividing the two numbers in the wrong order and then putting the decimal point in the wrong place.

(H) This answer is close to the correct answer and is placed here so that you cannot solve the problem by making a quick estimate.

(J) Note that $80\% = 100\% - 20\%$. This answer represents the percent of the whole that remains after 20% is removed.

(K) You have answered the wrong question. 500% represents the percent of 15 that 75 is! Not answering the question asked is a common test-taking error.

13. **The correct answer is (D).** This problem may seem rather confusing at first, since it contains an equation with two "=" signs. However, realize that the equation simply tells you that $7a = 45$ and $5b = 45$. Using these two equations, you can solve for a and b.

To find a in $7a = 45$, divide by 7:

$$a = \frac{45}{7}$$

To find b in $5b = 45$, divide by 5:

$$b = 9$$

Therefore, $14ab = 14\left(\frac{45}{7}\right)(9) = 2(45)(9) = 810$

(A) The number 90 is the value of $14a$. If you got this answer, you were rushing and didn't find the expression you were asked for.

(B) The answer is the value of ab. If you obtained this answer, you neglected to multiply the value of ab by 14 to get the value of $14ab$.

(C) This is the value of $7ab$. Somehow, in solving the problem, you missed a factor of 2.

(E) If you got this answer, you correctly found the value of a and b but made an error in computing $14ab$. You treated the expression $14ab$ as if it meant $(14a)(14b)$.

14. **The correct answer is (H).** To solve this problem, you need to remember that all four sides of a square have the same length. Because the six squares in the drawing are congruent, all of the sides of all of the squares in the diagram have the same length.

The longer side of the rectangle, which is 9, has been partitioned into three congruent "square sides." The length of each of these sides must be $9 \div 3 = 3$. This tells you that the only thing that you really need to know in order to answer the question is: the length of a side of a square is 3.

The perimeter of a square is the distance around it, and this consists of four sides of length 3. Since $4 \times 3 = 12$, the perimeter is 12.

(F) This answer choice represents half the perimeter. It is the sum of the lengths of two sides, not four.

(G) This answer represents a common error. The number 9 represents the area of a square, not the perimeter.

(J) Choosing this answer would result from misreading the problem and taking 9 to represent the shorter side of the rectangle. In this case, the side of the square would be $4\frac{1}{2}$, and the perimeter would be 18.

(K) This is another case of misreading the problem. This answer represents the perimeter of the entire rectangle, not the perimeter of one of the squares.

15. **The correct answer is (D).** There are two common techniques for simplifying this complex fraction. The first is to find common denominators for the fractions in the numerator and common denominators for the fractions in the denominator and add them. In both the numerator and the denominator, the least common denominator is 8. Therefore:

$$\frac{\frac{3}{8}+\frac{3}{4}}{\frac{1}{8}+\frac{1}{4}} = \frac{\frac{3}{8}+\frac{6}{8}}{\frac{1}{8}+\frac{2}{8}} = \frac{\frac{9}{8}}{\frac{3}{8}} = \frac{9}{8} \div \frac{3}{8} = \frac{9}{8} \times \frac{8}{3} = \frac{9}{3} = 3$$

Another way to simplify the complex fraction is to recognize that the LCD of all the fractions involved is 8. Then multiply all the fractions within the complex fraction by 8:

$$\frac{\frac{3}{8}+\frac{3}{4}}{\frac{1}{8}+\frac{1}{4}} = \frac{8\left(\frac{3}{8}+\frac{3}{4}\right)}{8\left(\frac{1}{8}+\frac{1}{4}\right)} = \frac{3+2(3)}{1+2(1)} = \frac{3+6}{3} = \frac{9}{3} = 3$$

(A) This answer is the result of an illegal division. If you divide the $\frac{3}{8}$ in the numerator by the $\frac{1}{8}$ in the denominator, you get 3. If you then divide the $\frac{3}{4}$ in the numerator by the $\frac{1}{4}$ in the denominator, you also get 3. So $3 + 3 = 6$. However, you cannot divide out terms in a fraction; only factors can be divided.

(B) If you obtained this answer, you didn't add the fractions in the numerator and denominator. You multiplied them.

(C) If you got this answer, you began correctly, but when you obtained $\dfrac{\frac{9}{8}}{\frac{3}{8}}$, you multiplied the two fractions instead of multiplying by the reciprocal.

(E) This answer results from a combination of some of the computational errors above. The fractions in the numerator and denominator were multiplied instead of added, and then they weren't multiplied by the reciprocal in the division step.

16. **The correct answer is (H).** This is a straightforward geometry question. There really are only two facts that you need to know in order to solve the problem. The first is the meaning of the word *trisect*, and the second is the Vertical Angle Theorem. Trisect means just what it sounds like it should mean—to cut into equal thirds. Therefore, $\angle AHB$ has been partitioned into three congruent angles measuring 15° each.

Overall, the measure of this angle must be 3(15°) = 45°.

Because $\angle AHB$ and $\angle CHD$ are vertical angles and therefore have the same measure, the measure of $\angle CHD$ must be 45°.

(F) Several of the angles in the figure have measures of 15°, including $\angle FHG$ and $\angle GHB$. If you read the problem too quickly and answered the wrong question, then you might be led to this answer.

(G) Several of the angles in this figure have measures of 30° as well, including $\angle AHG$ and $\angle FHB$. Again, if you read too quickly and answered the wrong question, you might be led to this answer.

(J) In geometry questions with diagrams, some answer choices are included that are often close enough to the correct answer to make it difficult for you to estimate the answer based on the figure. The answer choice here of 50° is such an answer.

(K) There are two angles in the figure that have measures of 135°, $\angle AHC$ and $\angle BHD$. If you find the measure of the wrong angle, you might be led to this answer.

17. **The correct answer is (B).** This is a multistep problem. First, round the number 3.2782 to the nearest hundredth. Note that the digit in the thousandths place is 8. Therefore, the digit in the hundredths place must be rounded up. Thus, the correct rounding of 3.2782 is 3.28.

To round 7.8452 to the nearest tenth, note that the digit in the hundredths place is 4, so the tenths digit should not be rounded up. The correct rounding of 7.8452 is 7.8.

Thus, $x + y = 3.28 + 7.8 = 11.08$.

(A) If you neglect to "round up" when rounding 3.2782 and therefore obtained 3.27 instead of 3.28, then you would get 3.27 + 7.8 = 11.07 as the answer.

(C) If you mistakenly rounded both numbers to the nearest tenth, this would be your answer,

3.3 + 7.8 = 11.1.

(D) If you mistakenly rounded both numbers to the nearest hundredth, you would get this answer,

3.28 + 7.85 = 11.13.

(E) If you made the mistake of rounding up when you rounded 7.8452, thus obtaining 7.9, you would get this answer,

7.9 + 3.28 = 11.18.

18. **The correct answer is (J).** The measure of the angle that is vertical to the 40° angle is 40°, according to the Vertical Angle Theorem.

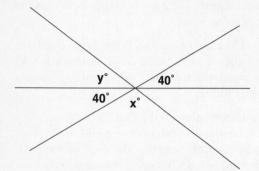

Because the angles labeled $x°$, $y°$, and 40° form a straight line, it must be true that $x + y + 40 = 180$. If you subtract 40 from both sides of this equation, the result is the equation $x + y = 140$.

(F) This answer would be the result if you mistakenly thought that the angles that form a straight line are complementary (add to 90) instead of supplementary (add to 180).

(G) If you concluded that the measures of the angles labeled $x°$, $y°$, and 40° were the same, then $x + y = 80$.

(H) This answer is close enough to the correct answer to make it more difficult for you to estimate the answer based solely on the diagram.

(K) This is another answer close enough to the correct answer to make estimating the answer a bit harder for you.

19. **The correct answer is (A).** In order to solve a quadratic equation, begin by writing it in standard form, $ax^2 + bx + c = 0$. In the case of the given equation, standard form is $y^2 + 3y - 10 = 0$. Next, see if the equation can be factored:

$(y + 5)(y - 2) = 0$

Now, set each factor separately equal to 0:

$y + 5 = 0$ and $y - 2 = 0$

The factor $y + 5 = 0$ means that $y = -5$. The factor $y - 2 = 0$ means that $y = 2$. This quadratic has two solutions, and the one that is given in the multiple-choice answers is –5.

(B) Almost! You made a sign error somewhere toward the end of the problem and determined that $y = -2$ was one answer, instead of $y = 2$.

(C) You made a computational error in solving this problem, eliminating the 5s from both sides of the equation and solving $y^2 + 3y = 0$. The 5s can be subtracted off only if they both have the same sign.

(D) Again, it seems as if you made a sign error somewhere near the end of the problem. The solution is –5, not 5.

(E) This solution results from using the Quadratic Formula to solve the equation $y^2 + 3y - 5 = 0$. But the equation you were given to solve is $y^2 + 3y - 5 = 5$.

20. **The correct answer is (F).** Don't let yourself get confused trying to find the individual values of a, b, c, and d. Given the information in the problem, it is not possible to find the values of these unknowns individually. However, it is possible to find their sum, and that is what you are being asked to do.

The key fact that you need to remember in order to answer this question is that a full circle contains 360°.

Note that the sum $40 + 50 + 60 + 70 = 220$. Therefore, $220 + a + b + c + d$ must be equal to 360:

$220 + a + b + c + d = 360$

Subtract 220: $a + b + c + d = 140$.

(G) This answer, which is close to the correct answer, is placed here to make it more difficult for you to find the answer by estimating the sizes of the angles in the diagram.

(H) This answer is the sum of the four given angles. This would be a likely guess for someone who wasn't certain how to find the answer.

(J) This answer would be obtained if you mistakenly thought that there are 540° in a full circle and, therefore, subtracted the 220° from the 540°. The number of degrees in a full circle is 2 x 180°. If you thought that the number of degrees in a full circle was 3 x 180° = 540°, you would be led to this answer.

(K) This is another error in logic. There are four triangles in the figure, and each has 180°. Thus, the four triangles contain 4 x 180° = 720° in total. Subtracting the 220° from the 720° gives this answer. Note, however, that the number of degrees in the four triangles in the figure has nothing to do with the number of degrees in $a + b + c + d$. Think through the question. Don't be fooled by what appears to be a likely solution.

21. **The correct answer is (D).** Let P represent the amount of money Janet needs to put into her account at the start of the year. Then P must have the property that P + .06P = 4,770. Combining the like terms on the left-hand side gives you a simplified form of the equation that you can solve: 1.06P = 4,770.

Divide both sides by 1.06:

$P = \dfrac{4,770}{1.06} = 4,500$

Therefore, Janet must invest $4,500 at the start of the year to end with $4,770.

(A) This answer is obviously less than it should be to be correct. However, it is the result of the computation 4,770 x .06. If you don't think about the question when solving this problem and simply multiply the two given numbers, you might be led to pick this answer choice.

(B) This answer choice comes about because of a very common error. An easy mistake to make when solving this type of problem is to think that you can take the desired final value and simply decrease it by 6% to find the amount of money to invest. Note that $4,770 decreased by 6% results in the number $4,483.80. However, the 6% represents the amount that the initial investment is to

be increased by, not the amount that the final amount is to be decreased by.

(C) This answer choice is close enough to the correct answer to make it a bit more difficult for you to answer the question by estimation.

(E) Same as answer choice (C). Note that both of these incorrect answers are close to the correct answer.

22. **The correct answer is (J).** Remember that a negative exponent represents the fact that the base should be reciprocated and that, therefore, $8^{-1} = \dfrac{1}{8}$. Thus, $8^{-1}(12x - 24) = \dfrac{1}{8}(12x - 24) = \dfrac{12x - 24}{8}$. Note that each term in this expression is divisible by 4 and that when the 4 is divided out of each term, you obtain $\dfrac{3x - 6}{2}$.

(F) This answer results from the mistake of using 8 in the computation instead of $\dfrac{1}{8}$. Either you ignored the exponent of –1 or weren't certain what it meant.

(G) If you make the mistake of thinking that 8^{-1} means –8, you will get this answer.

(H) This answer results from a division error. Once you obtain the expression $\dfrac{12x - 24}{8}$, if you divide the 24 by the 8, you will get this answer. However, remember that both the 24 and the 12x are being divided by 8 in the expression $\dfrac{12x - 24}{8}$.

(K) This is another illegal division error. This answer results from taking the quotient $\dfrac{12x - 24}{8}$, factoring the 8 as 2 × 4, and dividing the 12 by the 4 and the 24 by the 2. Again, both the 24 and the 12x need to be divided by 8 in the expression $\dfrac{12x - 24}{8}$.

23. **The correct answer is (B).** This is a rather tricky question. On first reading, it seems as if choice I must be true. After all, how can the average be A if none of the numbers are greater than A?

However, if all of the numbers are equal to A, then the average would be A, and none of the numbers would be greater. Therefore, choice I is not necessarily true.

In the same way, choice III is not necessarily true. In fact, the only statement that must be true is II, because there is no way the average can be A if all of the numbers are greater than A.

(A) Choosing this answer is the result of two errors in judgment. The first is that one of the numbers had to be greater than A. Second, you made the error of thinking that II, for some reason, was not necessarily true.

(C) You have already seen that choice I is not necessarily true. However, if you made the error of thinking it was necessarily true and also correctly selected choice II as true, you would be led to this answer.

(D) This is a very common wrong answer, because all of the choices seem as though they could be true.

(E) This would be your choice answer if you correctly identified choice I and choice III as not necessarily true but made an error and also concluded that choice II was not necessarily true.

24. **The correct answer is (G).** There are a variety of ways to determine the value of x, and they all hinge on a knowledge of the properties of parallel lines cut by a transversal. Perhaps the most direct way to find the answer is to realize that $\angle CBA$ and $\angle BCD$ are alternate interior angles and, therefore, must have the same measure. Since the measure of $\angle CBA$ is $90°$, then the measure of $\angle BCD$ is also $90°$.

You also need to note that $\angle ACD$ is vertical to the angle labeled $125°$, which means that $\angle ACD$ has a measure of $125°$ also.

Finally, since the measure of $\angle ACD$ would be the same as the sum of the measures of $\angle ACB$ and $\angle BCD$, you have:

$m\angle ACD = m\angle ACB + m\angle BCD$

$125 = m\angle ACB + 90$

Subtract 90:

$35 = m\angle ACB$

(F) Perhaps you selected this answer because you mistakenly concluded that triangle ABC had to be a 30-60-90 triangle. Another way of coming to this answer, because it is very close to the correct answer, is if you tried to estimate the answer based on the diagram.

(H) This is another answer choice that is close enough to the correct answer and might be chosen by trying to estimate the answer based on the diagram.

(J) This measure is equal to the complement of the correct answer and so could result from a variety of computational errors. It is also the measure of $\angle CAB$, so you might have chosen this answer if you misread the question.

(K) The value of $125 - 55 = 70$, so mistakenly computing that the measure of $\angle BCD$ is 55 would lead to choosing this answer.

25. **The correct answer is (E).** There really isn't any computational work to be done in solving this problem. You simply need to recognize that the equation $3x = -7$ represents a vertical line. Slope is undefined for a vertical line. In essence, a vertical line is of "infinite steepness."

(A) 0 is the slope of a horizontal line, but the line you were given in this problem is vertical.

(B) The equation $x = -\dfrac{7}{3}$ is the equation that you would get if you solved the equation for x. This might be something a person would try if he or she had no idea what else to do, but it does not fit in the context of the problem.

(C) As with answer choice (B), a person might try this answer because it involves the numbers that are in the given equation, but in the context of the problem, this answer does not make sense.

(D) As with answer choice (C), this answer involves the numbers that are contained in the problem but makes no sense in the context of the problem.

26. **The correct answer is (K).** In order to find the area of the rectangle, you need to determine the length and the width of the rectangle. Note first that the length of the rectangle is the distance between the two points (–2, 0) and (5, 0). Because the line connecting these two points is horizontal, the distance is simply the distance between the x-coordinates, which is:

$$5 - (-2) = 5 + 2 = 7$$

In the same way, the width of the rectangle is the distance between the two points (5, 0) and (5, –4). Since the width is vertical, the distance is simply the distance between the y-coordinates, which is:

$$0 - (-4) = 4$$

Therefore, the rectangle is 7 by 4, and the area is $7 \times 4 = 28$.

(F) This represents the sum of the length and the width of the rectangle. In other words, this answer results from adding 7 and 4, instead of multiplying them.

(G) This answer represents the perimeter of the rectangle to the right of the y-axis, with the y-axis serving as the rightmost side. Nice answer—but not what the problem is asking for.

(H) This is the area of the rectangle described in answer choice (G). The problem, however, asks for the area of the entire rectangle.

(J) This is the perimeter of the rectangle in the figure. The problem, however, asks for the area. Remember to answer the question that the problem is asking.

27. **The correct answer is (B).** This is an Order of Operations problem. The numerical expression con-

tains four different arithmetic operations. In order to evaluate the expression correctly, the operations must be performed in the correct order.

The first step is to perform all multiplications and divisions in the order they occur from left to right. This means that the multiplication must be performed first and then the division:

$$9 + 3 \times 12 \div 6 - 2$$

Multiply 3×12:

$3 \times 12 = 36$, resulting in $9 + 36 \div 6 - 2$

Divide 36 by 6:

$36 \div 6$, resulting in $9 + 6 - 2$

To finish up, perform the addition and then the subtraction:

$$9 + 6 - 2$$

Add $9 + 6$, resulting in:

$$15 - 2$$

Subtract $15 - 2$, resulting in 13.

All of the incorrect answer choices result from performing the four operations in various incorrect orders.

(A) In this case, the division is performed first, $12 \div 6 = 2$. If you then subtract, you get $2 - 2 = 0$. Next, multiply and the result is $3 \times 0 = 0$, which leaves you with 9.

(C) Performing the operations in order from right to left yields an answer of 18.

(D) This is likely the most common wrong answer. The answer 22 is the result of performing the operations in order from left to right.

(E) This answer is the result of adding and subtracting first and then multiplying and dividing.

28. **The correct answer is (H).** To solve this problem, you need to remember that the formula for the area of a rectangle is $A = lw$, where l is the length and w is the width.

If the length of the rectangle increases by 10%, it becomes 1.11. If the width of the rectangle decreases by 20%, it becomes $0.8w$. Overall, then, the area of the "new" rectangle is:

$A = (1.1l)(0.8w) = 0.88lw$

Therefore, the new rectangle has an area equal to 88% of the original area; thus, the area has been decreased by:

$100\% - 88\% = 12\%$

(F) This is likely the most common wrong answer and is obtained by making the incorrect assumption that an increase of 10% followed by a decrease of 20% leads to an overall change of $10\% - 20\% = -10\%$—that is, a decrease of 10%.

(G) This answer is midway between the common wrong answer of 10% and the correct answer of 12%. As such, it might be a tempting option to anyone trying to estimate the correct answer.

(J) Read carefully! The problem states that the length increases by 10%. This answer is the result of basing your computation on a length decrease of 10% and a width decrease of 20%.

(K) Again, read carefully! The problem states that the width decreases by 20%. This answer is the result of basing your computation on a length increase of 10% and a width increase of 20%.

29. **The correct answer is (C).** The most straightforward way to handle this problem is to write an algebraic equation that expresses the relationship given in the problem statement. The two appearances of the word *of* indicate multiplication, so the equation would be:

$20\% \times 50\% \times 30a = 21$

Express the percents as decimals:

$0.20 \times 0.50 \times 30a = 21$

Multiply the numbers on the left side:

$0.10 \times 30a = 21$

$3a = 21$

Divide both sides by 3:

$a = 7$

(A) If you mistakenly interpret the word *of* in the problem to represent addition instead of multiplication, you would choose this answer.

(B) This is a common wrong answer. If you interpret "20% of 50%" to mean 70% (that is, if you add instead of multiply), you will get this answer:

$70\% \times 30a = 21$

$21a = 21$

$a = 1$

(D) If you make the same error described in choice (B) and in addition make a decimal point error, you could end up with this answer.

(E) If you got this answer, you did everything correct—except you made a decimal point error when dividing. This has resulted in an answer ten times greater than it should be.

30. **The correct answer is (J).** Side $\overline{XY}$ is also a radius of the circle. Since $\overline{XY}$ has length 8 and the formula for the circumference of a circle is $C = 2\pi r$, the circumference of the full circle is:

$C = 2\pi r = 2\pi(8) = 16\pi$

Remember that a full circle contains 360°. Since arc XY is associated with a central angle of 120°, its length is $\dfrac{120}{360} = \dfrac{1}{3}$ of the circumference of the circle, which is equal to $\dfrac{1}{3}(16\pi) = \dfrac{16\pi}{3}$.

(F) This answer represents the length of side $\overline{XZ}$. The problem does not ask for the length of the side of the triangle, but rather for the length of the arc of the circle.

(G) This is the circumference of the entire circle, instead of the arc.

(H) This is the area of the sector of the circle cut off by the arc XZ, which, once again, is not what you were asked for.

(K) This is equal to half of the length of the arc, an error that could have been made by thinking that a circle contains 180° instead of 360°.

Day 18

Practice Math Test: Questions 31 through 60

Assignment for Today:

- Take a sample of the ACT Assessment Math Test under actual test conditions. For the real test, you will have 60 minutes to complete 60 items. The questions progress in difficulty, so for these 30 questions, set your timer for 30 minutes, but see if you can finish them in less than 30 minutes.

DIRECTIONS: *Solve each problem below and choose the correct answer.*

Be careful not to spend too much time on any one question. Instead, solve as many questions as possible, and then use any remaining time to return to those questions you were unable to answer at first.

You may use a calculator on any problem; however, not every problem requires the use of a calculator.

Note: Unless otherwise indicated, assume all of the following to be true:

- *Diagrams that accompany problems are not necessarily drawn to scale.*

- *All figures lie in a plane.*

- *A line indicates a straight line.*

- *Average refers to arithmetic mean.*

31. For which values of x is the function $f(x) =$ $\dfrac{\sqrt{3x+6}}{x^2+2x-3}$ undefined in the real number system?

    (A) $x = 1$ and $x = -3$

    (B) $x = 1$ and $x \le -2$

    (C) $x = 1$ and $x \le -3$

    (D) $x = 1$ and $x < -2$

    (E) $x < -2$

32. Which of the following represents the equation of a line with an x-intercept of 5 and y-intercept of -10?

    (F) $y = -\dfrac{1}{2}x - 10$

    (G) $y = -2x + 10$

    (H) $y = \dfrac{1}{2}x - 10$

    (J) $y = -2x - 10$

    (K) $y = 2x - 10$

33. If $x^2 - 4 = 45$ and $y - x = 12$, then which of the following represents the possible values of $x + y$?

    (A) -2

    (B) 5

    (C) 26

    (D) 19 and 5

    (E) 26 and -2

34. What are the coordinates of the center of the ellipse given by the equation $\dfrac{(x-2)^2}{16} + \dfrac{(y+9)^2}{25} = 1$?

    (F) $(-2, 9)$

    (G) $(2, -9)$

    (H) $(4, 5)$

    (J) $(-4, -5)$

    (K) $(2, 9)$

35. Which of the following represents the equation of the line that contains the points (2, 5) and (2, –5)?

    (A) $y = 2$

    (B) $x = 2$

    (C) $x + y = 7$

    (D) $x - 2y = -8$

    (E) $x + y = 4$

36. If the area of the triangle below is 24, what is the length of side $\overline{XZ}$?

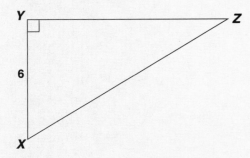

    (F) 4

    (G) 6

    (H) 8

    (J) 10

    (K) 12

37. Which of the answer choices below describes the roots of the quadratic equation $3x^2 - 5x + 3 = 0$?

    (A) Two different rational roots

    (B) Two different irrational real roots

    (C) One double rational root

    (D) One double irrational real root

    (E) Two imaginary complex conjugate roots

38. Which of the following statements is true about the triangle whose vertices are at (4, –4), (3, –1), and (0, 0)?

    (F) The triangle is scalene.

    (G) The triangle is equilateral.

    (H) The triangle is isosceles but not right.

    (J) The triangle is right but not isosceles.

    (K) The triangle is right and isosceles.

39. In the figure below, all intersecting line segments are perpendicular. What is the area of the shaded region?

USE THIS SPACE FOR YOUR FIGURING.

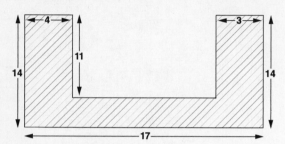

   (A) 84

   (B) 118

   (C) 128

   (D) 139

   (E) 238

40. Which of the following answer choices represents the equation of the line that has an x-intercept of -1 and is perpendicular to the line $8x - 4y = 5$?

   (F) $y = 2x + 2$

   (G) $y = \dfrac{1}{2}x - \dfrac{1}{2}$

   (H) $y = -\dfrac{1}{2}x - 1$

   (J) $y = -\dfrac{1}{2}x + \dfrac{1}{2}$

   (K) $y = -\dfrac{1}{2}x - \dfrac{1}{2}$

41. If $-32 = \left(-\dfrac{1}{2}\right)^{k}$, what is the value of k?

   (A) -16

   (B) -6

   (C) -5

   (D) 5

   (E) 16

42. In triangle XYZ, the value of tan a is the same as the value of _____.

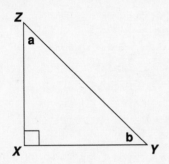

(F) sin b

(G) cos b

(H) tan b

(J) cot b

(K) csc b

43. Which of the following represents the product of $5 + 3i$ and $5 - 3i$?

(A) 10

(B) $-6i$

(C) $6i$

(D) 16

(E) 34

44. Which of the following is the equation for the perpendicular bisector of the segment with endpoints $(4, 6)$ and $(6, 0)$?

(F) $x - 3y = 14$

(G) $x - 3y = 6$

(H) $x - 3y = -4$

(J) $x + 3y = 14$

(K) $x + 3y = 22$

45. What is the common solution of the system of equations

$$y = x^2 + 6$$
$$y = 5x ?$$

   (A) $(1, 5)$

   (B) $(2, 10)$

   (C) $(3, 15)$

   (D) $(2, 10)$ and $(3, 15)$

   (E) $(-2, -10)$ and $(-3, -15)$

USE THIS SPACE FOR YOUR FIGURING.

46. What is the distance between the midpoint of the line segment with endpoints $(10, 4)$ and $(0, 0)$ and the midpoint of the line segment with endpoints $(-6, 10)$ and $(0, 6)$?

   (F) $2\sqrt{29}$

   (G) $2\sqrt{13}$

   (H) $2\sqrt{10}$

   (J) 10

   (K) 12

47. If $\sin \theta = \dfrac{12}{13}$, what is the value of $\sec \theta$?

   (A) $\dfrac{5}{13}$

   (B) $\dfrac{13}{5}$

   (C) $\dfrac{13}{12}$

   (D) $\dfrac{12}{5}$

   (E) $\dfrac{5}{12}$

48. What is the range of the function $f(x) = -x^2 + 2x$, if the domain is all real numbers?

   (F) $\{y \mid y \geq 1\}$

   (G) $\{y \mid y > 1\}$

   (H) $\{y \mid y \leq 1\}$

   (J) $\{y \mid y < 1\}$

   (K) $\{y \mid y \geq -3\}$

49. $5^n + 5^n + 5^n + 5^n + 5^n =$

    (A) 25^n

    (B) 25^{5n}

    (C) 5^{5n}

    (D) 5^{n+1}

    (E) 5^{n+5}

50. Which of the following is equivalent to the expression $\dfrac{\sqrt{9x^2} - \sqrt{9y^2}}{12x - 12y}$? Assume that $x > 0$ and $y > 0$.

    (F) $\dfrac{1}{4}$

    (G) 1

    (H) $\dfrac{x+y}{4}$

    (J) $\dfrac{\sqrt{x^2 - y^2}}{4x - 4y}$

    (K) 0

51. A model rocket is shot straight up in the air from ground level. Its height, h, in feet after t seconds is given by the formula $h = 80t - 16t^2$. In how many seconds will the rocket be 64 feet high?

    (A) 1 second

    (B) 4 seconds

    (C) 5 seconds

    (D) 1 second and 4 seconds

    (E) 1 second and 5 seconds

52. If x is an acute angle, and $4\sin x - 2\sqrt{2} = 0$, what is the measure of x?

    (F) $15°$

    (G) $30°$

    (H) $45°$

    (J) $60°$

    (K) $75°$

USE THIS SPACE FOR YOUR FIGURING.

53. Which of the graphs below correctly represents the solution set of the inequality $|x - 6| \le 4$?

USE THIS SPACE FOR YOUR FIGURING.

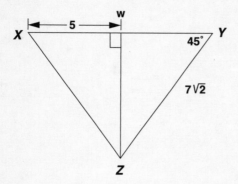

54. What is the area of triangle *XYZ* shown in the figure below?

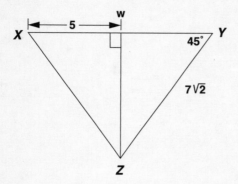

(F) 42

(G) 49

(H) 35

(J) $\dfrac{49\sqrt{2}}{2}$

(K) $42\sqrt{2}$

55. The graph of the equation $(x - 2)^2 + (y + 3)^2 = 20$ represents which of the following?

(A) A straight line with *x*-intercept 2 and *y*-intercept 3

(B) A circle with center at (2, –3) and radius 20

(C) A circle with center at (2, –3) and radius $\sqrt{20}$

(D) A circle with center at (–2, 3) and radius 20

(E) A circle with center at (–2, 3) and radius $\sqrt{20}$

56. In the figure below, if the length of the hypotenuse of triangle ABC is 10, what is the length of altitude AD?

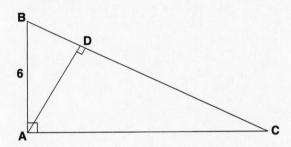

   (F) 5

   (G) $\dfrac{24}{5}$

   (H) 6

   (J) 8

   (K) 10

57. If n is the least of a group of six consecutive even integers, what is the median of the six consecutive even integers?

   (A) n

   (B) $n + 3$

   (C) $n + 4$

   (D) $n + 5$

   (E) $n + 6$

58. A road is inclined at an angle of 15° to the horizontal. Which of the expressions below represents the distance that must be driven along this road in order to be at a height of 50 feet above the horizontal?

   (F) $\dfrac{50}{\sin 15°}$

   (G) $50\sin 15°$

   (H) $50\cos 15°$

   (J) $\dfrac{50}{\cos 15°}$

   (K) $50\cos 15°$

59. In the figure below, the two circles have the same center, O. If $OP = 4$ and $PQ = 2$, what is the ratio of the area of the larger circle to the area of the smaller circle?

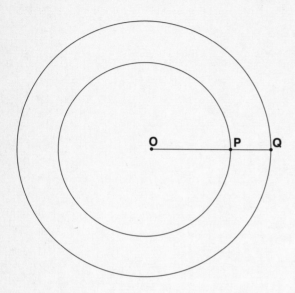

(A) $\dfrac{3}{2}$

(B) $\dfrac{4}{1}$

(C) $\dfrac{9}{4}$

(D) 20π

(E) $\dfrac{5}{4}$

60. The annual profit p that the Mega Computer Corporation makes from the sale of x computers is given by the formula $p = -x^2 + 400x + 5{,}000$. What is the maximum profit that Mega can make in a year from the sale of computers?

(F) $5,000

(G) $20,000

(H) $45,000

(J) $125,000

(K) $200,000

QUICK ANSWER GUIDE: QUESTIONS 31 THROUGH 60

31. D
32. K
33. E
34. G
35. B
36. J
37. E
38. H
39. C
40. K
41. C
42. J
43. E
44. H
45. D
46. J
47. B
48. H
49. D
50. F
51. D
52. H
53. A
54. F
55. C
56. G
57. D
58. F
59. C
60. H

For explanation to these problems, see Day 19.

Math Test: Questions 31 through 60
Explanations and Answers

Assignment for Today:

- Review the explanations for the second 30 math problems that you solved. See which answer is correct and learn what makes the other choices incorrect.

31. **The correct answer is (D).** There are two situations that can lead to undefined values for this function. First, any values that would lead to a denominator of 0 must be excluded, since division by 0 is undefined. In order to determine the values for which the denominator of the function is 0, you need to solve the quadratic equation $x^2 + 2x - 3 = 0$.

Factor the left-hand side:

$(x - 1)(x + 3) = 0$

Set each factor equal to 0:

$x - 1 = 0 \qquad x + 3 = 0$

Solve the resulting equations:

$x = 1 \qquad x = -3$

Therefore, the values of 1 and –3 must be excluded.

In addition, square roots of negative numbers are undefined in the real number system, so any numbers for which $3x + 6 < 0$ must also be excluded.

Subtract 6 from both sides:

$3x + 6 < 0$

$3x < -6$

Divide both sides by 3:

$x < -2$

Therefore, any numbers that are *less than* –2 must also be excluded.

Note that the number –3 is included in the numbers that are less than –2, so you can summarize all of the excluded values by simply saying that $x = 1$ and any value of $x < -2$ must be excluded.

(A) This answer represents the values that must be excluded from the denominator of the function, but it does not include the values that must be excluded from the numerator of the function.

(B) This answer is almost right, but note that it indicates that $x = -2$ should be excluded. The value $x = -2$ leads to a numerator of 0 and, therefore, an overall function value of 0.

(C) You might have selected this answer if you made the mistake of thinking that $x < -2$ and $x \leq -3$ represent the same set of numbers. They do not. For example, for the above function, you must exclude the value $x = -2\frac{1}{2}$, which *is* in the set $x < -2$ but is not in the set $x \leq -3$.

(E) This represents the set of excluded values for the numerator but doesn't include $x = 1$, which must be excluded from the denominator.

32. **The correct answer is (K).** The first step in determining the equation of a line is to find its slope.

That the x-intercept of the line is 5 tells you that the line contains the point $(5, 0)$. That the y-intercept of the line is -10 tells you that the line contains the point $(0, -10)$. Therefore, the slope is:

$$m = \frac{y_2 - y_1}{x_2 - x_1} = \frac{0 - (-10)}{5 - 0} = \frac{10}{5} = 2$$

Because you already know that the y-intercept of the line is $(0, -10)$, it will be easiest to use the slope-intercept form to express the equation of the line. The slope-intercept form is $y = mx + b$, where m is the slope and b is the y-intercept. Therefore, the equation of the line is $y = 2x - 10$.

(F) This answer results from two errors—using the incorrect formula for the slope (the reciprocal of the formula) and making a sign error along the way.

(G) To choose this answer, the signs of both of the terms on the right-hand side of the equation have to be reversed. Always be careful to compute correctly and to substitute values correctly.

(H) If you got this answer, you probably made the mistake of using the reciprocal of the slope formula to compute the slope.

(J) A sign error was made during the computation of the slope of the line. Remember that the order in which the y-coordinates are subtracted and the order in which the x-coordinates are subtracted must be the same.

33. **The correct answer is (E).** Begin by noting that the equation $x^2 - 4 = 45$ contains only one unknown and can, therefore, be solved for x.

Add 4 to both sides:

$x^2 - 4 = 45$

$x^2 = 49$

Take the square root of both sides:

$x = \pm 7$

Therefore, x has two different values. If $x = 7$, then the equation $y - x = 12$ can be solved for y.

Substitute $x = 7$:

$y - x = 12$

$y - 7 = 12$

Add 7 to both sides:

$y = 19$

In this case, the value of $x + y = 7 + 19 = 26$.

However, if $x = -7$, you get another solution.

Substitute $x = -7$:

$y - x = 12$

$y - (-7) = 12$

$y + 7 = 12$

Subtract 7 from both sides:

$y = 5$

In this case, $x + y = -7 + 5 = -2$.

(A) This is one of the possible values for $x + y$, but as you have just seen, there are *two* possible solutions.

(B) This is one of the possible values for y, but the problem asks for the value of $x + y$.

(C) This is one of the possible values for $x + y$, but as you have seen, there are *two* possible solutions.

(D) These are the two possible values for y, but the problem asks for the values of $x + y$.

34. **The correct answer is (G).** The general formula for the equation of an ellipse is:

$$\frac{(x-h)^2}{a^2} + \frac{(y-k)^2}{b^2} = 1$$

In this formula, the center of the ellipse is given by (h, k).

If you rewrite the equation that you are given in the question as: $\dfrac{(x-2)^2}{16} + \dfrac{(y-(-9))^2}{25} = 1$

you can see that the coordinates of the center are $(2, -9)$.

(F) This would be the answer you would obtain if you got the signs of the two coordinates "backward."

(H) Note that 4 is the value of a, and 5 is the value of b. However, these numbers are related to the lengths of the axes of the ellipse and have nothing to do with the location of the center.

(J) This result is similar to the answer to choice (H), but again the numbers 4 and 5 have nothing to do with the location of the center.

(K) Almost! If you got this answer, you made an error on the sign of the y-coordinate of the center.

35. **The correct answer is (B).** Note that the x–coordinates of the two given points are the same. This means that the line through the two points must be vertical. The equation for a vertical line has the form $x = a$, where a is the x-intercept of the line. Since the x-intercept is 2, the correct equation is $x = 2$.

(A) If you selected this answer, you have the right idea, but the graph of $y = 2$ is horizontal, not vertical.

(C) This answer is tempting because it is satisfied by the point $(2, 5)$; however, it is not satisfied by $(2, -5)$ and, therefore, cannot be correct.

(D) This solution is the result of making a sign error while attempting to compute the slope of the line. If you dropped one of the negative signs

in the denominator, you would obtain a slope of $\dfrac{10}{4} = \dfrac{5}{2}$, which would lead to this answer choice. But you *shouldn't* be trying to find the slope of this line in the first place, because it is a vertical line, which, therefore, has no slope.

(E) This equation is thrown in for a likely looking guess, because both points and the equation itself contain the number 2.

36. **The correct answer is (J).** To begin, recall that the formula for the area of a rectangle is $A = \dfrac{1}{2}bh$. Now, in a right triangle, one of the legs can be considered the base, and the other leg can be taken as the height. That is, in order to find the area of this triangle, you can take $\overline{YX}$ and $\overline{YZ}$ as the base and the height. If you let h stand for the length of $\overline{YZ}$, then you have $A = \dfrac{1}{2}bh$.

Substitute:

$24 = \dfrac{1}{2}(6)h$, or $24 = 3h$

Divide both sides by 3:

$8 = h$

Therefore, the length of $\overline{YZ}$ is 8.

The triangle that you are given, then, is a right triangle with legs of 6 and 8. You can use the Pythagorean Theorem to compute the length of the hypotenuse, but it is easier if you just recognize that this triangle has sides corresponding to the common Pythagorean Triple 6-8-10. The length of the missing side is 10.

(F) This answer results from taking the area of 24 and dividing it by the length of the given side: $24 \div 6 = 4$. If you did this, you made two mistakes. First, the area of a triangle is $\dfrac{1}{2}bh$, not bh. Second, even after making this mistake, the length 4 would represent the length of side $\overline{YZ}$, not the length of side $\overline{XZ}$.

(G) The length 6 is the length of side $\overline{XY}$. If, for some reason, you guessed that $\overline{XZ}$ had the same length as $\overline{YX}$, this would be the answer.

(H) If you selected this answer, you probably started the problem correctly and found the length of side YZ. However, the problem wanted the length of side XZ.

(K) This answer is close to the correct answer and is placed here to make it more difficult for you to guess the missing length based on the figure.

37. **The correct answer is (E).** The quickest way to determine the nature of the roots of a quadratic equation is to compute the discriminant $b^2 - 4ac$. In the given equation, $a = 3$, $b = -5$, and $c = 3$. Therefore:

$$b^2 - 4ac = (-5)^2 - 4(3)(3) = 25 - 36 = -9$$

Since the value of the discriminant is negative, the two roots are imaginary complex conjugates.

(A) The roots of a quadratic equation are rational if, and only if, the discriminant is a perfect square.

(B) The roots of a quadratic equation are real and irrational if, and only if, the discriminant is positive and not a perfect square.

(C) The only way for a quadratic equation to have a double root is if the discriminant is 0.

(D) The only way for a quadratic equation to have a double root is if the discriminant is 0.

38. **The correct answer is (H).** The first step in solving this problem is to use the distance formula to find the lengths of the sides. Recall that the distance formula for the distance between two points is:

$$d = \sqrt{(x_2 - x_1)^2 + (y_2 - y_1)^2}$$

Thus, for the points $(4, -4)$ and $(3, -1)$:

$$d = \sqrt{(4-3)^2 + (-4-(-1))^2} = \sqrt{1^2 + (-3)^2} = \sqrt{1+9} = \sqrt{10}$$

For the points $(4, -4)$ and $(0, 0)$:

$$d = \sqrt{(4-0)^2 + (-4-0)^2} = \sqrt{4^2 + (-4)^2} = \sqrt{16+16}$$
$$= \sqrt{32} = 4\sqrt{2}$$

For the points $(3, -1)$ and $(0, 0)$:

$$d = \sqrt{(3-0)^2 + (-1-0)^2} = \sqrt{3^2 + (-1)^2} = \sqrt{9+1} = \sqrt{10}$$

Therefore, the lengths of the sides of the triangle are $\sqrt{10}$, $\sqrt{10}$, and $4\sqrt{2}$. Since the lengths of two sides are the same, the triangle is isosceles.

It is easy to see that the triangle is not right, because if it were, the triangle would have to be a 45-45-90 triangle. In such a triangle, the length of a leg times $\sqrt{2}$ is equal to the length of the hypotenuse. Since $\sqrt{10} \times \sqrt{2} \leq 4\sqrt{2}$, the triangle is not right.

(F) The likely way to have obtained this answer was to have made a mistake in using the distance formula so that you did not determine that two sides were of the same length.

(G) This answer results from making a mistake using the distance formula and, therefore, determining that all three sides are the same length.

(J) This answer is the result of having made two mistakes. The first was an error in using the distance formula and, therefore, finding that all three sides were of different lengths. The second error was in applying the Pythagorean Theorem and computing that the triangle is right.

(K) If you got this answer, you correctly computed that the triangle was isosceles but made an error working with the Pythagorean Theorem and, thus, determined that the triangle was also a right triangle.

39. **The correct answer is (C).** While there are several ways to find the area of the shaded region, probably the quickest way is to consider the shaded area as what remains when a rectangular shape is cut out of a larger rectangle:

The area of the entire figure without the "cut-out" is $14 \times 17 = 238$.

The "cut-out" rectangle has a length of 11.

The width is equal to $17 - 4 - 3 = 10$.

Thus, the area of the "cut-out" rectangle is $11 \times 10 = 110$.

The area of the shaded region is $238 - 110 = 128$.

Note that the answer could also be found by partitioning the shaded region into three smaller rectangles, as shown in the figure below, and summing the area of each. The result is also 128.

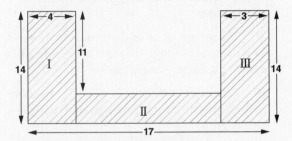

(A) If you chose this answer, you needed to read the problem more carefully. This is the *perimeter* of the shaded region, whereas you were asked for the area.

(B) This answer is the result of finding the area by the second method described above but mistakenly using the value of 3 for the width of both the left and the right rectangles. Note that the rectangle on the left has a width of 4.

(D) If you got this answer, you made a mistake similar to the one made in choice (B), only this time, you used 4 as the width of both the left and right rectangles. The width of the rectangle on the right is 3!

(E) This is the area of the *entire* 14×17 rectangle, without taking the "cut-out" portion into account.

40. **The correct answer is (K).** The first step in solving this problem is to find the slope of the line $8x - 4y = 5$. The easiest way to do this is to rewrite the equation in the slope-intercept form, $y = mx + b$. In this form, the value of m represents the slope of the line:

$$8x - 4y = 5$$

Subtract $8x$ from both sides:

$$-4y = -8x + 5$$

Divide both sides by –4:

$$y = 2x - \frac{5}{4}$$

Therefore, the slope of the given line is 2. Since perpendicular lines have slopes that are negative reciprocals of each other, the slope of the line that you are looking for is $-\frac{1}{2}$.

Expressing the equation you are looking for in slope-intercept form gives you the equation $y = -\frac{1}{2}x + b$.

Now, you are told that the x-intercept of this line is –1, which means the line contains the point $(-1, 0)$. Substituting $(-1, 0)$ into $y = -\frac{1}{2}x + b$ results in:

$$0 = -\frac{1}{2}(-1) + b \text{ or } 0 = \frac{1}{2} + b$$

This means that b must equal $-\frac{1}{2}$. Substituting this value for b in the equation $y = -\frac{1}{2}x + b$ gives you the correct equation $y = -\frac{1}{2}x - \frac{1}{2}$.

(F) If you selected this answer, you read the problem too quickly and found the slope of the line *parallel* to $8x - 4y = 5$, instead of perpendicular to it.

(G) This is the answer that results by mistakenly using the *reciprocal* as the slope of the perpendicular line, instead of the *negative reciprocal*.

(H) If you obtained this answer, you read the problem too quickly and found the equation of the line that has a y-intercept of –1 instead of an x-intercept of –1.

(J) This is the equation that will result if you mistakenly work with an x-intercept of 1 instead of –1.

41. **The correct answer is (C).** This problem is asking you to determine the power that $-\frac{1}{2}$ must be raised to in order to obtain –32. To begin, note that $(-2)^5 = -32$, so the answer to the problem must involve the number 5. However, the 2 in the number $\frac{1}{2}$ is in the denominator, and you must "move" it to the numerator. Recall that a negative exponent reciprocates the base. Therefore, $\left(-\frac{1}{2}\right)^{-5} = -32$.

(A) This answer is incorrect because an exponent cannot be evaluated by multiplying the exponent by the base! For example, 2^{16} is *not* 32.

(B) If you made the mistake of thinking that $2^6 = 32$, then you would have selected this answer. Note, however, that $2^6 = 64$, not 32.

(D) $(-2)^5 = -32$, but you need to raise the $-\frac{1}{2}$ to the –5 power in order to reciprocate it as well.

(E) If you selected this choice, you made the same mistake as discussed in choice (A). However, you made a sign error as well.

42. **The correct answer is (J).** To solve this problem, you need to remember that the tangent of an angle is equal to the ratio of the side opposite the angle to the side adjacent to the angle.

Therefore, for the given triangle, $\tan a = \frac{XY}{XZ}$.

The cotangent of an angle is the ratio of the side adjacent to the angle to the side opposite the angle. Again, for the given triangle, $\cot b = \frac{XY}{XZ}$. Therefore, $\tan a = \cot b$.

You could get the answer to this problem more easily by noting that tangent and cotangent are "co-functions," which means that the tangent of

one of the acute angles in a right triangle is equal to the cotangent of the other acute angle.

(F) The sine of an angle is equal to the ratio of the side opposite the angle to the hypotenuse—that is, $\sin b = \frac{XZ}{YZ}$. If you selected this answer (or any of the other incorrect answers), be certain to review the definitions of the trigonometric functions.

(G) The cosine of an angle is equal to the ratio of the side adjacent to the angle to the hypotenuse—that is, $\cos b = \frac{XY}{YZ}$.

(H) The tangent of an angle is equal to the ratio of the side opposite to the angle to the side adjacent to the angle—that is, $\tan b = \frac{XZ}{XY}$.

(K) The cosecant of an angle is equal to the ratio of the hypotenuse to the side opposite the angle—that is, $\csc b = \frac{YZ}{XY}$.

43. **The correct answer is (E).** The first step in solving this problem is to correctly identify the operation that you are being asked to perform on the two quantities. The word *product* refers to multiplication. Therefore, you need to perform the multiplication $(5 + 3i)(5 - 3i)$. This multiplication can be performed the way any other binomial multiplication is performed—by using the FOIL method.

$(5 + 3i)(5 - 3i) =$

$(5)(5) - 15i + 15i - (3i)(3i) =$

$25 - 9i^2 = 25 - 9(-1) = 25 + 9 = 34$

(A) If you added the two expressions instead of multiplied them, you would have gotten this answer. Remember that *product* refers to multiplication. If the intention were to have you add, you would have been asked for the sum.

(B) If you subtracted $5 + 3i$ from $5 - 3i$, you would get this answer. Remember that *product* refers to multiplication. If the intention was to have you subtract, you would have been asked for the difference.

(C) This is the answer you would have obtained by subtracting $5 - 3i$ from $5 + 3i$. Once again, remember that *product* refers to multiplication. If the intention were to have you subtract, you would have been asked for the difference.

(D) This answer results from making a sign error while multiplying. From the point where you had $25 - 9i^2$, you likely missed a minus sign and computed $25 - 9 = 16$.

44. **The correct answer is (H).** The perpendicular bisector of a line segment is the line that is perpendicular to the line segment and goes through the midpoint of the line segment.

The midpoint of the line segment through $(4, 6)$ and $(6, 0)$ is $\left(\dfrac{4+6}{2}, \dfrac{6+0}{2} \right) = (5, 3)$. In order to find the equation of the line through $(5, 3)$, which is perpendicular to the given line segment, you need to find the slope of the line segment.

The slope is $m = \dfrac{6-0}{4-6} = \dfrac{6}{-2} = -3$.

The slope of the perpendicular line is given by the negative reciprocal of -3, which is $\dfrac{1}{3}$.

To finish, you need the equation of the line through $(5, 3)$ with slope $\dfrac{1}{3}$. Using the point-slope form, compute:

$y - 3 = \dfrac{1}{3}(x - 5)$

Multiply both sides by 3:

$3y - 9 = x - 5$

Write in standard form:

$x - 3y = -4$

(F) If you got this answer, you correctly found the slope of the perpendicular bisector but then found the equation through $(4, 6)$, instead of through $(5, 3)$.

(G) If you got this answer, you correctly found the slope of the perpendicular bisector but then found the equation through $(6, 0)$, instead of through $(5, 3)$.

(J) This answer is the result of working with a slope that is the reciprocal, instead of the *negative reciprocal*, of -3.

(K) This answer is the result of two errors: first, working with a slope that is the reciprocal, instead of the *negative reciprocal*, of -3; and second, finding the equation through $(4, 6)$, instead of through $(5, 3)$.

45. **The correct answer is (D).** The easiest way to solve this system of equations is to use the substitution method. Since the second equation tells you that $y = 5x$, you can substitute $5x$ for y in the first equation. This will give you a quadratic equation that you can then solve for x:

$5x = x^2 + 6$

Write in standard form:

$x^2 - 5x + 6 = 0$

Factor the left-hand side:

$(x - 2)(x - 3) = 0$

Set the factors equal to 0:

$x - 2 = 0, \ x - 3 = 0$

Solve the equations:

$x = 2, x = 3$

Now, if $x = 2$, $y = 5(2) = 10$, so $(2, 10)$ is a solution. Also, if $x = 3$, $y = 5(3) = 15$, so $(3, 15)$ is a solution.

Therefore, there are two common solutions to the given system.

(A) This solution is tempting because it clearly solves the second equation, but if you check, you will see that it does not solve the first.

(B) This is another tempting solution. This ordered pair solves both equations, but it offers only one of the two solutions. Be careful if you try to solve this problem by testing the answer choices.

Because one of the equations is quadratic, there is the possibility of two solutions!

(C) This solution has the same flaw as answer choice (B). This is the other of the two solutions.

(E) If you commit a sign error when factoring or solving the quadratic equation, you could end up with these ordered pairs.

46. **The correct answer is (J).** This problem is asking you to find the distance between the midpoints of two line segments. In order to solve this problem, then, you need to know two things: the midpoint formula and the distance formula.

First, you need to remember that to find the coordinates of the midpoint of a line segment, you have to average the x-coordinates of the endpoints and the y-coordinates of the endpoints. In other words, the midpoint of the line segment with endpoints (x_1, y_1) and (x_2, y_2) is $\left(\dfrac{x_1 + x_2}{2}, \dfrac{y_1 + y_2}{2} \right)$.

Therefore, in the case of the endpoints $(10, 4)$ and $(0, 0)$, the midpoint is $\left(\dfrac{10+0}{2}, \dfrac{4+0}{2} \right)$, or $(5, 2)$.

In the same way, for the endpoints $(-6, 10)$ and $(0, 6)$, the midpoint is $\left(\dfrac{-6+0}{2}, \dfrac{10+6}{2} \right)$, or $(-3, 8)$.

Now, you need to find the distance between the two points $(5, 2)$ and $(-3, 8)$. The distance between the two points (x_1, y_1) and (x_2, y_2) is given by the formula:

$$d = \sqrt{(x_2 - x_1)^2 + (y_2 - y_1)^2}$$

For the two points you have:

$$d = \sqrt{(5 - (-3))^2 + (2 - 8)^2} = \sqrt{8^2 + (-6)^2} =$$
$$\sqrt{64 + 36} = \sqrt{100} = 10$$

(F) This answer results from a misreading of the problem. It is the distance between the two points $(10, 4)$ and $(0, 0)$. You want the distance between the midpoints of the line segments.

(G) This is another misreading. This is the distance between the two endpoints $(-6, 10)$ and $(0, 6)$.

(H) This answer results from a sign error in the use of the distance formula. Note that in the solution above when using the distance formula, you needed to compute $5 - (-3) = 5 + 3 = 8$. If you made a sign error and concluded that $5 - (-3) = 2$, you would have come up with this answer.

(K) This answer represents a number close to the correct answer and is designed to make it tougher for you to guess the right answer through estimation.

47. **The correct answer is (B).** This is a problem for which drawing a figure will help you. Begin by drawing a picture of a triangle with $\sin \theta = \dfrac{12}{13}$. Since the sine of an angle is the ratio of the side opposite the angle to the hypotenuse, your triangle should look like the one drawn here.

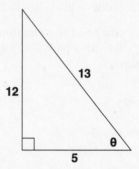

Note that the third side must be of length 5 according to the Pythagorean Theorem.

Now, the secant of an angle is the ratio of the hypotenuse to the adjacent side, so $\sec \theta = \dfrac{13}{5}$.

If you selected any one of the wrong answers for this problem, make certain to review the definitions of the trigonometric functions.

(A) In the triangle shown above, $\frac{5}{13}$ is the ratio of the adjacent side to the hypotenuse, which is equal to the cos θ.

(C) In the triangle shown above, $\frac{13}{12}$ is the ratio of the hypotenuse to the opposite side, which is equal to the csc θ.

(D) In the triangle shown above, $\frac{12}{5}$ is the ratio of the opposite side to the adjacent side, which is equal to the tan θ.

(E) In the triangle shown above, $\frac{5}{12}$ is the ratio of the adjacent side to the opposite side, which is equal to the cos θ.

48. **The correct answer is (H).** The graph of the given function is a parabola that opens down. The first step in determining the range is to find the maximum point of the parabola. The range then is all values of y less than or equal to the y-coordinate of the maximum point.

The x-coordinate of the maximum point is given by $x = \frac{-b}{2a} = \frac{-2}{2(-1)} = \frac{-2}{-2} = 1$.

The y-coordinate, then, is $f(1) = -(1)^2 + 2(1) = -1 + 2 = 1$.

This tells us that the greatest value the function can have is 1 and that anything less than 1 is also possible. Therefore, the range is $\left\{y \mid y \le 1\right\}$.

(F) This answer is likely the result of finding the correct extreme point but concluding that the parabola "opens up," instead of "opens down." In this case, (1, 1) would be the minimum point, and any value of y that is greater than 1 would be possible.

(G) This answer results from the same mistake as in choice (F), along with the additional error of concluding that the extreme point itself is not a part of the range.

(J) This answer is almost correct, but it neglects to include the extreme point itself as a part of the range.

(K) If you selected this answer choice, you may have made a sign error when you computed $f(1)$,

perhaps computing $-1 - 2 = -3$ instead of $-1 + 2 = 1$. Be sure to carefully keep track of signs when making variable substitutions.

49. **The correct answer is (D).** This problem is asking you to add together five terms of 5^n. To begin, when you add up the five terms, you get 5×5^n. This expression can be further simplified by using the Multiplication Property of Exponents: In general, $x^a \times x^b = x^{a+b}$. Rewriting 5 as 5^1, you can use this property to write:

$5 \times 5^n = 5^1 \times 5^n = 5^{n+1}$

All of the incorrect answers result from combining the five terms in incorrect ways.

(A) This particular answer choice is obtained by adding the bases of the five terms and retaining the common exponent. This, however, is not the way to add these terms. As discussed above, the sum of five terms of 5^n is actually 5×5^n.

(B) This answer results from adding the bases and adding the exponents of the five numbers. Again, this is not how terms with exponents are combined.

(C) To choose this answer, you added the exponents but kept the base the same.

(E) In this answer, the base has been left the same, and somehow the five exponents of n have been combined to yield an overall exponent of $n + 5$.

50. **The correct answer is (F).** Since you are told that $x > 0$ and $y > 0$, you can conclude that $\sqrt{9x^2} = 3x$, and $\sqrt{9y^2} = 3y$.

Therefore:

$$\frac{\sqrt{9x^2} - \sqrt{9y^2}}{12x - 12y} = \frac{3x - 3y}{12x - 12y}$$

Next, factor the numerator and denominator and divide out the $x - y$:

$$\frac{3x - 3y}{12x - 12y} = \frac{3(x - y)}{12(x - y)} = \frac{3}{12} = \frac{1}{4}$$

All of the common incorrect answers to this problem are the result of incorrect factoring or incorrect division.

(G) To reach this answer, you would have made it correctly as far as the expression $\frac{3x-3y}{12x-12y}$. You then mistakenly concluded that $3x - 3y = x - y$ because the 3s "subtract out" and that $12x - 12y = x - y$ because the 12s "subtract out." That results in $\frac{x-y}{x-y}=1$.

(H) The error here was forgetting to find the square roots of the variables when computing $\sqrt{9x^2} - \sqrt{9y^2}$. If you incorrectly computed that $\sqrt{9x^2} - \sqrt{9y^2} = 3x^2 - 3y^2 = 3(x-y)(x+y)$, you would get as your answer $\frac{3(x-y)(x+y)}{12(x-y)} = \frac{x+y}{4}$.

(J) This answer is the result of thinking that the difference of two square roots is equal to the square root of the differences. If you mistakenly concluded that

$$\sqrt{9x^2} - \sqrt{9y^2} =$$
$$\sqrt{9x^2 - 9y^2} = \sqrt{9(x^2 - y^2)} = 3\sqrt{x^2 - y^2}$$

you would get as your answer

$$\frac{3\sqrt{x^2 - y^2}}{12(x-y)} = \frac{\sqrt{x^2 - y^2}}{4(x-y)} = \frac{\sqrt{x^2 - y^2}}{4x - 4y}$$

(K) This answer is the result of another incorrect division. If you took $\frac{3x-3y}{12x-12y}$ and divided the $12x$ by the $3x$ and the $12y$ by the $3y$, you would get $\frac{3x-3y}{12x-12y} = \frac{1-1}{4-4}$. While this expression evaluates to $\frac{0}{0}$, which is undefined, in a rush you might pick 0 as the answer.

51. **The correct answer is (D).** The problem is asking for the value of t when h is equal to 64. Therefore, you need to solve the equation $64 = 80t - 16t^2$.

This equation is quadratic in the variable t, and to solve it, you must begin by writing it in the standard form $ax^2 + bx + c = 0$. In this case, the standard form is $16t^2 - 80t + 64 = 0$.

Solving the equation will become easier if you notice that all terms can be divided by 16, leaving you with the equation:

$$t^2 - 5t + 4 = 0$$

Factor the left-hand side:

$$(t - 4)(t - 1) = 0$$

Set each factor equal to 0:

$$t - 4 = 0, \ t - 1 = 0$$

Solve the equations:

$$t = 1, 4$$

Therefore, the rocket is at a height of 64 feet after 1 second and again after 4 seconds. It reaches a height of 64 feet after one second on its way up and again, after 4 seconds, on its way down.

(A) Selecting this answer would be a very common error since $t = 1$ *does* solve the equation. However, the equation is a quadratic, and quadratics typically have two solutions. If you got this answer by substituting the answer choices into the equation, instead of solving the equation, you should remember that when substituting into a quadratic, there might be two different solutions.

(B) The value $t = 4$ is the other solution to the equation. Again, because quadratics typically have two solutions, you must be careful when substituting into a quadratic.

(C) This answer would possibly be the result of incorrectly factoring the equation.

(E) This incorrect answer could also result from incorrectly factoring the equation.

52. **The correct answer is (H).** In order to solve this trigonometric equation, begin by solving for $\sin x$:

$$4\sin x - 2\sqrt{2} = 0$$

Add $2\sqrt{2}$ to both sides:

$4\sin x = 2\sqrt{2}$

Divide both sides by 4:

$\sin x = \dfrac{2\sqrt{2}}{4} = \dfrac{\sqrt{2}}{2}$

There are an infinite number of angles x for which $\sin x = \dfrac{\sqrt{2}}{2}$. However, only one of them is in the first quadrant, and that is 45°.

It is helpful for the test to memorize the values of all the trigonometric functions for angles of 0°, 30°, 45°, 60°, and 90°.

(F) If you have a scientific calculator, you can confirm that the value of sin 15° is about .26. This value does not solve the equation.

(G) The value of sin 30° is $\dfrac{1}{2}$. This is one of the fundamental trigonometric values that should be memorized. However, it does not solve the given equation.

(J) The value of sin 60° is $\dfrac{\sqrt{3}}{2}$. This is another of the fundamental trigonometric values that you should know. However, it does not solve the given equation.

(K) If you have a scientific calculator, you can confirm that the value of sin 75° is about .97, a value that does not solve the equation.

53. **The correct answer is (A).** In order to solve an absolute value inequality, you must remove the absolute value signs from the inequality. Doing this results in two inequalities, and the solution set of the original inequality is the intersection of the two inequalities.

The first inequality is:

$x - 6 \le 4$

Add 6 to both sides:

$x \le 10$

The second inequality is:

$-(x - 6) \le 4$

Multiply both sides by −1 and remember to flip the inequality sign:

$x - 6 \ge -4$

Add 6 to both sides:

$x \ge 2$

The common solution to these two inequalities is $2 \le x \le 10$.

On the number line, then, shade the region between 2 and 10, and put solid dots above the 2 and the 10 to represent that these numbers are also part of the solution set.

(B) This is the solution to the inequality $|x - 6| < 4$. Remember that if the inequality contains a "≤" sign, the endpoints are included and must be shaded on the number line.

(C) This graph contains the correct endpoints but is shaded "in the wrong direction." This likely results from flipping the inequality signs at the wrong time or just misreading them.

(D) This answer is the result of making a sign error when solving the inequality $-(x - 6) \le 4$ and ending up with −2 on the right instead of 2.

(E) This graph is the result of making both the error described in choice (C), shading in the wrong direction, and in choice (D), making a sign error.

54. **The correct answer is (F).** This question is not as difficult so it might initially appear. Begin by noting that triangle WYZ is an isosceles right triangle.

You are told that the length of the hypotenuse is $7\sqrt{2}$. Therefore, by the properties of the 45-45-90 triangle, the other two sides are of length $\dfrac{7\sqrt{2}}{\sqrt{2}} = 7$.

You now know that the length of $\overline{WZ}$, which is an altitude of the triangle, is 7 and that the length of the associated base is $XW + WY = 5 + 7 = 12$.

Therefore, the area of the triangle is:

$$A = \frac{1}{2}bh = \frac{1}{2}(12)(7) = 42$$

(G) This answer is the result of mistakenly concluding that the base and the height of the triangle are both $7\sqrt{2}$. The area, then, is $A = \frac{1}{2}bh = \frac{1}{2}(7\sqrt{2})(7\sqrt{2}) = 49$.

(H) This is the result of concluding that since $\overline{XW}$ is of length 5, the length of the entire base of the triangle is 10. The area is then $A = \frac{1}{2}bh = \frac{1}{2}(10)(7) = 35$.

(J) This answer is the result of having mistakenly concluded that the base of the triangle is $7\sqrt{2}$, so that the area is $A = \frac{1}{2}bh = \frac{1}{2}(7\sqrt{2})(7) = \frac{49\sqrt{2}}{2}$.

(K) If you got this answer, you correctly computed the length of the base of the triangle as 12 but incorrectly computed the height of the triangle to be $7\sqrt{2}$, leading to an area of $A = \frac{1}{2}bh = \frac{1}{2}(7\sqrt{2})(12) = 42\sqrt{2}$.

55. **The correct answer is (C).** The standard form for the equation of a circle with center (h, k) and radius r is given by the equation $(x - h)^2 + (y - k)^2 = r^2$.

The equation that you are given can be rewritten as $(x - 2)^2 + (y - (-3))^2 = \left(\sqrt{20}\right)^2$. Therefore, the center of the circle is at $(2, -3)$, and the radius is $\sqrt{20}$.

(A) The equation will represent a straight line only if *neither* of the variables is squared.

(B) This answer correctly identifies the equation as representing a circle and has the correct center. However, the radius is not 20, it is $\sqrt{20}$.

(D) This answer correctly identifies the equation as a circle but has the wrong radius and the wrong center.

(E) This time the radius is correct, but the center is incorrect.

56. **The correct answer is (G).** This is a rather tricky geometry problem, because it is an area problem that doesn't really seem like an area problem. In order to find the answer, you need to find the area of the triangle two different ways.

To begin, note that triangle ABC is a right triangle. You are given that the length of one leg is 6 and that the hypotenuse is 10. According to the Pythagorean Theorem, then, the other leg is 8.

Using the two legs of the triangle as the height and base, you can find the area of the triangle:

$$A = \frac{1}{2}bh = \frac{1}{2}(6)(8) = 24$$

Now, use the fact that the area is 24 and the hypotenuse is 10 to find the length of $\overline{AD}$. Simply consider the hypotenuse as the base of the triangle and AD as the height, and you can compute:

$$A = 24 = \frac{1}{2}bh = \frac{1}{2}(10)(AD) = 5(AD)$$

Simplifying, you see that $24 = 5(AD)$.

Divide both sides by 5:

$$AD = \frac{24}{5}$$

(F) The number 5 represents half of the length of the hypotenuse, so this incorrect answer could possibly have occurred when computing with the hypotenuse. In addition, this answer is close to the correct answer, which makes estimating your answer using the figure more difficult.

(H) The number 6 is the length of one of the legs of the triangle, and if you made the mistake of concluding that triangle ABD was isosceles, you would conclude that $AD = 6$. Again, this number is close to the correct answer, which makes it more difficult to estimate your answer using the figure.

(J) The number 8 is the length of side $\overline{AC}$, which you computed by using the Pythagorean Theorem. If you rushed and misread the question, you might have picked this answer.

(K) The length 10 is the length of the hypotenuse, and, if for some reason, you concluded that the hypotenuse and its associated height were the same length, you would be led to this answer.

57. **The correct answer is (D).** The six consecutive even integers are $n, n + 2, n + 4, n + 6, n + 8$, and $n + 10$. In order to find the median of a group consisting of an even number of numbers, you need to write the numbers in numerical order and then find the arithmetic mean of the two numbers in the middle.

In this case, the two numbers in the middle are $n + 4$ and $n + 6$, and the arithmetic mean of these numbers is:

$$\frac{(n+4)+(n+6)}{2} = \frac{2n+10}{2} = n+5$$

(A) This is the smallest of the numbers in the group of six. This would be the answer you would select if you somehow misread the problem and concluded that all six of the numbers were the same.

(B) This is the arithmetic mean of the second and third numbers in the group, but you need to find the arithmetic mean of the third and fourth numbers.

(C) This is the third number in the group, but because it is not the number in the "middle," it is not the median. Remember, you can't find the median of an even number of numbers without some computation.

(E) This is the fourth number in the group, but because it is not the number in the "middle," it is not the median.

58. **The correct answer is (F).** The best way to begin this problem is to make a quick sketch of the situation described:

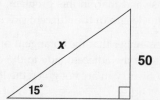

You need to find the length represented by the x in the diagram. This length represents the hypotenuse of the triangle, and because you know the length of the side opposite the 15° angle, the sine function is the one you should use to find the length of the missing side. Recall that the sine of an angle is defined to be the ratio of the side opposite to the angle to the hypotenuse. Therefore:

$$\sin 15° = \frac{50}{x}$$

Cross-multiply:

$$x \sin 15° = 50$$

Divide by sin 15°:

$$x = \frac{50}{\sin 15°}$$

All of the incorrect answer choices are the result of either solving the equation incorrectly or setting up the incorrect trigonometric formula. Be sure to review trigonometric formulas for the test.

(G) This answer involves the correct trigonometric function, but this answer contains the 50 and the sin 15° as a product instead of a quotient. If you obtained this answer, you likely made a mistake solving the equation.

(H) This answer not only contains the incorrect function, but it also contains the two numbers as a product instead of a quotient. Remember that the cosine is the ratio of the adjacent side to the hypotenuse and that, in this problem, you are not given the length of the adjacent side.

(J)   This answer involves an incorrect trigonometric function. Remember that the cosine of an angle is the ratio of the adjacent side to the hypotenuse and that, in this problem, you are not given the length of the adjacent side.

(K)   Remember that the cotangent of an angle is the ratio of the adjacent side to the opposite. In this problem, you are not given the length of the adjacent side.

59. **The correct answer is (C).** The line segment $\overline{OP}$ is a radius of the smaller circle and, therefore, is equal to 4. Therefore, the area of the smaller circle is $A = \pi r^2 = \pi(4^2) = 16\pi$.

The radius of the larger circle is equal to the length of $\overline{OP}$ plus the length of $\overline{PQ}$, which is $4 + 2 = 6$. The area of the larger circle, then, is $A = \pi r^2 = \pi(6^2) = 36\pi$. The ratio of the areas is $\frac{36\pi}{16\pi} = \frac{36}{16} = \frac{9}{4}$.

(A)   This is the answer to a different question. The given ratio is the ratio of the circumferences of the two circles. It is also the ratio of the diameters of the two circles, as well as the ratio of the radii of the two circles. You were asked, however, for the ratio of the areas.

(B)   This answer results from using 2 as the radius for the larger circle and then finding the ratio of the area of the smaller circle to the area of the "circle" with radius 2.

(D)   The number 20π represents the *difference* of the areas of the two circles, as opposed to the ratio of the two areas.

(E)   This answer is the ratio of the area of the "ring" surrounding the smaller circle to the area of the smaller circle.

60. **The correct answer is (H).** The given profit formula is a quadratic. The key piece of mathematical information needed to solve this problem is the fact that the x-coordinate of the extreme point

of a quadratic equation is given by the formula $x = \frac{-b}{2a}$. In the profit formula, $b = 400$ and $a = -1$, so the maximum point is at:

$$x = \frac{-b}{2a} = \frac{-400}{-2} = 200$$

Therefore, the maximum profit is made when 200 computers are sold. This, however, is only the first step in finding the answer.

Now you need to find the profit when 200 computers are sold. To do this, substitute 200 into $p = -x^2 + 400x + 5,000$.

$$p = -(200)^2 + 400(200) + 5,000$$

$$p = -40,000 + 80,000 + 5,000$$

$$p = 45,000$$

Therefore, the biggest profit Mega Computer Corporation can make is $45,000.

(F)   This answer results from incorrectly remembering the formula for the extreme point of a quadratic as $x = \frac{-b}{a}$, instead of $x = \frac{-b}{2a}$.

(G)   This answer results from determining that the maximum point is at 200 but not realizing that this number needs to be substituted back into the profit formula. Since $200 is obviously less than it should be to represent the profit made from the sale of the computers, this answer represents a more likely "guess" that "looks like" the $200 figure.

(J)   This incorrect answer results from making a sign error. When you evaluated the expression $-(200)^2$, you got $-(200)^2 = -40,000$. Treating this expression as if it were $(-200)^2$ would be equal to $+40,000$.

(K)   This answer results from the same logic that leads to choosing incorrect answer choice (G). The test-taker is trying to find a likely looking answer—one that "looks like" it fits with $200.

Practice Reading Test: Passages I and II

Assignment for Today:

- Take a sample of the ACT Assessment Reading Test under actual test conditions. For the real test, you will have 35 minutes to answer 40 questions. For this practice, set your timer for 17 minutes. Remember to skim to decide which passage to do first. Then use the ACT Assessment Reading Strategies to answer the questions.

DIRECTIONS: This test consists of two passages, each followed by several questions. Read each passage, select the correct answer for each question, and mark the oval representing the correct answer on your answer sheet. Refer to the passages as needed.

Passage I

NATURAL SCIENCE: This passage is adapted from two sources: "Black Holes," an article presented on NASA's Imagine the Universe Web site, and a press release from NASA announcing an astronomical discovery.

Line   A black hole is an object in space the
density of which is so great that nothing can
evade its gravity—not even light, the fastest-
traveling entity in the universe. Black holes
(5) usually occur at the end of the lifetime of stars
that have a mass of at least ten to fifteen times
greater than the Sun. If a star of such great
mass experiences a supernova—an explosion
at the end of a star's lifecycle that creates a
(10) temporary increased level of brightness, and
then fades gradually—it could leave a large
scrap of burned-out mass.

Eventually, the burned-out mass collapses
to the point at which its volume decreases to
(15) zero and its density increases infinitely. As the
star's density rises, the rays of light that the
star emits bend and wrap around it, trapping
any photons into its powerful field of gravity.
Once the star reaches the point of infinite
(20) density, neither light nor any other object in its
orbit can escape, categorizing the object as a
"stellar-mass" black hole.

In addition to stellar-mass black holes,
"supermassive" black holes have been
(25) discovered in space. These entities are the size
of entire galaxies, with masses ranging from
about 10 to 100 billion Suns. Scientists theorize
that supermassive black holes are formed as
smaller black holes grow and merge with one
(30) another. Supermassive black holes are found
in active galactic nuclei, which are galaxies
that spew massive amounts of energy from
their centers, far more than ordinary galaxies
(such as the Milky Way). Many astronomers
(35) believe supermassive black holes may lie at

the center of these galaxies and power their explosive energy output.

Recently, scientists have discovered that two supermassive black holes exist together in (40) the same galaxy. According to data retrieved by NASA's Chandra X-ray Observatory, these black holes are orbiting one another and in hundreds of millions of years will eventually merge. When this occurs, these entities will (45) create an even larger supermassive black hole and the result will be disaster. This catastrophic event will set off tremendous amounts of radiation and gravitational waves throughout the universe.

(50) The images collected by Chandra reveal that the two giant black holes are in the nucleus of an unusually bright galaxy, referred to as NGC 6240. Data from the observatory shows that the supermassive black holes are (55) currently accreting matter from their environment. As the black holes accumulate more matter, they grow in mass.

This breakthrough discovery proves that supermassive black holes have the ability to (60) grow and merge in the centers of galaxies, and that future gravitational wave observatories will be able to detect such previously unfathomable events.

The observatory was able to discriminate (65) between the two black holes, also referred to as nuclei, and measure the level of x-radiation from each nucleus. Both nuclei demonstrated an excess of high-energy photons from gas swirling around a black hole, and X rays from fluorescing (70) iron atoms in gas near black holes—all characteristics of supermassive black holes.

Previous X-ray observatories had shown that the central region of the galaxy produces X rays, while radio, infrared, and optical observations (75) had detected two bright nuclei; however, the nature of this region remained a mystery. Scientists did not know the location of the X-ray source or the nature of the two bright nuclei.

Astronomers had hoped that with Chandra, (80) they would be able to determine which one, if

either, of the nuclei was an active supermassive black hole. They were surprised to discover that both nuclei were indeed supermassive black holes.

(85) At a distance of about 400 million light-years, NGC 6240 is a prime example of a massive galaxy in which stars are forming at an exceptionally rapid rate as a result of a recent collision and subsequent merger of two (90) smaller galaxies. Because of the large amount of dust and gas in such galaxies, it is difficult to peer deep into their central regions with optical telescopes. However, X rays emanating from the galactic core can penetrate the veil of (95) gas and dust.

Over the course of the next few hundred million years, the two black holes in NGC 6240, which are about 3,000 light-years apart, will drift toward one another and merge to (100) form an even larger supermassive black hole. Toward the end of this process, an enormous burst of gravitational waves will be produced.

These gravitational waves will spread through the universe and produce ripples in (105) the fabric of space, which would appear as minute changes in the distance between any two points. NASA's planned space-based detector, LISA (Laser Interferometer Space Antenna), will search for gravitational waves (110) from black-hole mergers. These events are estimated to occur several times each year in the observable universe.

1. The passage states that a stellar-mass black hole is formed when
   I.   a massive star explodes at the end of its lifecycle.
   II. a massive galaxy has collapsed and increased its density infinitely.
   III. a burned-out mass has collapsed to zero volume and infinite density.

   (A) I only
   (B) II only
   (C) I and III only
   (D) I, II, and III

2. As it is used in line 55, the word *accreting* most nearly means
   (F) gathering.
   (G) depleting.
   (H) transporting.
   (J) collapsing.

3. According to the passage, the concept of active galactic nuclei is related to black holes in that
   (A) no object can evade the gravitational pull of active galactic nuclei.
   (B) supermassive black holes may be the reason active galactic nuclei emit so much energy.
   (C) their infinite level of density contributes to the collapse of end-of-lifecycle stars in their orbit.
   (D) they are the only type of galaxy in which black holes occur.

4. The passage suggests that stellar-mass black holes have which of the following characteristics in common with a supermassive black hole?
   I. Existence within the same galaxy
   II. Zero volume and infinite density
   III. The inability for any object, including light, to escape from its gravitational pull
   (F) I only
   (G) II only
   (H) II and III only
   (J) I, II, and III

5. The passage suggests that the discovery of the supermassive black holes in NGC 6240
   (A) was an unexpected turn of events for astronomers.
   (B) was the primary reason for building the Chandra X-ray Observatory.
   (C) proves that there must be additional galaxies in the universe with more than one supermassive black hole.
   (D) threatens the existence of common galaxies, such as the Milky Way.

6. Astronomers were able to discover the supermassive black holes in NGC 6240 through the use of
   I. X-ray technology.
   II. radio and infrared observations.
   III. optical observations.
   (F) I only
   (G) I and II only
   (H) III only
   (J) I, II, and III

7. The main purpose of the first three paragraphs is
   (A) to contrast the characteristics of stellar-mass black holes to supermassive black holes.
   (B) to list multiple theories on how black holes are created.
   (C) to provide the reader with background on black holes for a better understanding of NASA's discovery.
   (D) to discuss the concept of active galactic nuclei and the significance of their relation to black holes.

8. As it is used in line 46, the word *catastrophic* most nearly means
   (F) flood-like.
   (G) destructive.
   (H) final.
   (J) tragic.

9. The information provided in paragraph 9 (lines 79–84) suggest that
   (A) all galaxies form rapidly and collide.
   (B) the greater the amount of dust particles and gas in a galaxy, the easier it is to observe the galaxy optically.
   (C) X-ray technology is the only type of technology that allows scientists to detect galaxies at such a great distance.
   (D) scientists have previously researched other galaxies that have characteristics similar to NGC 6240.

10. The passage states that in a few hundred million years,

I. the Laser Interferometer Space Antenna will detect any gravitational waves emitted from the merger of the supermassive black holes in NGC 6240.

II. a colossal explosion of gravitational waves will be propelled from the supermassive black hole, thus modifying the distance between any two locations in the universe.

III. the two supermassive black holes will drift apart from one another, diminishing to stellar-mass black-hole status.

(F) II only

(G) III only

(H) I and II only

(J) I, II, and III

Passage II

PROSE FICTION: This passage is adapted from the short story "The Return of a Private," by Hamlin Garland (1890).

Line   The nearer the train drew toward La Crosse, the soberer the little group of "vets" became. On the long way from New Orleans they had beguiled tedium with jokes and friendly chaff;
(5)   or with planning with elaborate detail what they were going to do now, after the war. The journey was long, slow, irregular, yet persistently pushing northward. When they entered on Wisconsin Territory they gave a cheer, and
(10)   another when they reached Madison, but after that they sank into a dumb expectancy. Comrades dropped off at one or two points beyond, until there were only four or five left who were bound for La Crosse County.
(15)   Three of them were gaunt and brown, the fourth was gaunt and pale, with signs of fever and ague upon him. One had a great scar down his temple; one limped; and they all had unnaturally large bright eyes, showing emacia-
(20)   tion. There were no bands greeting them at the stations, no banks of gaily dressed ladies waving handkerchiefs and shouting "Bravo!" as they came in on the caboose of a freight train

into the towns that had cheered and blared at
(25)   them on their way to war. As they looked out or stepped upon the platform for a moment, as the train stood at the station, the loafers looked at them indifferently. Their blue coats, dusty and grimy, were too familiar now to excite
(30)   notice, much less a friendly word. They were the last of the army to return, and the loafers were surfeited with such sights.

The train jogged forward so slowly that it seemed likely to be midnight before they
(35)   should reach La Crosse. The little squad of "vets" grumbled and swore, but it was no use, the train would not hurry; and as a matter of fact, it was nearly two o'clock when the engine whistled "down brakes."
(40)   All of the group were farmers, living in districts several miles out of the town, and all were poor.

"Now, boys," said Private Smith, he of the fever and ague, "we are landed in La Crosse
(45)   in the night. We've got to stay somewhere till mornin'. Now, I ain't got no two dollars to waste on a hotel. I've got a wife and children, so I'm goin' to roost on a bench and take the cost of a bed out of my hide."
(50)   "Same here," put in one of the other men. "Hide'll grow on again, dollars come hard. It's goin' to be mighty hot skirmishin' to find a dollar these days."

Smith went on: "Then at daybreak we'll
(55)   start for home—at least I will."

The station was deserted, chill, and dark, as they came into it at exactly a quarter to two in the morning. Lit by the oil lamps that flared a dull red light over the dingy benches, the
(60)   waiting room was not an inviting place. The younger man in the group went off to look up a hotel, while the rest remained and prepared to camp down on the floor and benches. Smith was attended to tenderly by the other men,
(65)   who spread their blankets on the bench for him, and by robbing themselves made quite a comfortable bed, though the narrowness of the bench made his sleeping precarious.

It was chill, though August, and the two
(70) men sitting with bowed heads grew stiff with
cold and weariness, and were forced to rise
now and again, and walk about to warm their
stiffened limbs. It didn't occur to them,
probably, to contrast their coming home with
(75) their going forth, or with the coming home of
the generals, colonels, or even captains—but
to Private Smith, at any rate, there came a
sickness at heart almost deadly, as he lay there
on his hard bed and went over his situation.
(80)   In the deep of the night, lying on a board
in the town where he had enlisted three years
ago, all elation and enthusiasm gone out of
him, he faced the fact that with the joy of
homecoming was mingled the bitter juice of
(85) care. He saw himself sick, worn out, taking up
the work on his half-cleared farm, the inevi-
table mortgage standing ready with open jaw
to swallow half his earnings. He had given
three years of his life for a mere pittance of
(90) pay, and now—
     Morning dawned at last, slowly, with a
pale yellow dome of light rising silently above
the bluffs which stand like some huge
battlemented castle, just east of the city. Out to
(95) the left the great river swept on its massive
yet silent way to the south. Blue jays called
across the river from hillside to hillside,
through the clear, beautiful air, and hawks
began to skim the tops of the hills. The two
(100) vets were astir early, but Private Smith had
fallen at last into a sleep, and they went out
without waking him. He lay on his knapsack,
his gaunt face turned toward the ceiling, his
hands clasped on his breast, with a curious
(105) pathetic effect of weakness and appeal.
     An engine switching near woke him at last,
and he slowly sat up and stared about. He
looked out of the window and saw that the
sun was lightening the hills across the river.
(110) He rose and brushed his hair as well as he
could, folded his blankets up, and went out to
find his companions.

11. It is most reasonable to infer that the word *sober*,
    as it is used in line 2, most nearly means

    (A) abstaining from alcohol.

    (B) subdued.

    (C) indulgent.

    (D) cheerful.

12. The details and events in the passage suggest that
    the war from which the privates are returning

    (F) enlisted only farmers.

    (G) caused sickness among most of its soldiers.

    (H) ended months ago.

    (J) took place in the Wisconsin Territory.

13. How do Private Smith's feelings about going to
    war contrast with his feelings about coming
    home?

    (A) Private Smith entered the war with a
        feeling of responsibility and commitment,
        but he returned home feeling reckless and
        unreliable.

    (B) Private Smith entered the war with hopes
        of rising through the ranks, but he returned
        home disappointed because he had not
        been promoted.

    (C) Private Smith entered the war with
        enthusiastic anticipation, but he returned
        home jaded and disillusioned.

    (D) Private Smith entered the war with a
        feeling of guilt and obligation, but he came
        home feeling noble and righteous.

14. Given the description of the soldiers provided by
    the author, it is reasonable to infer that the sol-
    diers

    (F) have become stronger and more muscular
        after three years on the battlefield.

    (G) slept well on the train ride.

    (H) have not eaten well during their tour of
        duty.

    (J) survived the war without injury.

15. How do most of the other characters in the story regard Private Smith?

    (A) They respect him and follow his lead.

    (B) They believe he is too sick to continue his travel home.

    (C) They look upon him as an unsung hero.

    (D) They think he is pathetic and weak.

16. In order to portray the soldiers as simple and uneducated, the author

    (F) contrasts the soldiers with the poise and dignity of the generals, colonels, and captains.

    (G) depicts the soldiers as grumbling and swearing.

    (H) uses simple, colloquial dialogue when the soldiers speak.

    (J) comments that their clothing is dusty and grimy.

17. The main reason Private Smith mentions his wife and children in line 47 is that he

    (A) believes his situation is more dire than that of the soldiers who do not have a family.

    (B) doesn't want to spend money for a hotel room because he needs his money for his family.

    (C) is disappointed that his family has not come to meet him at the train station.

    (D) is concerned that his poor health will leave his family without a provider.

18. The dialogue and narration used in the passage suggest that the business of farming during the time in which the story is set was

    (F) laborious and unrewarding.

    (G) simple and prosperous.

    (H) enterprising and fulfilling.

    (J) tedious and effortless.

19. You can determine from the passage that the word *precarious*, as it is used in line 68, means

    (A) unattainable.

    (B) peaceful.

    (C) insufficient.

    (D) dangerous.

20. At what point does Private Smith contemplate his return to the farm?

    (F) Before the train pulls into the station

    (G) Before falling asleep

    (H) After the blue jays called across the river

    (J) Before the young man went to find a hotel

QUICK ANSWER GUIDE

Passage I

1. C
2. F
3. B
4. H
5. A
6. J
7. C
8. G
9. D
10. F

Passage II

11. B
12. H
13. C
14. H
15. A
16. H
17. B
18. F
19. D
20. G

For explanations to these questions, see Day 21.

Day 21

Reading Test: Passages I and II
Explanations and Answers

Assignment for Today:

- Review the explanations for the answers to the 20 questions for Passages I and II. See which answer is correct and learn what makes the other choices incorrect.

Passage I

1. **The correct answer is (C).** This is a detail question, and the first two paragraphs describe the formation of a stellar-mass black hole. In the first paragraph, it is stated that stars can experience a supernova, or explosion, at the end of their lifecycle. The first sentence of the second paragraph states that once the star burns out, it collapses to zero volume and infinite density. However, the passage never mentions the collapse of a galaxy. Therefore, whereas both I and III are correct, option II is incorrect. To correctly answer a question when more than one choice may be correct, you need to choose the answer that is *most accurate*, in this case the one that includes both I and III. This is also a good reminder to read all the answer options and answer choices.

   (A) This answer choice is only partially correct. While it is true that a stellar-mass black hole is formed when a massive star explodes at the end of its lifecycle, another valid point is made in choice III.

   (B) The passage doesn't mention the collapse of an entire galaxy, only the collapse of stars. Later in the passage, the concept of supermassive black holes, which can be the *size* of galaxies, is discussed; however, the collapse of galaxies has nothing to do with the formation of stellar-mass black holes.

   (D) Although options I and III are correct, option II is not and therefore makes this answer choice incorrect. The passage doesn't mention the collapse of an entire galaxy, only the collapse of stars.

2. **The correct answer is (F).** The word *accreting* is defined in the sentence that follows the cited word in the passage: "As the black holes accumulate more matter, they grow in mass." The context clue for *accrete* is "accumulate." Another word for "accumulate" is "gather."

   (G) While *depleting* fits logically in the sentence's structure (one can *deplete* an environment of its natural resources, for example), the context in which the word *accrete* appears does not suggest that the black holes are draining or exhausting the environment.

(H) *Transporting* is the act of moving objects from one place to another. Although matter is moving from one environment to another environment, this is not the closest meaning to the word *accrete*.

(J) *Collapsing* is the act of falling. Although it is stated earlier in the passage that when a star collapses onto itself it may form a black hole, the context in which the word *accrete* is used does not suggest that the black hole is falling.

3. **The correct answer is (B).** This question asks you to recall details explicitly stated in the passage. The concept of active galactic nuclei is the main idea in paragraph 3, which then discusses details about the concept. The paragraph states that supermassive black holes are found in these types of galaxies and may be the reason active galactic nuclei spew, or emit, so much energy.

(A) While it is true that active galactic nuclei have excessive energy, the passage doesn't discuss the gravitational pull of these types of galaxies.

(C) The concept of infinite density is mentioned in the passage as it relates to the density of black holes and stars, not entire galaxies.

(D) The passage states that supermassive black holes occur in active galactic nuclei; however, it doesn't state in what type of galaxies stellar-mass black holes form. Therefore, one cannot assume that simply because supermassive black holes occur in active galactic nuclei that *all* black holes occur only in active galactic nuclei.

4. **The correct answer is (H).** The characteristics of stellar-mass black holes and supermassive black holes are discussed in the first three paragraphs of the passage. Stellar-mass black holes are described as having a mass of ten to fifteen times greater than the Sun, zero volume, and infinite density (option II) and the inability for any object to escape their gravitational pull (option III). Supermassive black holes form from the merger of stellar-mass black holes, so one can infer from

the passage that they also have zero volume and infinite density (option II), along with the inability for objects to escape their gravity (option III). Option I refers to two particular supermassive black holes that were found in the same galaxy. This question requires that you find information in the passage and then combine it to draw a new conclusion, or inference.

(F) This choice is incorrect because it refers to two supermassive black holes that scientists discovered in the same galaxy. It has nothing to do with the concept of black holes and supermassive black holes in general.

(G) This answer choice is only partially correct. While it is true that stellar-mass black holes and supermassive black holes both have zero volume and infinite density, option III is also true and should be included in the correct answer choice.

(J) Options II and III are correct; however, option I is incorrect because it refers to two supermassive black holes scientists discovered in the same galaxy. It has nothing to do with the concept of black holes and supermassive black holes in general.

5. **The correct answer is (A).** Paragraph 9 states that the astronomers were surprised to discover that both black holes in NGC 6240 were supermassive black holes. Therefore, you can infer that it was an unexpected turn of events for them.

(B) The reason that the Chandra X-ray Observatory was built is not discussed in the passage.

(C) Although scientists may discover in the future another galaxy with more than one supermassive black hole, nothing in the passage suggests that the discovery of the supermassive black holes in NGC 6240 proves that other galaxies also have more than one supermassive black hole.

(D) Although the Milky Way is mentioned as a "common" galaxy, the passage doesn't state that its existence is threatened by these supermassive black holes.

6. **The correct answer is (J).** Paragraph 8 states that X-ray technology had detected the X rays coming from the central region of the galaxy, while radio, infrared, and optical observations found the two bright nuclei in the galaxy. According to these three details provided in the passage, all three options (I, II, and III) are correct.

(F) This answer choice is incomplete because it omits options II and III, which are also true.

(G) This answer choice is incomplete because it omits option III, which is also true.

(H) This answer choice is incomplete because it omits options I and II, which are also true.

7. **The correct answer is (C).** The reason the author of the passage included the first three paragraphs of this article was to provide the reader with background on stellar-mass and supermassive black holes. Without this background, the reader may not understand the significance of the discovery discussed later in the passage.

(A) When an author contrasts two or more concepts or objects, he or she will generally point out the major differences between them. However, in this passage, the author simply describes the two types of black holes.

(B) Only one theory is provided for the formation of each type of black hole.

(D) Active galactic nuclei are mentioned only in the third paragraph and thereafter. Hence, this cannot be the reason for the inclusion of the first three paragraphs in the passage.

8. **The correct answer is (G).** In this context, the word *catastrophic* means "destructive," or "disastrous." The context clue within the paragraph is "disaster," which appears in the sentence before *catastrophic*. Remember to read a line or two above and below the cited word in order to understand the context in which it is used.

(F) Although a flood can cause damage and even catastrophes in some instances, it is not synonymous with the word *catastrophic*.

(H) A catastrophe can be the final act of a tragic drama; however, this is not the context in which the word *catastrophic* is used in the passage.

(J) A tragic event, such as the overthrow of a popular king, can be considered a catastrophe to some people; however, this is not the context in which the word *catastrophic* is used in the passage.

9. **The correct answer is (D).** The paragraph states that NGC 6240 is a prime example of a massive galaxy in which stars form rapidly because two galaxies have collided and merged. If the astronomers list this galaxy as an example, then you can infer that they have seen merged galaxies similar to this before.

(A) This is a blanket statement that is not made in the passage. The paragraph doesn't suggest that all galaxies collide and merge, just that there are galaxies that have collided and merged in the past. Remember that warning about absolutes like *all* and *never*. Read questions carefully for qualifiers.

(B) The paragraph states that the dust and gas make it *difficult* to view the central regions of such galaxies with optical (visual) telescopes.

(C) The paragraph states that X-ray technology allows astronomers to detect X rays that are emitted from the core of the galaxy, not that X-ray technology is the only way to detect an entire galaxy at such a far distance.

10. **The correct answer is (F).** Lines 91–105 state that within a few hundred million years, the black holes will merge, and at the end of the merger, the newly formed black hole will produce a huge explosion of gravitational waves. The last paragraph goes on to state that the effect of these waves will affect the distance between any two points in the universe. So option II is correct.

(G) This answer choice is incorrect because the passage never states that the black holes will drift apart and become smaller, option III. Read the choices carefully. In a rush, you could easily have chosen this choice.

(H)   Although option II is correct, option I is incorrect. Option I refers to the Laser Interferometer Space Antenna, which is being designed to search for gravitational waves from black-hole mergers. It has nothing to do with what will happen a few hundred million years from now.

(J)   Both options I and III are incorrect, so answer choice (J) must also be incorrect.

Passage II

11.   **The correct answer is (B).** You can determine through context clues that the word *sober* suggests that the soldiers are subdued or calm. The sentence that follows describes their journey as one that had included jokes and friendly banter, but as they approached La Crosse, the group became more sober, or subdued. Be sure to read a line or two above and below the cited word.

(A)   Remember to refer to the passage. If you had not done that with this question, you might have mistakenly selected choice (A). Although abstaining from alcohol is a definition of *sober*, this is not the context in which the word is used here. The passage does not mention alcohol, so it is not logical to infer that the meaning of *sober* in this context has anything to do with liquor.

(C)   The word *indulgent* means lenient or tolerant. Nothing in the passage suggests that the soldiers became more lenient during their trip.

(D)   The word *cheerful* means happy; this is not the meaning of the word *sober* as it is used in the passage. The word *cheerful* is an antonym of *sober*.

12.   **The correct answer is (H).** The passage states in the second paragraph that the men's grimy blue coats were a familiar sight to the people of the town and no longer elicited excitement from them. Hence, you can infer that soldiers had been coming home for some time.

(F)   Although the passage states that the four soldiers from La Crosse were all farmers, you cannot deduce that *all* of the soldiers in the war were farmers. Here's another qualifying word again,

only. Beware of absolute statements like this one that *only* farmers were recruited.

(G)   Only one of the soldiers in the story is ill. It is not logical to infer that because one soldier is ill, all of the soldiers must be ill.

(J)   The soldiers are returning to their home in the Wisconsin Territory from New Orleans. The soldiers most likely fought somewhere in the south.

13.   **The correct answer is (C).** Paragraph 10 states that Private Smith had entered the war with elation and enthusiasm and is now sick and tired, with a farm to get up and running. It is reasonable to infer that he is now jaded and disillusioned, or tired and disappointed.

(A)   Although Private Smith may have felt responsible in his position as a soldier, he did not return home feeling like a rebel who couldn't be counted on by his family.

(B)   The passage doesn't mention anything about Private Smith's dreams about a military career.

(D)   Nothing in the passage suggests that Private Smith felt guilty about becoming a soldier. He entered the war with enthusiasm.

14.   **The correct answer is (H).** In the second paragraph, the author describes the soldiers as gaunt and emaciated, which means excessively thin. You can infer that if they were thin, they probably did not eat very well.

(F)   If the soldiers came home excessively thin, they were probably not stronger and more muscular.

(G)   The author does not indicate whether the soldiers slept on the train.

(J)   The second paragraph mentions that one of the soldiers had a large scar on his head and that another soldier limped. These injuries most likely happened on the battlefield.

15.   **The correct answer is (A).** In the fifth paragraph, Private Smith speaks up to the group, announc-

ing that he will stay at the train station and leave for home in the morning. Two of his group members follow his lead. Later in the story, the two men who stay with him make a bed with their belongings for Private Smith, which indicates that they must respect him.

(B) While it is true that Private Smith is ill, nothing in the passage suggests that his companions think he is too sick to carry on.

(C) An unsung hero is someone who hasn't been praised for all the good deeds he has done. Although the soldiers do not praise Private Smith, it is not clear in the passage that he has done anything heroic in the war.

(D) The author describes Private Smith as appearing pathetic and weak but appealing as he sleeps; however, the author does not indicate that this is how Private Smith's companions observe him.

16. **The correct answer is (H).** You can tell by the way the soldiers speak that they are uneducated and simple people. The author uses colloquialisms in the dialogue to convey that the characters are simple people.

(F) The author contrasts the soldiers' coming home to that of generals, colonels, and captains, meaning that the generals, colonels, and captains were probably met with celebration by their communities, whereas the soldiers were not. The author doesn't specifically mention the poise and dignity of the officers.

(G) While it is true that the soldiers were grumbling and swearing, this does not indicate that they are uncomplicated and uneducated.

(J) Most soldiers and officers probably returned home in grimy, dusty uniforms. It is not logical to infer that because one's clothes are dirty that one is simple and uneducated.

17. **The correct answer is (B).** Private Smith mentions his family in the context of money. He states that he doesn't have two dollars to waste on a hotel because he has a wife and children to think about.

(A) Although he may think his situation is more serious than that of soldiers who do not have a family, he doesn't compare his situation with theirs.

(C) While it is true that his family has not come to meet him at the train station, the passage doesn't mention how Private Smith feels about that. Remember, it was nearly 2:00 a.m. when the train finally arrived in La Crosse.

(D) Although it is true that Private Smith has a fever and is sick, he doesn't mention his illness when he speaks of his family, nor the effect it will have on them.

18. **The correct answer is (F).** You learn from the passage that all four soldiers are farmers and that all of them are poor. They discuss the value of a dollar, and only one of the four soldiers/farmers is willing to spend $2 on a hotel room. Later in the passage, you read about Private Smith's thoughts on returning to his farm. He sees himself "sick, worn out, taking up the work on his half-cleared farm," with a mortgage that will take half of his earnings. The hard work, or labor, is unrewarding because he has practically nothing to show for it except for a large mortgage bill.

(G) Although farm life can appear to be simple or uncomplicated, the passage doesn't suggest that it was so at the time the events in this passage are set. Because most of the soldiers returning home to their farms are concerned about money, you can conclude that farming most likely didn't provide much income.

(H) While it is true that farming is an enterprise, the word *enterprising* means "marked by an independent energetic spirit and readiness to take on work." That is not the case with Private Smith or the other men in the passage.

(J) Farming may seem tedious or boring to Private Smith, but nothing in the passage suggests that it is effortless.

19. **The correct answer is (D).** You can determine the meaning for *precarious* by the context in which the

word is used. The soldiers made a comfortable bed for Private Smith on a narrow bench. Sleeping on a narrow bench can be precarious, or dangerous, because one can easily roll off.

(A) *Unattainable* means "unreachable." If the bed were uncomfortable, sleep may have been unattainable for Private Smith. But this is not the case.

(B) If the bench weren't so narrow, sleep might be more *peaceful*; but because of the narrowness of the bench, the best choice is (D), dangerous.

(C) *Insufficient* means "not enough." While it is true that the soldiers may feel that they have had insufficient sleep, that is not the meaning of *precarious*.

20. **The correct answer is (G).** This question asks you to determine the sequence of events. Before falling asleep, Private Smith thinks about his return to the farm.

(F) The train pulls into the station before Private Smith thinks about his return to the farm.

(H) The blue jays called across the river after Private Smith thought about his farm.

(J) The young man went to find a hotel before Private Smith thought about the farm.

Practice Reading Test: Passages III and IV

Assignment for Today:

- Take a sample of the ACT Assessment Reading Test under actual test conditions. For the real test, you will have 35 minutes to answer 40 questions. For this practice, set your timer for 17 minutes. Remember to skim to decide which passage to do first. Then use the ACT Assessment Reading Strategies to answer the questions.

DIRECTIONS: This test consists of two passages, each followed by several questions. Read each passage, select the correct answer for each question, and mark the oval representing the correct answer on your answer sheet. Refer to the passages as needed.

Passage III

HUMANITIES: This passage is adapted from Literary Taste: How to Form It, *by Arnold Bennett (1909).*

Line   In discussing the value of particular books,
      I have heard people say—people who were
      timid about expressing their views of litera-
      ture in the presence of literary men: "It may
(5)   be bad from a literary point of view, but there
      are very good things in it." Or: "I dare say the
      style is very bad, but really the book is very
      interesting and suggestive." Or: "I'm not an
      expert, and so I never bother my head about
(10) good style. All I ask for is good matter. And
      when I have got it, critics may say what they
      like about the book." And many other similar
      remarks, all showing that in the minds of the
      speakers, there existed a notion that style is

(15) something supplementary to, and distinguish-
      able from, matter; a sort of notion that a writer
      who wanted to be classical had first to find
      and arrange his matter, and then dress it up
      elegantly in a costume of style, in order to
(20) please beings called literary critics.

          This is a misapprehension. Style cannot be
      distinguished from matter. When a writer
      conceives an idea, he conceives it in a form of
      words. That form of words constitutes his
(25) style, and it is absolutely governed by the
      idea. The idea can only exist in words, and it
      can only exist in one form of words. You
      cannot say exactly the same thing in two
      different ways. Slightly alter the expression,
(30) and you slightly alter the idea. Surely it is
      obvious that the expression cannot be altered
      without altering the thing expressed! A writer,
      having conceived and expressed an idea, may,
      and probably will, "polish it up." But what
(35) does he polish up? To say that he polishes up
      his style is merely to say that he is polishing
      up his idea, that he has discovered faults or
      imperfections in his idea, and is perfecting it.

An idea exists in proportion as it is expressed;
(40) it exists when it is expressed, and not before.
It expresses itself. A clear idea is expressed
clearly, and a vague idea vaguely.

You need but take your own case and your
own speech. For just as science is the develop-
(45) ment of common sense, so is literature the
development of common daily speech. The
difference between science and common sense
is simply one of degree; similarly with speech
and literature. When you "know what you
(50) think," you succeed in saying what you think,
in making yourself understood. When you
"don't know what to think," your expressive
tongue halts. And note how in daily life the
characteristics of your style follow your mood;
(55) how tender it is when you are tender, how
violent when you are violent. You have said to
yourself in moments of emotion: "If only I
could write——." You were wrong. You ought to
have said: "If only I could *think* on this high
(60) plane." When you have thought clearly, you
have never had any difficulty in saying what
you thought, though you may occasionally
have had some difficulty in keeping it to
yourself. And when you cannot express
(65) yourself, depend upon it that you have nothing
precise to express, and that what incommodes
you is not the vain desire to express, but the
vain desire to *think* more clearly. All this just to
illustrate how style and matter are co-existent,
(70) and inseparable, and alike.

You cannot have good matter with bad
style. Examine the point more closely. A man
wishes to convey a fine idea to you. He
employs a form of words. That form of words
(75) is his style. Having read, you say: "Yes, this
idea is fine." The writer has therefore achieved
his end. But in what imaginable circumstances
can you say: "Yes, this idea is fine, but the
style is not fine"? The sole medium of
(80) communication between you and the author
has been the form of words. The fine idea has
reached you. How? In the words, by the
words. Hence the fineness must be in the

words. You may say, superiorly: "He has
(85) expressed himself clumsily, but I can *see* what
he means." By what light? By something in
the words, in the style. Moreover, if the style
is clumsy, are you sure that you can see what
he means? The "matter" is what actually
(90) reaches you, and it must necessarily be
affected by the style.

In judging the style of an author, you must
employ the same canons as you use in judging
men. If you do this, you will not be tempted
(95) to attach importance to trifles that are negligible. There can be no lasting friendship
without respect. If an author's style is such
that you cannot *respect* it, then you may be
sure that, despite any present pleasure that
(100) you may obtain from that author, there is
something wrong with his matter, and that the
pleasure will soon cloy.

If you are undecided upon a question of
style, whether leaning to the favorable or to
(105) the unfavorable, the most prudent course is to
forget that literary style exists. For, indeed, as
style is understood by most people who have
not analyzed their impressions under the
influence of literature, there *is* no such thing
(110) as literary style. You cannot divide literature
into two elements and say: this is matter and
that style. Further, the significance and the
worth of literature are to be comprehended
and assessed in the same way as the signifi-
(115) cance and the worth of any other phenom-
enon: by the exercise of common sense.
Common sense will tell you that nobody, not
even a genius, can be simultaneously vulgar
and distinguished, or beautiful and ugly, or
(120) precise and vague, or tender and harsh. And
common sense will therefore tell you that to
try to set up vital contradictions between
matter and style is absurd.

21. When the author refers to "a writer who wanted to be classical" in lines 16–17, he means that a writer

    (A) aspires to have his work published.

    (B) hopes that reviewers will consider his work excellent.

    (C) of a literary piece hopes that his work outlives him.

    (D) wants his book to be a bestseller.

22. As it is used in line 66, the word *incommodes* most nearly means

    (F) distresses.

    (G) interrupts.

    (H) ridicules.

    (J) inspires.

23. The main point of the second paragraph (lines 21–42) is that

    (A) matter and style are vital to literary success.

    (B) authors revise their work in order to perfect their idea.

    (C) matter and style are equivalent to one another.

    (D) in reviewing literature, you must use common sense.

24. The author suggests that "literature is the development of common daily speech" (lines 45–46) to convey that

    (F) you should write the way you speak.

    (G) how well you write depends upon how clearly you think.

    (H) literature is based on dialogue.

    (J) it is impossible to say the exact same thing in different ways.

25. According to the fourth paragraph (lines 71–91), a writer has achieved his end if

    (A) his reader enjoys what the writer has written.

    (B) his work is acclaimed by critics.

    (C) he is pleased with the manner in which he has expressed himself.

    (D) his reader understands the point he is making.

26. When the author refers to a style as clumsy, he suggests that

    (F) the writer confuses the concepts of matter and style.

    (G) an idea is not expressed clearly and succinctly.

    (H) the writer has used words that are not graceful.

    (J) the writer has a good idea, but the way he conveys it is poor.

27. As it is used in line 95, the word *trifles* most nearly means

    (A) desserts.

    (B) important ideas.

    (C) insignificant matters.

    (D) rare mushrooms.

28. The author compares science and literature (lines 44–46) in order to

    (F) demonstrate the simplicity of the two subjects.

    (G) show how the two subjects differ vastly from one another with regard to logic.

    (H) illustrate how a scientific experiment is similar to writing a book.

    (J) explain why literary critics are often disregarded by scientists.

29. You can infer from the passage that the author feels that most people who read literature
    (A) depend entirely too much on the opinions of literary critics.
    (B) believe that there is no such thing as literary style.
    (C) do not understand the relationship between matter and style.
    (D) cannot express their ideas clearly.

30. The passage states that the best way to evaluate a piece of literature is to
    (F) observe the work scientifically.
    (G) understand that the matter may be conveyed poorly through the style the writer has used.
    (H) be respectful of the writer's ideas.
    (J) use the same criteria you would use in evaluating a person.

Passage IV

SOCIAL SCIENCE: *This passage is adapted from* The Railroad Builders: A Chronicle of the Welding of the States, *by John Moody (1919).*

Line   After the opening of the Erie Canal in 1825, the Legislature of New York directed a survey of a state road that was to be constructed at public expense through the southern tier of
(5)   counties from the Hudson River to Lake Erie. The unfavorable profile exhibited in the survey apparently caused the project to be abandoned. But the idea still held sway over the minds of many people; and the great benefits brought to
(10)   the Mohawk Valley and surrounding country by the Erie Canal led the southern counties to demand a transportation route that would work similar wonders in that region. This growing sentiment finally persuaded the
(15)   Legislature to charter, in April 1832, the New York and Erie Railroad Company, and to give it authority to construct tracks and to regulate its own charges for transportation.
    During the following summer, a survey of
(20)   the route was made by Colonel De Witt Clinton Jr., and in 1834 a second survey was made of

the whole of the proposed route. When the probable cost was estimated, many opponents arose who declared that the undertaking was
(25)   "chimerical, impractical, and useless." The road, they declared, could never be built and, if built, would never be used; the southern counties were mountainous, sterile, and worthless, and afforded no products requiring
(30)   a market; and, in any case, these counties should find their natural outlet in the valley of the Mohawk. This antagonism was successfully opposed, however, and the construction of the railroad was begun in 1836.
(35)   The Panic of 1837 [the first depression in United States history] interfered with the work, but in 1838 the state Legislature came forward with a construction loan of $3 million, and the first section of line, extending from
(40)   Piermont on the Hudson to Goshen, was put into operation in September 1841. In the following year, the company became insolvent and was placed in the hands of receivers. This disaster delayed further progress for several
(45)   years, and it was not until 1846 that sufficient new capital was raised to continue the work. The original estimate for building the entire line of 485 miles had been $3 million, but already the road had cost over $6 million and
(50)   only a small portion had been finished. The final estimate now rose to $15 million, and, although some money was raised from time to time and new sections were built, there was no certainty that the entire road would ever be
(55)   completed. Ultimately the State of New York canceled its claim against the property, new subscriptions of some millions were secured, and additional money was raised by mortgaging the finished sections.
(60)   Finally, in 1851, after eighteen years of effort, the line was opened to Lake Erie. In addition, various feeders, or branches, had been added, giving the railroad entry into Scranton, Pennsylvania, and Geneva and Buffalo, New
(65)   York. It had its western terminus on Lake Erie at Dunkirk and its eastern terminus at

Piermont, near Nyack on the Hudson, about 25 miles by boat from New York City.

(70) Although the original estimate had been $3 million and the highest estimate of the cost during construction had been $15 million, the company, in 1851, started its career with capital obligations of no less than $26 million—a very large sum for those days.

(75) The fact that these initial obligations constituted a heavy burden became apparent when the Erie Railroad began operations. Freight rates were so high that shippers held indignant meetings and again and again made appeals for

(80) legislative relief. Although much money had been raised after 1849 for improvements, the condition of the Erie steadily grew worse. It soon became notorious for its many accidents because of carelessness in running trains and of

(85) the breaking of the brittle iron rails.

In spite of these drawbacks, the business of the Erie grew. In 1852 it acquired the Ramapo and Paterson and the Paterson and Hudson River Railroads and in this way it obtained a

(90) more direct connection with New York City.

31. As it is used in line 25, the word *chimerical* most nearly means
    (A) commercial.
    (B) improbable.
    (C) realistic.
    (D) virtuous.

32. It is reasonable to infer that the author of this passage most likely would agree that
    (F) the State of New York made a terrible blunder when it decided to build the Erie Railroad.
    (G) the Erie Railroad is the example after which all other railroads should be modeled.
    (H) the Erie Canal is one of the greatest engineering marvels in American history.
    (J) despite the financial hardships the Erie Railroad experienced, the project was ultimately a success.

33. The original plan for building a state road through the Hudson River to Lake Erie was discarded because the
    (A) residents of New York didn't want to pay for it.
    (B) survey that was conducted showed that it was a bad idea.
    (C) project would put the state in an enormous amount of debt.
    (D) legislature was still paying for the cost of constructing the Erie Canal.

34. Which of the following statements best describes Moody's method and purpose for addressing his subject?
    (F) He has relayed a series of personal anecdotes and memories in an attempt to demonstrate to the reader the difficulty the State of New York encountered as it built the Erie Railroad.
    (G) He has presented his personal opinion supported by factual information to present an accurate depiction of the construction of the Erie Railroad.
    (H) He has presented a series of chronological facts to present a precise history of the Erie Railroad.
    (J) He has compared the construction of the Erie Railroad with the accomplishments and failures of railroads that had preceded it in history.

35. According to the passage, the final cost of building the Erie Railroad was
    (A) $3 million.
    (B) $6 million.
    (C) $15 million.
    (D) $26 million.

36. It is most reasonable to infer that when Moody states that the "Panic of 1837 interfered with the work" (lines 35–37), he means that

    (F) a lack of money halted construction temporarily.

    (G) the company was in such a frenzy to complete the project that it was unable to function efficiently.

    (H) the company was dealing with the issue of creditors wanting their investment back, thus ending the project prematurely.

    (J) they had underestimated the original cost of the project and panicked.

37. As it is used in line 83, the word *notorious* most nearly means

    (A) revered.

    (B) ill-famed.

    (C) popular.

    (D) forgotten.

38. The section of railroad extending from Piermont on the Hudson to Goshen was completed

    (F) after the extension into Scranton, Pennsylvania.

    (G) before the Panic of 1837.

    (H) before Colonel De Witt Clinton Jr. completed the survey.

    (J) before the State of New York canceled its claim against the railroad property.

39. It can reasonably be inferred that through the acquisition of two additional railroad companies, the Erie Railroad

    (A) became a more nationally recognized railroad company.

    (B) increased its number of passengers and routes.

    (C) was the most popular railroad connection into New York City.

    (D) was able to pay off its debt more quickly as a result of the increased income from fares.

40. Which of the following reasons were argued for NOT building the Erie Railroad?

    I. The terrain through which the railroad would pass was too rough.

    II. The southern counties, which the railroad would serve, had no products to offer, and the road would never be used.

    III. The Erie Canal provided a sufficient transportation route for all the residents and businesses of New York State.

    (F) I only

    (G) III only

    (H) I and II only

    (J) I, II, and III

QUICK ANSWER GUIDE

Passage III
21. B
22. F
23. C
24. G
25. D
26. G
27. C
28. F
29. C
30. J

Passage IV
31. B
32. J
33. B
34. H
35. D
36. F
37. B
38. J
39. B
40. H

For explanations to these questions, see Day 23.

Day 23

Reading Test: Passages III and IV
Explanations and Answers

Assignment for Today:

- Review the explanations for the answers to the 20 questions for Passages III and IV. See which answer is correct and learn what makes the other choices incorrect.

Passage III

21. **The correct answer is (B).** The author refers to classical literature in the first paragraph of the passage, stating that some writers want their work to be classical, so they dress it up for literary critics to praise. Hence, you can infer that the author intends the word *classical* to mean excellent as perceived by critics or reviewers. It is important to remember to refer to the passage when you are asked the meaning of a word. Had you simply answered the question based on the usual meaning of *classical*, you would have probably selected answer choice (C).

(A) While it is true that most writers aspire to have their work published, this concept is not mentioned at all in the passage.

(C) Classic literature usually outlives its writer; however, the author of the passage does not discuss this topic in the passage.

(D) The author does not mention the idea of best-selling literature anywhere in the passage. There-

fore, it is not logical to conclude that this is what the author means by *classical* in the essay.

22. **The correct answer is (F).** The meaning of the word *incommodes* is found within the context of the paragraph in which the word is used. The paragraph discusses the author's concept that being able to think clearly and precisely works with being able to communicate those thoughts effectively. According to the author, writers often misunderstand the notion of expressing themselves clearly; what they really want to do is *think* more clearly. This confusion can often distress, or incommode, a writer.

(G) *Interrupt* means to stop the flow of something. This is not the meaning of incommode.

(H) To *ridicule* is to make fun of someone. Although the author ridicules people who do not understand how to interpret literature in this passage, this is not the meaning of *incommode*.

(J) *Inspire* means to move or influence a person. While it is true that writers are often inspired to

155

express themselves through writing, this isn't the meaning of the word *incommode*.

23. **The correct answer is (C).** Main ideas are usually introduced in the beginning of a passage or paragraph. Sometimes there is an exception to this rule, but not in this case. The main idea is expressed clearly in the second sentence of the second paragraph: "Style cannot be distinguished from matter." The remainder of the paragraph is simply details that support this idea.

    (A) While you can determine that matter and style can affect the success of a literary work, this is not the main idea of the second paragraph.

    (B) The author does, in fact, state in the second paragraph that writers often revise their work to "polish up" an idea; however, this is not the main idea of the paragraph.

    (D) In this paragraph, the concept of common sense is used in the context of thinking and writing clearly, not evaluating literature.

24. **The correct answer is (G).** The author defines literature as the "development of common speech" and supports this definition by stating, "when you know what you think, you succeed in saying what you think." The paragraph goes on to say that if you have difficulty expressing yourself, it is because you are not sure of what you think.

    (F) The author is not being literal in the use of his expression. It is important to look to the text that introduces an idea and then to the text that follows an idea to get a clear understanding of what the author means.

    (H) While dialogue is a form of speech and is often used in literature, the author of this passage doesn't specifically mention this method of writing in the passage.

    (J) Although the author does indeed state that one cannot say the exact same thing using different words, he says so well before he mentions the concept of common sense and common daily speech.

25. **The correct answer is (D).** This question is a simple matter of recalling details. The writer specifically states in the fourth paragraph that if a man uses words to convey his idea to you and you consider the idea fine (meaning you understand it), then the writer has achieved his end.

    (A) The author mentions nothing in this paragraph about the reader enjoying the work.

    (B) The author mentions literary critics at the end of the first paragraph; however, the notion of critics is not discussed in the fourth paragraph.

    (C) Whether or not a writer is pleased with the way he has expressed himself has nothing to do with whether or not the reader has understood the writer's idea, nor is it mentioned in the paragraph.

26. **The correct answer is (G).** The author discusses the idea of clumsy style in the fourth paragraph. At the end of the paragraph, the author states that if a style is clumsy, then a reader cannot be sure that he understands what a writer means; in other words, matter is affected by style.

    (F) The author claims that readers, not writers, often confuse matter with style.

    (H) While it is true that the word *clumsy* often refers to people who are not graceful, this is not what the author means by *clumsy style*.

    (J) The author clearly states that if a writer expresses himself clumsily, there is no way you can determine whether you understand his meaning. If you don't understand the writer's meaning, then you cannot say whether or not the idea is good.

27. **The correct answer is (C).** The meaning of the word *trifle* can be found within the context of the paragraph in which it is used. The words *importance* and *negligible* are your context clues: The author says that one shouldn't be tempted to attach importance to trifles that are negligible. Negligible means unimportant, so trifles must be insignificant matters or things.

    (A) *Trifle* is a multiple-meaning word and in some contexts is a type of dessert; however, that is not the meaning of the word in the context in which it is used in this passage.

(B) This answer choice does not make sense if you insert it in place of the word *trifle* in the sentence, "If you do this, you will not be tempted to attach importance to important idea." Remember to go back and substitute your answer choice in the sentence to see if it makes sense.

(D) A *truffle* is a type of rare mushroom. A trifle is something else entirely.

28. **The correct answer is (F).** The end of paragraph 3 discusses how an idea is expressed clearly or vaguely. The author mentions science as the development of common sense and compares it to literature, which is the development of common speech. Hence, you can infer that the reason the author mentions science and literature together is that they are both common, or simple, when you break them down.

(G) The author discusses how the two subjects are similar, not different.

(H) The author doesn't mention specifically in the paragraph either scientific experimentation or writing a book; therefore, it is not logical to conclude that conducting an experiment is like writing a book.

(J) Literary critics are mentioned in the first paragraph; however, they have nothing to do with scientists in the passage.

29. **The correct answer is (C).** You can determine the author's point of view by assessing the points he makes in the passage. In the first paragraph, he states that people who are not versed in literature tend to separate the concepts of matter and style. In the second paragraph, he blatantly states that this is a misapprehension, or misunderstanding, and that the two are indistinguishable. Therefore, it is logical to infer that the author believes that most people do not understand the relationship between matter and style.

(A) The first paragraph mentions writers wanting to please literary critics, not "most people."

(B) The author himself believes there is no such thing as literary style, as stated in the final paragraph. However, he does not imply that most people believe this.

(D) The author discusses the notion of expression in the second paragraph. However, he is referring to how writers express themselves, not most readers of literature.

30. **The correct answer is (J).** The answer to this question is found within the details of the passage. The beginning of paragraph 5 states that "[I]n judging the style of an author, you must employ the same canons as you use in judging men." In other words, evaluate an author the same way you would evaluate a person.

(F) Science is mentioned in the passage only to compare it to literature, not to use it to evaluate literature.

(G) While it is true that an idea may be expressed poorly because the words that a writer used are unclear, this has nothing to do with evaluating a piece of literature.

(H) One does not necessarily have to respect a writer's ideas; however, the author states that if you do not respect a writer's *style*, then you most likely won't appreciate that writer's writing.

Passage IV

31. **The correct answer is (B).** The meaning of the word *chimerical* is found within the context of the second paragraph. The sentence in which the word *chimerical* appears is: " . . . many opponents arose who declared that the undertaking was '*chimerical*, impractical, and useless.' " The paragraph then goes on to say that the opponents declared the road could never be built. Even if you have never seen the word *chimerical* before, you can infer from the context that it most likely means "improbable."

(A) Although *chimerical* may look similar to the word *commercial*, the word *commercial* refers to "buying and selling" and doesn't fit within the context of the sentence in which chimerical is used. Always remember to read a line or two above and below the cited word to be sure you understand how it's used—its context.

(C) *Realistic* means that something seems very true or real. The paragraph in which the word *chimerical* is used states that the railroad could never be built, so chimerical can't mean realistic.

(D) *Virtuous* means that someone or something is morally correct or righteous. This word does not make sense in the context of the paragraph in which the word *chimerical* is used.

32. **The correct answer is (J).** This question asks you to identify the author's point of view. The author provides numerous facts about the construction of the Erie Railroad. He includes the problems that the railroad incurred before, during, and after the railroad was built. However, the passage concludes that in spite of all the drawbacks or problems the railroad had, it still managed to grow and acquire other railroads. It is reasonable to infer, then, that the author thinks the railroad was ultimately successful.

(F) If the author thought that the State of New York made a mistake by building the Erie Railroad, his tone would have been more negative throughout the passage. The tone in this passage is matter-of-fact, not negative.

(G) The author doesn't mention other railroads in the passage. Hence, it is not reasonable to infer that the author thinks all other railroads should have been built like the Erie Railroad.

(H) The author mentions the Erie Canal only briefly in the beginning of the passage. Although it is true that the Erie Canal is considered an engineering marvel by some people, this is outside the context of the passage. The author doesn't mention what he thinks about the Erie Canal.

33. **The correct answer is (B).** The details in the first paragraph state that "the unfavorable profile exhibited in the survey apparently caused the project to be abandoned." In other words, the

survey concluded that the project shouldn't be completed.

(A) While it is true that the road would be constructed at public expense, the passage doesn't state that the residents of New York didn't want to pay for it.

(C) The debt load of New York State is not the reason stated in the passage for discarding the original plan for a state road.

(D) The passage doesn't mention whether the cost of building the Erie Canal had been paid off.

34. **The correct answer is (H).** The author of the passage tells the history of the construction of the Erie Railroad through facts in the order in which they occurred. The passage begins at the planning stage and ends at the conclusion of the railroad's construction and its acquisition of other railroads. This is a sequence-of-events question.

(F) The author does not include any personal stories about the Erie Railroad in the passage.

(G) The author offers no opinions in the passage. All of his statements are factual.

(J) The author doesn't mention any other railroad in the passage; therefore, it is not reasonable to state that he has made any comparisons.

35. **The correct answer is (D).** Details in paragraph 5 state that the railroad owed "no less than $26 million" at the end of its construction. You can infer, then, that the cost of constructing the railroad was at least $26 million.

(A) The passage states that the original estimate of building the railroad was $3 million. However, more financial information is provided later in the passage.

(B) The third paragraph states that the railroad company spent $6 million for building only a small portion of the railroad. However, this was not the final cost of constructing the railroad.

(C) The fifth paragraph states that the highest estimate for building the railroad was $15 million. However, the same paragraph goes on to state that the company owed much more than that upon completion of the railroad.

36. **The correct answer is (F).** The passage tells you that the Panic of 1837 was the first depression in United States history. Even if you did not know what a depression is, you can infer from the second part of the sentence ["… but in 1838 the state Legislature came forward with a construction loan of $3 million"] that it has to do with a lack of money.

    (G) While it is true that the word *panic* can mean "frenzy," the context in which the word panic is used tells you something different.

    (H) While the company may have had to deal with creditors during the Panic, or depression, of 1837, the passage doesn't state that the project had ended prematurely. In fact, it discusses its completion.

    (J) Although it is true that the cost of constructing the railroad was grossly underestimated, this has nothing to do with the Panic of 1837.

37. **The correct answer is (B).** You can determine the meaning of *notorious* from its context. The word *notorious* is used in the sixth paragraph and refers to the many accidents the railroad experienced. If something is *notorious*, it is generally remembered, or "ill-famed," for something negative.

    (A) To *revere* means "to deem something worthy of being honored." Most people wouldn't honor a railroad that has had many accidents.

    (C) *Popular* means "well liked" or "approved." Most people wouldn't approve of a railroad that had a great number of accidents.

    (D) To forget means "not to remember." The word *forgotten* doesn't fit within the context of the sentence in which the word *notorious* is used. Remember to substitute your answer choice into the sentence to make sure it makes sense. Had you done that with answer choice (D), you would see that it's illogical.

38. **The correct answer is (J).** This question asks you to recall the sequence of events in the passage. The section of railroad referred to in the question was completed before the State of New York canceled its claim against the railroad company.

    (F) The extension into Scranton, Pennsylvania, was completed *after* the Piermont–Goshen section was completed.

    (G) The Panic of 1837 took place *before* the Piermont–Goshen section of the railroad was completed.

    (H) Colonel De Witt Clinton Jr. completed his survey *before* the Piermont–Goshen section was completed.

39. **The correct answer is (B).** You can infer that by acquiring, or buying, two additional railroads that the number of passengers and routes increased. The company bought additional trains that were used by different (additional) passengers and additional railroad lines that traveled to different (additional) places.

    (A) Nothing in the passage suggests that the Erie Railroad became more nationally recognized when it bought two additional railroad lines.

    (C) The passage states that through the purchase of the two additional railroads, the Erie Railroad gained a more direct route into New York City. However, the passage doesn't suggest that this route was the most popular route.

    (D) Nothing in the passage suggests that by purchasing the additional railroads, the Erie Railroad was able to pay off its debts more quickly. You might infer that, but answer choice (B) is a more accurate inference in terms of what is in the passage.

40. **The correct answer is (H).** The second paragraph states that the reasons people argued against building the Erie Railroad was because the southern counties were "mountainous" (suggesting that the terrain is rough), "sterile, and worthless, and afforded no products requiring a market."

Earlier in the paragraph, the passage states that even if the railroad were built, it would never be used. Hence, it is reasonable to select both options I and II and then choice (H) as the correct answer to this question.

(F)   This answer choice is only partially correct. While it is true that the terrain was mountainous or rough, there is another answer choice that is also correct. When working with questions like this one, you should choose the *most accurate* answer.

(G)   According to the first paragraph, the Erie Canal provided a transportation route that helped the Mohawk Valley, not the entire state of New York.

(J)   This answer choice is incorrect because option III is incorrect. The Erie Canal provided a transportation route that helped the Mohawk Valley, not the entire state of New York.

Day 24

Practice Science Reasoning Test: Passages I and II

Assignment for Today:

- Take a sample of the ACT Assessment Science Reasoning Test under actual test conditions. For the real test, you will have 35 minutes to answer 40 questions. For this practice, set your timer for 9 minutes. Remember to skim to decide which passage to answer first. Then use the ACT Assessment Science Reasoning Strategies to answer the questions.

DIRECTIONS: *This test consists of two passages, each followed by several questions. Read each passage, select the best answer for each question, and mark the oval representing the correct answer on your answer sheet. Refer to the passage as needed.*

Note: You may NOT use a calculator on this test.

Passage I

Soil is composed of a combination of sand, silt, and clay. The relative percentages of each particle type in soil are referred to as its texture. The diagram below is used to identify the soil types for various textures. Soils classified as loams contain organic matter.

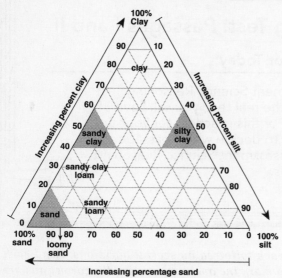

Soil samples were collected from a forest and a grassy field. The samples were dried and then weighed. The dried samples were then separated by particle size. The particles of each size were weighed and the percentages of each size was calculated. The results are presented in Study 1 and Study 2.

Study 1

Sample No.	% Sand	% Silt	% Clay
Forest 1	45	5	50
Forest 2	20	60	20 .
Forest 3	43	28	15

repeat

Study 2

Sample No.	% Sand	% Silt	% Clay
Grass 1	12.5	54.5	33
Grass 2	57	37	6
Grass 3	82	7	11

1. What determines the texture of the soil?
   - (A) The percentage of sand, clay, and silt
   - (B) The ratio of sand to silt
   - (C) The ratio of silt to sand
   - (D) The percentage of clay

2. The smallest component by percent of silty clay loam is
   - (F) silt.
   - (G) clay.
   - (H) loam.
   - (J) sand.

3. What is the soil type of sample Grass 2?
   - (A) Silty clay
   - (B) Sandy loam
   - (C) Loamy sand
   - (D) Loam

4. How do the percentages of clay in the Forest samples compare with those of the Grass samples?
   - (F) The percentages of clay are higher in the Forest samples than in the Grass samples.
   - (G) The percentages of clay in the Forest samples fall within the loam soil type, whereas those of the Grass samples fall within the silty loam soil type.
   - (H) The percentages of clay in the Forest samples fall within the sandy loam soil type, whereas those of the Grass samples fall within the silty clay loam soil type.
   - (J) The percentages of clay account for less than half of the soil particles in the forest sample, but account for a third or less in the grass samples.

5. What would be the best way to determine the moisture content of each sample?

    (A) Measure the amount of water needed to saturate the soil.

    (B) Weigh the samples before and after they are dried.

    (C) After placing each sample in a container with holes at the bottom, pour an equal amount of water through the samples to measure and compare how quickly the water moves through each.

    (D) Expose the samples to a heat lamp or sunlight and measure the amount of time it takes the samples to dry.

6. What would be the best way to determine the relation between soil texture and its permeability (the ability of water to pass through it)?

    (F) Fill cups (with holes in the bottom) separately with sand, silt, and clay, and measure the amount of time it takes for a certain amount of water to pour through each particle type.

    (G) Fill a cup (with holes in the bottom) with a mixture of equal amounts of sand, silt, and clay, and measure the amount of time it takes for a certain amount of water to pour through.

    (H) Fill separate cups (with holes in the bottom) with a mixture of varying amounts of sand, silt, and clay. Measure the amount of time it takes for a certain amount of water to pour through each sample.

    (J) Fill separate jars with a mixture of varying amounts of sand, silt, and clay. Add enough water to cover each sample. Shake each jar vigorously and allow to settle for 24 hours. Measure the height of each layer of the three particles that have formed.

Passage II

The diagrams below show typical changes in temperature and dissolved oxygen levels in two lakes from season to season. The two lakes have very similar temperature (T) and dissolved oxygen (DO) levels in the spring and fall, so only one graph is shown. One lake is eutrophic, and the other is oligotrophic. A eutrophic lake is one that is rich in nutrients with many microorganisms, fish, and plants, including algae. An oligotrophic lake is one that is nutrient-poor with little plant or animal life. The water of oligotrophic lakes is generally quite clear.

The diagrams show the dissolved oxygen (DO; bottom scale) and temperature (T; top scale) of the two lakes during each season.

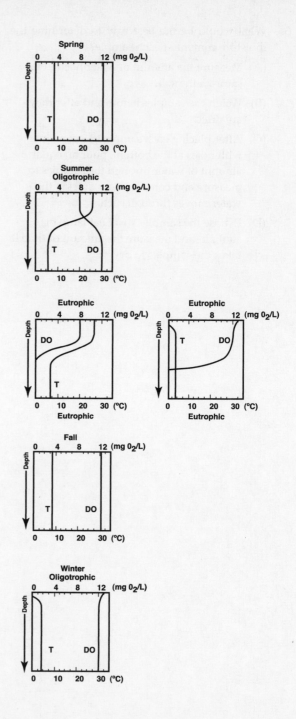

7. During fall and spring, the lakes have

   (A) a variable temperature and dissolved oxygen level throughout.

   (B) a constant temperature and dissolved oxygen level throughout.

   (C) a variable temperature and constant dissolved oxygen level throughout.

   (D) a constant temperature and variable dissolved oxygen level throughout.

8. What is the DO level near the eutrophic lake bottom during the summer?

   (F) About 0 mg O_2/L

   (G) 8 mg O_2/L

   (H) 10 mg O_2/L

   (J) It's impossible to tell from the data given in the graph.

9. From spring to summer, how do the dissolved oxygen levels in eutrophic lakes vary?

   (A) The levels increase in the upper layer.

   (B) The levels do not change in the upper layer.

   (C) The levels increase in the lower layer.

   (D) The levels decrease in the lower layer.

10. What accounts for the difference in the DO levels between oligotrophic lakes and eutrophic lakes during the summer?

    (F) The colder water of the oligotrophic lake

    (G) The larger population of animals in the oligotrophic lake

    (H) The larger amount of decomposing algae in the eutrophic lake

    (J) The mixing of surface waters in the eutrophic lake

11. What might explain the oxygen levels near the surface of the lakes in the winter?

    (A) Plants near the surface may be getting just enough sunlight to produce oxygen.

    (B) Plants near the surface may be getting just enough sunlight to remove oxygen.

    (C) Plants near the surface may be getting just enough sunlight to produce carbon dioxide.

    (D) Plants near the surface may be getting just enough sunlight to decrease temperatures there.

QUICK ANSWER GUIDE

Passage I

1. A
2. J
3. B
4. J
5. B
6. H

Passage II

7. B
8. F
9. D
10. H
11. B

For explanations to these questions, see Day 25.

Science Reasoning Test: Passages I and II
Explanations and Answers

Assignment for Today:

- Review the explanations for the test you just took.

Passage I

1. **The correct answer is (A).** Texture is determined by the percentage of all three particle sizes—sand, silt, and clay.

   (B) The ratio in choice (B) only accounts for one of the three particle components of soil.

   (C) The ratio in choice (C) only accounts for one of the three particle components of soil.

   (D) The percentage of clay alone does not determine soil texture, which must include the percentage of the other two particle sizes.

2. **The correct answer is (J).** According to the triangle diagram, the range of silt in silty clay loam is 60% to 71%, clay is 80% to 100%, and sand is 28% to 60%.

   (F) There is more clay present than sand.

   (G) Clay is present in the highest percentage.

   (H) The term *loam* only indicates that organic matter is present but does not refer to a particle size.

3. **The correct answer is (B).** According to Study 2, sample Grass 2 is 57% sand, 37% silt, and 6% clay. These percentage lines on the triangle diagram intersect within the sandy loam range.

   (A) Silty clay contains at least 40% clay.

   (C) Loamy sand contains at least 70% sand.

   (D) Loam containing 37% silt contains less than 55% sand and more than 8% clay.

4. **The correct answer is (J).** The highest percentage of clay in the Forest soils is 49%, or less than half. The highest percentage of clay in the Grass soils is 33%, or a third or less.

   (F) Grass sample 1 contains more clay than either Forest samples 2 or 3.

   (G) The 15% to 50% clay range of the Forest soil falls within numerous different soil types.

   (H) The 6% to 33% Grass soil falls within numerous different soil types.

5. **The correct answer is (B).** The difference in weight before and after drying will indicate how much of the soil by weight was moisture.

    (A) This procedure would only indicate the amount of water a soil can hold, not how much it was holding at the time the sample was collected.

    (C) This procedure would only show how quickly water can move through each soil type, not how much water was in each sample.

    (D) Whereas this procedure might indicate the comparative moisture content among the samples, it would not determine how much of each sample was moisture.

6. **The correct answer is (H).** By varying the percentages of the particles in each soil sample, you will be able to determine which combination is most permeable.

    (F) Whereas this procedure would provide some information on permeability, it would not show the permeability of soils that are a mixture of the three particle types.

    (G) Similar to the reason given for choice (F), this procedure would only indicate the permeability of one type of soil.

    (J) This procedure would only indicate the relative amounts of each particle size.

Passage II

7. **The correct answer is (B).** To answer this question, you must understand how to read the graph. When reading for temperature on the graph, ignore the DO scale along the top axis and the DO graph line. When reading for the DO level, ignore the temperature scale at the bottom and the T graph line. This leaves a simple two-axes graph: the vertical axis for depth and either the top horizontal axis for DO or the bottom horizontal axis for temperature. The straight vertical lines for both T and DO indicate a temperature of a little more than 6°C at all depths and a DO level of about 12 mg O_2/L. Note that depth decreases from the top of the graph to the bottom.

    (A) The straight line indicates that at all depths, the temperature and dissolved oxygen level are the same. A variable temperature or dissolved oxygen level would be indicated by a curve in the graph.

    (C) See choice (A).

    (D) See choice (A).

8. **The correct answer is (F).** Note that depth decreases downward along the vertical edge of the graph. At a certain depth, the graph line for DO crosses the 0 mg O_2/L tic mark. Any level that is deeper than that has no oxygen.

    (G) This is the reading at the surface of the lake. Depth decreases downward on the scale, not upward.

    (H) You may have chosen this answer if you looked at the wrong (temperature) graph line. If you did that, you would have seen that it crosses the top (DO) scale at 10. However, you should actually be reading along the bottom scale (27°C).

    (J) Although you cannot know if the scale shows all the way to the lake bottom, you can see from the trend of the DO graph line that the DO levels have decreased to 0 mg O_2/L at a certain depth.

9. **The correct answer is (D).** You need only read the graph to find the DO levels. As shown, the lower layer DO declines during the summer.

    (A) Whereas DO levels are high in the summer, they have decreased from their spring levels.

    (B) Although the straight lines of both graphs in the upper layer indicate a constant temperature, the graph shows that the DO changes from 8 mg to 12 mg O_2/L from spring to summer.

    (C) The graph shows a decrease, not an increase.

10. **The correct answer is (H).** The graphs show that the oligotrophic lake's DO level increases with depth below the warm upper layer and remains at a high level with depth. The eutrophic lake's DO is present only in the upper layer and has none in the lower level. The temperatures of both lakes are basically the same, with both decreasing with depth to about 6°C. Therefore, the difference must be in the amount of DO used up by the decomposing algae.

    (F) As shown on the two graphs, the temperatures are almost identical and, therefore, could not cause the great difference.

    (G) According to the passage, oligotrophic lakes are notable in that they do not have large populations of either plants or animals.

    (J) As shown on the two graphs, the conditions of the surface waters are almost identical in the two lakes, and, therefore, actions affecting only the lake surface are unlikely to cause the difference.

11. **The correct answer is (B).** The lakes show a slight increase (from 12 mg to 13 mg O_2/L) in DO near the surface.

    (A) The graph indicates an increase in oxygen levels, not a decrease.

    (C) The graph does not give any indication as to the carbon dioxide levels at any depth.

    (D) The graph indicates that the water is slightly warmer, not colder, near the lake surface.

Day 26

Practice Science Reasoning Test: Passages III and IV

Assignment for Today:

- Take a sample of the ACT Assessment Science Reasoning Test under actual test conditions. For the real test, you will have 35 minutes to answer 40 questions. For this practice, set your timer for 9 minutes. Remember to skim to decide which passage to answer first. Then use the ACT Assessment Science Reasoning Strategies to answer the questions.

DIRECTIONS: *This test consists of two passages, each followed by several questions. Read each passage, select the best answer for each question, and mark the oval representing the correct answer on your answer sheet. Refer to the passage as needed.*

Note: *You may NOT use a calculator on this test.*

Passage III

The first graph below shows the number of maternal deaths from 1979 to 1986. The term *maternal death* refers to the deaths of women whose pregnancies ended in a live birth. The second graph shows the percentage of pregnancy-related deaths by the number of days from the end of the preg-

nancy until death. Pregnancy-related deaths include those deaths that occur while a woman is pregnant or up to one year from the end of the pregnancy and are from any cause related to or aggravated by the pregnancy, excluding accidental deaths.

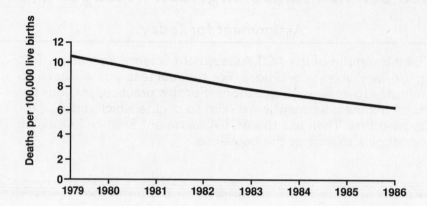

Percentage of pregnancy deaths, by number of days from time of end of pregnancy to death–United States, 1979-1986

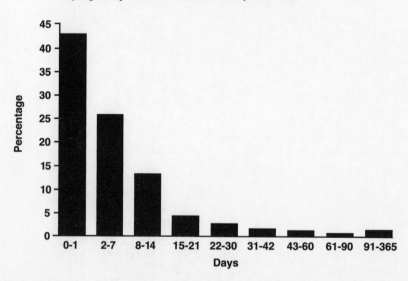

12. From 1979 to 1985, pregnancy-related deaths decreased by about

    (F) 3 per 100,000 live births.

    (G) 5 per 100,000 live births.

    (H) 8 per 100,000 live births.

    (J) 11 per 100,000 live births.

13. Which graph best represents the relation between the percentage of pregnancy-related deaths and the number of days after the end of pregnancy for the period of 0–90 days?

    (A)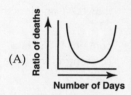

    (B)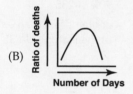

    (C)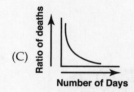

    (D)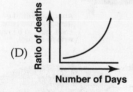

14. In 1981, there were 3,629,000 live births in the United States. Approximately how many maternal deaths were there that year?

    (F) 363

    (G) 327

    (H) 3,629

    (J) 3,266

15. Why does the last bar of the graph show a change in the trend for percentage of pregnancy-related deaths versus days?

    (A) Deaths rise significantly after ninety days.

    (B) Deaths rise only slightly after ninety days.

    (C) Deaths after ninety days are not considered a result of pregnancy.

    (D) None of the above

16. Suppose that 50% of the pregnancy-related deaths that occur within the first week after the end of a pregnancy could be prevented. What approximate percentage of all pregnancies that would have ended in death would not?

    (F) 43%

    (G) 34%

    (H) 26%

    (J) 13%

Passage IV

The nuclei of atoms consist of protons and neutrons. The total number of protons and neutrons in an atom's nuclei is its mass number. Atoms of the same element can have different mass numbers, depending on the number of neutrons in each atom. Atoms of the same element with different mass numbers are identified by their mass number. The three isotopes of uranium are U-234, U-235, and U-238. Uranium is used to produce energy through fission, which is the process in which the nuclei of atoms are split to release energy.

The diagram below summarizes the processes of the Nuclear Fuel Cycle in which naturally occurring uranium is converted to usable fuel. Table 1 explains some of the terms used in the processing of Uranium.

Table 1

Term	Definition
UF_6	uranium hexafluoride gas
U_3O_8	solid concentrate uranium oxide
UO_2	solid uranium dioxide
Natural Uranium	contains 99.3% U-238 and 0.7% U-235
Low Enriched Uranium	contains U-235 in a concentration higher than 0.7% and less than 20%
Highly Enriched Uranium	contains U-235 in a concentration above 20%
Weapons-Grade Uranium	enriched to more than 90% U-235
Depleted Uranium	contains less than 0.7% of the isotope U-235

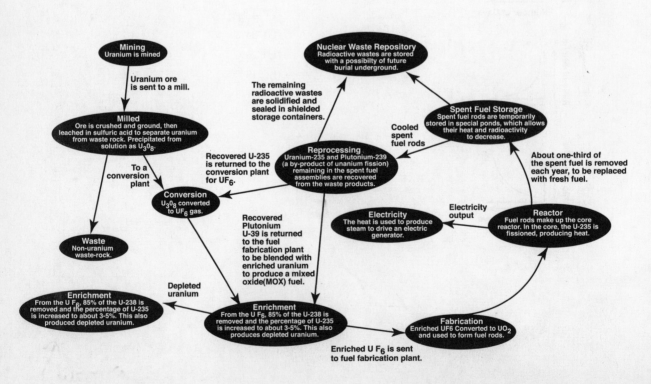

17. The type of uranium used in fuel rods is

    (A) natural uranium.

    (B) low enriched uranium.

    (C) highly enriched uranium.

    (D) depleted uranium.

18. Uranium is useful as a fuel because

    (F) the enrichment of U-235 produces electricity.

    (G) uranium gives off electricity.

    (H) its radioactivity gives off heat.

    (J) the fission of its nuclei gives off heat.

19. Spent fuel assemblies are stored in ponds because they are

    (A) worth too much money to throw out.

    (B) too highly radioactive to store safely.

    (C) used to produce electricity.

    (D) used to convert U_3O_8 to UF_6 gas.

20. The sequence in which uranium is converted from ore to fuel is uranium ore converted to

    (F) uranium hexafluoride to uranium oxide to uranium dioxide.

    (G) uranium oxide to uranium hexafluoride to uranium dioxide.

    (H) uranium oxide to uranium dioxide to plutonium.

    (J) uranium hexafluoride to plutonium.

21. Why are spent fuel rods reprocessed?

    (A) The cost of recovering the uranium-235 remaining in the rods is less than the price of the recovered uranium.

    (B) There is no way to store the spent rods so they must be reused.

    (C) The spent fuel rods must be placed in shielded containers.

    (D) They have a higher percentage of U-235 than U-238, making them very valuable.

QUICK ANSWER GUIDE

Passage III
12. F
13. C
14. F
15. D
16. G

Passage IV
17. B
18. J
19. B
20. G
21. A

For explanations to these questions, see Day 27.

Science Reasoning Test: Passages III and IV
Explanations and Answers

Assignment for Today:

- Review the explanations for the test you just took.

Passage III

12. **The correct answer is (F).** According to the figure, the mortality rate in 1979 was about 11 per 100,000. By 1985, it had decreased to 8 per 100,000, so 11 − 8 = 3.

    (G) 5 is a random wrong number.

    (H) 8 is the number for 1985.

    (J) 11 is the number for 1979.

13. **The correct answer is (C).** From the figure in this answer choice, you can see that the death ratio decreases as time increases.

    (A) This figure shows the death ratio decreasing then increasing, which it does not do.

    (B) This figure shows the death ratio decreasing then increasing, which it does not do.

    (D) This figure shows the ratio increasing rather than decreasing over time.

14. **The correct answer is (F).** The answer is calculated using the total of 10 per 100,000 deaths/births in 1981 and multiplying by 3,629,000 births.

(G) This answer is calculated as 9 deaths per 100,000 births.

(H) This answer is calculated as 10 deaths per 1,000,000 births.

(J) This answer is calculated as 9 deaths per 1,000,000 births.

15. **The correct answer is (D).** The trend shown by the graph is a decrease over time. The last bar appears to go against that trend; that is, it increases from the previous time period. However, the most likely reason for this change is that the time period accounted for by the last bar is significantly longer, 274 days, than the earlier bars, 1 to 20 days.

(A) If averaged over the 274 deaths, the bar would be far lower than the previous 90 days.

(B) If averaged over the 274 deaths, the bar would be far lower than the previous 90 days.

(C) The paragraph states that pregnancy-related deaths include those up to 1 year after the pregnancy ends, so this answer can't be correct.

16. **The correct answer is (G).** First, you must determine from the bar graph the percentage of deaths that occur within the first week. This is the first bar (0–1 days) or 43% plus the second bar (2–7) or 26%, or 69% of all pregnancy-related deaths. Fifty percent, or half, of this number is 34.5%, or approximately 34%.

    (F)   This answer uses the percentages in the graph for days 0–1.

    (H)   This answer uses the percentages in the graph for days 2–7.

    (J) This is half of the percentage of deaths on days 2–7.

Passage IV

17. **The correct answer is (B).** According to Table 2, low-enriched uranium is higher than 0.7% but lower that 20%. The *Enrichment* step of the diagram states that the U-235 is enriched to 3% to 5% of the total, thus falling into the low-enrichment category.

    (A)   Natural uranium is less than 0.7% U-235.

    (C)   Highly enriched uranium is more than 20% U-235.

    (D)   Depleted uranium is less than 0.7% U-235.

18. **The correct answer is (J).** The *Reactor* step states that the nuclei are fissioned, producing heat. The *Electricity* step states that the heat is used to produce steam, which is used to produce electricity.

    (F)   Enrichment only increases the amount of U-235 in the uranium product. It does not produce any energy.

    (G)   Electricity is not produced directly from uranium.

    (H)   Although radioactivity does produce heat, it is the controlled fission of the uranium, as stated in the *Reactor* step, that gives off the heat used to produce electricity.

19. **The correct answer is (B).** As stated in the *Spent Fuel Storage* step, the fuel rods are stored in ponds to allow the radioactivity to decrease before moving them to the next step, either disposal or reprocessing.

    (A) No mention is made anywhere in the diagram about the fuels' cost.

    (C)   The fuel has already been used to produce energy in the previous step. The useful atoms have already been spent.

    (D)   Spent fuel is neither needed nor used to convert U_3O_8 to UF_6 gas.

20. **The correct answer is (G).** Table 2 shows that U_3O_8 is uranium oxide; UF_6 is uranium hexafluoride; and UO_2 is uranium dioxide. Following the steps in sequence, ore is converted to U_3O_8 at *Milling*, followed by *Conversion* where U_3O_8 is converted to UF_6, followed several steps later by *Fabrication* where UF_6 is converted to UO_2. UO_2 is used to form the fuel rods.

    (F)   The sequence is incorrect; ore is converted to U_3O_8, not UF_6.

    (H) Plutonium is not a compound produced in the making of the fuel. Plutonium is not produced until after the fuel is fissioned.

    (J) See answer choice (H).

21. **The correct answer is (A).** In the *Reprocessing* step, U-235 remaining in the spent fuel is recovered from the waste products. It is reasonable to deduce that this process would not be worthwhile if the process lost money.

    (B)   Spent fuel can be stored.

    (C)   Reprocessing draws out the usable U-235 from the spent rods; it is not the process in which the fuel is sent to storage.

    (D)   At no point anywhere in the fuel cycle is there ever more U-235 than U-238 in the uranium. Only uranium enriched for purposes other than fuel would have this proportion.

Day 28

Practice Science Reasoning Test:
Passages V, VI, and VII

Assignment for Today:

- Take a sample of the ACT Assessment Science Reasoning Test under actual test conditions. For the real test, you will have 35 minutes to answer 40 questions. For this practice, set your timer for 17 minutes. Remember to skim to decide which passage to answer first. Then, use the ACT Assessment Science Reasoning Strategies to answer the questions.

DIRECTIONS: *This test consists of three passages, each followed by several questions. Read each passage, select the best answer for each question, and mark the oval representing the correct answer on your answer sheet. Refer to the passage as needed.*

Note: *You may NOT use a calculator on this test.*

Passage V

Tests were conducted in two steps to determine which metals were present in a solution containing unknown metal ions. Tables 1 and 2 list tests performed in Steps 1 and 2. The tests show the presence of various metals. All reactions that *may* occur during the testing of the solution are listed. In the flow charts, the chemical next to an arrow indicates its addition to the substance in the box. Boxes with two arrows leading away indicate that a solution and precipitate were separated. If no precipitate is indicated, none was produced. Keep in mind that while testing, the dark color of some precipitates can mask the presence of other lighter precipitates.

Table 1: Step 1 Tests

Metal	Tested with	Result
Ag, Pb, or Hg ions	HCl	white precipitates (AgCl, Hg_2Cl, or $PbCl_2$)
Pb ion	K_2CrO_4 + acetic acid	yellow precipitate
AgCl	NH_4OH	dissolves (Ag ions)
Hg_2Cl	NH_4OH	black or gray precipitate
AgCl	NH_4OH then nitric acid	white precipitate
$PbCl_2$	H_2O +heat	dissolves
AgCl and Hg_2Cl	H_2O +heat	no reaction

Table 2: Step 2 Tests

Metal	Tested with	Result
Cu ions	H_2S	black precipitate (CuS)
Bi ions	H_2S	brown precipitate (Bi_2S_3)
Hg ions	H_2S	black precipitate (HgS)
Bi ions	NH_4OH	white precipitate ($Bi(OH)_3$)
Cu ions	NH_4OH	turns solution blue
Hg ions	NH_4OH	gray precipitate
Bi_2S_3, and CuS	Nitric acid + heat	dissolves (Bi and Cu ions)
HgS	Nitric acid + heat	no reaction

22. Was Hg present, and how could you tell?

    (F) Yes, first a white precipitate formed in Step 1a; then the white precipitate turned into a clear solution in Step 1d.

    (G) Yes, first a white precipitate formed in Step 1a; then the white precipitate turned into a clear solution in Step 1d; then a white precipitate formed in Step 1e.

    (H) No, first a white precipitate formed in Step 1a; then the white precipitate turned into a clear solution in Step 1d.

    (J) Yes, first a white precipitate formed in Step 1a; then the white precipitate turned into a clear solution in Step 1d; then a white precipitate Formed in Step 1e.

23. After which step can you be sure whether Pb is present?

    (A) Step 1a
    (B) Step 1b
    (C) Step 1c
    (D) It is not possible to tell.

24. What does the dark precipitate produced in Step 2a indicate?

    (F) Only HgS is definitely present.
    (G) HgS and Bi ions are definitely present.
    (H) HgS, Bi ions, and Cu ions may be present.
    (J) Only Bi and Cu ions may be present.

25. Step 2b was performed to test for the presence of

    (A) Hg.
    (B) Bi.
    (C) Cu and Bi.
    (D) Hg and Cu.

26. What are all the metals present in the unknown solution?

    (F) Pb, Hg, Ag, Cu, Bi
    (G) Hg, Ag, Cu, Bi
    (H) Ag, Cu, Bi
    (J) Pb, Ag, Cu

27. After the precipitate has been removed from the solution in Step 2a, the experimenter adds a few drops of H_2S to the remaining solution. A black precipitate forms. What does this show?

    (A) There were still Cu ions in the solution.
    (B) The H_2S became a solid.
    (C) Some HCl remained in the solution.
    (D) Too much H_2S had been added to the solution.

Passage VI

The diagram below, known as Bowen's Reaction Series, shows the temperature and the order in which minerals form as hot magma cools. The minerals present in rock indicate the temperature at which it formed. As shown in Table 1, the rocks are named depending on the proportion of certain minerals present and on the size of the mineral crystals, or grains. Two sets of rock samples were collected. These samples were brought back to the lab, and their mineral content was analyzed. Table 2 lists those collected from deposits on a volcanic island. Table 3 lists those collected from ancient mountains on a continent.

Table 1. Percent of Mineral by Volume*

Rock Color	Light		Intermediate		Dark		
Fine grain	Rhyolite	Dacite	Trachyte	Andesite	Basalt	—	—
Coarse grain	Granite	Granodiorite	Syenite	Diorite	Gabbro	Pyroxenite	Peridotite
Quartz	>20%	20–40%	<10%				
Orthoclase feldspar	>Plagioclase	<Plagioclase	65–95%				
Plagioclase feldspar	<Orthoclase	>Orthoclase	0–35%	>Pyroxene, mostly Sodium-rich	<Pyroxene, mostly Calcium-rich		<10%
Pyroxene			<10%	<30%	15% to >50%	>90%	10–60%
Olivine				<10%	<10%	>40%	
Amphibole		<10%	<10%	<30%	<10%		
Muscuvite mica	<10%						
Biotite mica	<10%	<10%	<10%				

Totals do not add to 100% because minerals in trace amounts are not listed.

Table 2. Volcanic Island*

Sample Coarse	1 Fine	2 Coarse	3 Coarse	4 Fine
Quartz				
Orthoclase feldspar				
Plagioclase feldspar	23%		9%	29%
Pyroxene	68%	97%	33%	62%
Olivine	7%	3%	58%	8%
Amphibole	1.5%			1%
Muscuvite mica				
Biotite mica				

Totals do not add to 100% because minerals in trace amounts are not listed.

Table 3. Continental Mountain Region*

Sample Grain	5 Fine	6 Coarse	7 Coarse	8 Coarse
Quartz	5%	23%	20%	3%
Orthoclase feldspar	68%	36%	22%	75%
Plagioclase feldspar	20%	29%	51%	15%
Pyroxene	4%			2%
Olivine				
Amphibole	3%		3%	2%
Muscuvite mica		6%		
Biotite mica		6%	4%	2%
Hornblende				

Totals do not add to 100% because minerals in trace amounts are not listed.

28. A rock with a composition of 28% quartz, 32% orthoclase feldspar, and 28% plagioclase feldspar is classified as a
    (F) granite.
    (G) granodiorite.
    (H) trachyte.
    (J) rhyolite.

29. What type of rock is Sample 1?
    (A) Gabbro
    (B) Basalt
    (C) Peridotite
    (D) Diorite

30. Which graph best represents the relation between temperature and dark mineral content?

(F)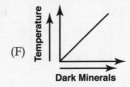

(G)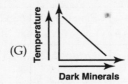

(H)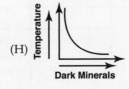

(J)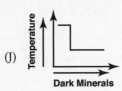

31. Which major difference between Sample 5 and Sample 8 indicates the difference in the way the two samples formed?

    (A) The percentage of plagioclase compared to orthoclase

    (B) The amount of biotite

    (C) The difference in rock color

    (D) The difference in grain size

32. Based on the rock samples collected, which of the following best describes the difference between the magma that formed the volcanic islands and the magma that formed the continental mountains?

    (F) The island magma was at high temperatures; the mountain magma, at low to intermediate temperatures.

    (G) The island magma was at low to intermediate temperatures; the mountain magma, at high temperatures.

    (H) The island magma and the mountain magma were both formed at low to intermediate temperatures.

    (J) The island magma and the mountain magma were both formed at high temperatures.

Rock Color	Light		Intermediate		Dark		
Fine grain	Rhyolite	Dacite	Trachyte	Andesite	Basalt	—	—
Coarse grain	Granite	Granodiorite	Syenite	Diorite	Gabbro	Pyroxenite	Peridotite
Quartz	>20%	20-40%	<10%				
Orthoclase feldspar	>Plagioclase	<Plagioclase	65-95%				
Plagioclase feldspar	<Orthoclase	>Orthoclase	0-35%				
Pyroxene			<10%				
Olivine							
Amphibole		<10%	<10%%				
Muscuvite mica	<10%						
Biotite mica	<10%	<10%	<10%				

33. Which two rock types are most similar in their composition?

    (A) Rhyolite: Granite

    (B) Dacite:Syenite

    (C) Trachyte: Dacite

    (D) Dacite:Granite

Passage VII

The fossil record shows that about 100,000 years ago, several species of hominids, including *Homo erectus*, *Homo sapiens*, and Neanderthals, populated Africa and Eurasia. However, by about 25,000 years ago, only *Homo sapiens* remained. Scientists are now debating the place and the time at which this change occurred. Following are the two major theories proposed to explain this transformation.

The Out-of-Africa Theory

Proponents of this theory agree that a migration of *Homo erectus* occurred 1.7 million years ago but contend that descendants of this early migration did not contribute to the genetics of modern humans. The out-of-Africa theory proposes that all *Homo erectus* populations originated in Africa, evolved into *Homo sapiens* in Africa, and about 100,000 to 200,000 years ago, spread across Europe and Asia replacing other human species without interbreeding.

There is much DNA evidence to support this theory. Scientists have calculated the rates at which DNA mutations occur. To estimate the time when two populations shared a common ancestor, the number of genetic differences between the two populations can be divided by the calculated rate of mutation. Many estimates of evolutionary ancestry rely on studies of the DNA in cell structures called mitochondria. This DNA is referred to as mtDNA. Most mtDNA is inherited solely from the mother. Because so little variation in mtDNA is found throughout worldwide populations, theorists have concluded that all human mtDNA came from a common ancestral female about 200,000 years ago. Scientists also found many more variations in African mtDNA than European or Asian, leading to the conclusion that mtDNA originated in Africa where it had more time to mutate. Both of these conclusions support the out-of-Africa theory.

Supporters of this theory also note that many modern human skeletal traits evolved within about the past 200,000 years, suggesting a single, common origin. Also, all modern humans share many more physical similarities than those shared by archaic and modern humans within particular geographic regions.

The Multi-Regional Theory

The multi-regional theory proposes that *Homo erectus* populations evolved in Africa and migrated to Europe and Asia around 1.7 million years ago. Then each population evolved separately into *Homo sapiens*. Occasionally, the *sapiens* populations mixed through migration. They also mixed with archaic species, so that no separate *Homo sapiens* species evolved.

Evidence in support of this theory includes the similarity in certain physical features of archaic and modern humans. For example, both archaic and modern skulls of eastern Asia have flatter cheek and nasal areas than do skulls from other regions. In archaic and modern European skulls, the cheeks and nasal areas of the face project forward. If these traits were inherited, then archaic humans may have given rise to modern humans, or interbred with modern human populations in those regions.

Proponents of this theory also argue that mtDNA evidence used to support the out-of-Africa theory is misleading. For example, some estimates of mtDNA mutation put the time of a common ancestor closer to 850,000 years ago, about the time of *Homo erectus*. Also, some evidence suggests that some mtDNA is inherited from the male and would therefore make tracing mtDNA to a common female impossible. Also, the smaller diversity of modern mtDNA in Europe and Asia could have resulted from drastic population declines in those regions.

34. According to the out-of-Africa theory,

    (F) all humans descended from a single female in Africa.

    (G) all mtDNA have descended from a single female.

    (H) all modern mtDNA originated in Africa.

    (J) All of the above

35. According to the multi-regional theory,

    (A) no separate species of *Homo sapiens* evolved, because the separate populations would sometimes interbreed.

    (B) no separate populations of *Homo sapiens* interbred.

    (C) *Homo sapiens* did not interbreed with *Homo erectus*.

    (D) all species of *Homo sapiens* originated in Africa.

36. Which of the following evidence would support the out-of-Africa theory?

    (F) Inheritance of some mtDNA from males

    (G) A *Homo sapiens* migration from Africa to Europe 800,000 years ago

    (H) Neanderthal mtDNA differed radically from modern humans.

    (J) 60,000-year-old *Homo sapiens* mtDNA differed radically from modern humans.

37. According to the multi-regional theory, if no mixing through migration of *Homo sapiens* populations had occurred,

    (A) a mixed species of *Homo erectus* and *Homo sapiens* would have evolved.

    (B) separate species would have evolved instead of a single *Homo sapiens* species.

    (C) all *Homo erectus* would have descended from the same African population.

    (D) all *Homo sapiens* would have descended from the same African population.

38. What is one main difference between the theories?

    (F) Whether *Homo erectus* evolved solely in Africa or evolved in several regions

    (G) Whether modern humans evolved solely in Africa and then migrated outward or evolved at the same time in several regions

    (H) Whether archaic and modern humans have a similarity in certain physical features

    (J) Whether modern human skeletal features evolved within about the last 200,000 years or within the last 500,000 years

39. On which of the following is there agreement among scientists who support the two theories?

    (A) Modern humans completely replaced archaic species of humans.

    (B) There was interbreeding between archaic and modern humans.

    (C) There was a migration of *Homo erectus* from Africa to Eurasia 1.7 million years ago.

    (D) Separate populations of *Homo erectus* evolved into *Homo sapiens*.

40. What might help settle the debate between the two theories?

    (F) If more advanced dating techniques are developed

    (G) If more *Homo erectus* and *Homo sapiens* fossils are found

    (H) If more genetic studies are made using a broad spectrum of the population and many subjects, with fewer statistical errors

    (J) All of the above

QUICK ANSWER GUIDE

Passage V

22. H
23. C
24. H
25. A
26. H
27. A

Passage VI

28. G
29. B
30. G
31. D
32. F
33. A

Passage VII

34. J
35. A
36. H
37. B
38. G
39. C
40. J

For explanations to these questions, see Day 29.

Science Reasoning Test: Passages V, VI, and VII Explanations and Answers

Assignment for Today:

- Review the explanations for the test you just took.

Passage V

22. **The correct answer is (H).** If Hg were present, it would produce a white precipitate in Step 1a, but when tested in Step 1d, only a clear solution formed. If Ag were present, it would have formed a black or gray precipitate.

    (F) This choice states that these same procedures show the presence of Hg, whereas, in fact, they show its absence.

    (G) The final Step 1e is unnecessary to show Hg's presence, because the previous step showed it wasn't present. This final step only confirms the presence of Ag.

    (J) Again, Step 1d proves Hg is *not* present, because no precipitate was left.

23. **The correct answer is (C).** According to Table 1, PbCl reacts with K_2CrOH and acetic acid (Step 1c) to form a yellow precipitate. If Pb were present, it would form PbCl (white precipitate) in Step 1a, dissolve in the solution in Step 1b, and then turn to yellow precipitate in Step 1c.

(A) There is no way to know what the white precipitate formed is until the other tests are done.

(B) There is no way to tell whether there was Pb in the clear solution formed.

(D) The test of adding acetic acid and K_2CrOH to the clear solution would clearly tell whether Pb is present.

24. **The correct answer is (H).** The words *may* and *definitely* are important in order to understand this answer. Using Table 2, you can see that precipitates that could form in Step 2a include HgS (black), Cu ions (black), and Bi ions (brown). Thus, a dark precipitate *may* indicate, but *not definitely* confirm, that all three ions are present.

(F) The presence of a dark precipitate *may* indicate HgS. However, this is not *definite*, because the precipitate may also indicate any combination of Bi ion, Cu ion, and HgS because these combinations would also form a dark precipitate.

(G) The presence of Hg and Bi *may* be indicated but is not definite for the same reason as choice (F).

(J) HgS may also be present for the same reason as choice (F).

25. **The correct answer is (A).** According to Table 2, adding nitric acid and heat dissolves precipitates of Bi and Cu. So if a precipitate dissolved, it would not be possible to tell which of the two metals was present. However, a precipitate of Hg will not dissolve in nitric acid and heat. Thus, if Hg is present, it will remain after nitric acid and heat are added.

(B) Bi precipitate dissolves in nitric acid and couldn't be detected if it were present.

(C) Bi and Cu precipitates dissolve in nitric acid and couldn't be detected if they were present.

(D) Cu precipitate dissolves in nitric acid and couldn't be detected if it were present.

26. **The correct answer is (H).** Step 1d and Step 1e confirm the presence of Ag. Step 2c proves the presence of Cu and Bi, respectively, because a blue solution and white precipitate formed.

(F) Step 1c disproves the presence of Pb, because no yellow precipitate formed with the addition of acetic acid and heat. Step 1d disproves the presence of Hg, because no precipitate formed with the addition of NH_4OH. Also, Step 2b disproves the presence of Hg because Hg would have formed a black precipitate, HgS, when H_2S was added. This precipitate would not have reacted with nitric acid and heat. However, when nitric acid and heat were added, a clear solution formed, showing no HgS precipitate is present.

(G) No Hg is present for the reasons stated in choice (F).

(J) Step 1c disproves the presence of Pb because no yellow precipitate formed.

27. **The correct answer is (A).** According to Table 2, adding H_2S to a solution of metal ions produces a

black precipitate if Cu is present. Since it was shown that Cu is present, some could very likely have been left in the solution after the first addition of H_2S, and by adding more, the rest of Cu formed a precipitate.

(B) The table shows that adding H_2S to a metal solution produces precipitates of S combined with the metals, not a precipitate of H_2S itself.

(C) If adding H_2S to HCl formed a precipitate, this would have occurred when the H_2S was originally added to the solution in Step 2a. According to Table 2, this did not happen.

(D) Adding more H_2S to the solution does not form a precipitate.

Passage VI

28. **The correct answer is (G).** By using Table 1, you can eliminate all the intermediate and dark rocks, because the quartz content is above 10%. Of the four light rock types, only granodiorite and dacite have more orthoclase than plagioclase.

(F) Granite has more plagioclase than orthoclase.

(H) Trachyte, although it has more orthoclase than plagioclase, has less than 10% quartz.

(J) Rhyolite, while it does meet the quartz content, has more plagioclase than orthoclase.

29. **The correct answer is (B).** Note that the sample is fine-grained and has no quartz or orthoclase. The sample has more pyroxene than plagioclase and small amounts of amphibole and olivine. According to Table 1, the only rock that meets these criteria is basalt.

(A) While having the same composition as basalt, this rock is coarse-grained, unlike the sample.

(C) Sample 1 has 8% too much pyroxene, more than 10% plagioclase, and not enough olivine (greater than 40%) to be peridotite.

(D) Diorite has more plagioclase than pyroxene, the inverse of Sample 1.

30. **The correct answer is (G).** According to the figure, as temperature (left side of figure) decreases, rock color (right side of figure) changes from dark to light. Rocks are composed of minerals, so rock color is determined by the minerals that a rock is made of. Thus, as temperature decreases, the amount of dark minerals decreases.

(F) This graph indicates that dark mineral content increases as temperatures decrease, whereas the inverse is true.

(H) This graph also indicates that dark mineral content increases as temperatures decrease, whereas the inverse is true.

(J) This graph indicates that dark mineral content continues to increase as the temperature remains stable and even when the temperature drops dramatically. A magma of a stable temperature would continue to produce rocks of the same mineral content.

31. **The correct answer is (D).** The two samples are almost identical in composition. The major difference is that Sample 5, trachyte, is fine-grained and Sample 8, syenite, is coarse-grained. The passage states that fine-grained igneous rocks form on the earth's surface, while coarse-grained rocks form beneath the surface.

(A) The mineral content in both samples, including the amounts of plagioclase and orthoclase, is very similar, thus indicating that there are no differences in their formation.

(B) Again, the mineral content is too similar to indicate a difference.

(C) Rock color is determined by the minerals present, and because the minerals in the samples are so similar, this again would not indicate a difference in the rocks' formation.

32. **The correct answer is (F).** By using Table 1, you can determine that the island samples are (1) basalt, (2) pyroxene, (3) peridotite, and (4) Basalt, and the mountain samples are (5) trachyte, (6) granite, (7) granodiorite, and (8) syenite. Accord-

ing to the table, the island samples are all dark rocks; the mountain samples, light- to intermediate-colored rocks. Looking at the figure, you can see that dark rocks form at higher temperatures, and intermediate to light rocks form at intermediate to low temperatures, respectively.

(G) The inverse is true.

(H) The two very different sets of rock types do not form at the same temperatures, as shown in the figure.

(J) The two very different sets of rock types do not form at the same temperatures, as shown in the figure.

33. **The correct answer is (A).** The first column of the table lists both Rhyolite and Granite having the same composition. The only difference between the two rock types is size of the grains.

(B) Dacite has more quartz than syenite. Also, dacite has more plagioclase than orthoclase, and syenite has more orthoclase than plagioclase.

(C) Trachyte has the same composition as syenite.

(D) Dacite has more plagioclase than orthoclase, and granite has more orthoclase than plagioclase.

Passage VII

34. **The correct answer is (J).** This question proves the need to go back and check the passage carefully. All three statements are true, so if you read the question too quickly and just took the first answer as true, you'd be wrong. Choices (F) and (G) are correct because the study of mtDNA concluded that all modern mtDNA was inherited from a single African female; therefore, all humans are descendants of this female. Choice (H) is also correct because there are many more variations in African mtDNA than in other regions, so mtDNA originated in Africa where it has had more time to mutate.

35. **The correct answer is (A).** The theory states that the interbreeding of separate populations maintained the *Homo sapiens* as a single species.

(B)   The theory specifically states that separate populations interbred.

(C)   The theory also states that there was some interbreeding with archaic species, of which *Homo erectus* is one.

(D)   The theory states that *Homo erectus* migrated to Europe and Asia where the populations then evolved to *Homo sapiens*.

36. **The correct answer is (H).** The large difference in Neanderthal and modern humans' mtDNA would support the idea that there was no interbreeding between the two species.

(F)   The out-of-Africa theory derives much of its support from the idea that only females contribute genetic material to mtDNA.

(G)   This statement does not necessarily counter the theory, because the *sapiens* in this earlier migration may not have interbred with later *sapiens*. However, this evidence does nothing to support the theory that the ancestors of modern humans emerged from Africa only 200,000 years ago.

(J)   This evidence would support the idea that there were divergent populations of *Homo sapiens* rather than just one from which all modern humans are descended.

37. **The correct answer is (B).** The mixing of separate populations was necessary to assure that the species did not become too divergent and thus unable to interbreed.

(A) If there were no mixing, then the two species wouldn't have interbred.

(C) Whether the populations mixed is unrelated to *Homo erectus* leaving Africa.

(D) Whether the populations mixed is unrelated to *Homo sapiens* leaving Africa.

38. **The correct answer is (G).** The theories differ greatly on this issue. The out-of-Africa theory contends that modern humans evolved solely in Africa. The multi-regional theory contends that they evolved in several regions at the same time.

(F) Both theories *agree* that *Homo erectus* evolved in Africa.

(H) This evidence is used only to support the multi-regional theory.

(J)   This evidence is used only to support the out-of-Africa theory.

39. **The correct answer is (C).** Both theories agree that *Homo erectus* migrated from Africa at this time—however, with differing results.

(A)   This is part of only the out-of-Africa theory.

(B)   This is part of only the multi-regional theory.

(D)   This is part of only the multi-regional theory.

40.   **The correct answer is (J).** Choice (F) is correct. Advanced dating techniques could be used to date more precisely fossils of archaic humans and *Homo sapiens*, giving credence to one evolutionary time line over another. Choice (G) is also correct. The more fossils available for study, the more likely useful DNA evidence and evidence of skeletal features can be discerned. Choice (H), too, is correct. The more genetic studies that are conducted, the more data are available for study and comparison among populations. The more precisely the data are calculated, the less likely there is to be contention over the results.

Day 30

Final Review
and
Last-Minute Preparation

Day 30

Final Review and Last-Minute Preparation

Assignments for Today:

- Prepare what you'll need for test day.
- Review the overall strategies for taking the ACT Assessment.
- Review the specific strategies for each subtest of the ACT Assessment.

You're almost there—Day 30. It's the night before the test, and you need to gather together a few things for the test. There are also some things you can do for yourself to help you feel calm and confident as you walk into the test site.

ASSEMBLE WHAT YOU'LL NEED FOR TEST DAY

The night before the test, get together those things that you will need for the test. The following are your "must haves":

- Your official admission ticket, which you will receive by mail after you have registered
- Photo identification, which can be:
  - a photo driver's license
  - your school photo ID
  - your passport
  - your picture in the yearbook with your name identified (not a group shot with no one identified)

- a letter with a physical description of you from the guidance counselor on school letterhead
- A half dozen sharpened number-2 pencils with clean erasers
- A watch, even if there is a clock in the room where the test is given
  - You may not be able to see a wall clock easily, and it takes less time to glance at the watch on your desk than on the wall. A digital watch will be more help in pacing than one with hands.

The following are some "doesn't hurt to haves":

- Battery-operated four-function scientific, or graphing, calculator
  - Put fresh batteries in your calculator and make sure it works.
- Snack for break time
  - There is a break halfway through the test, and you might want some juice, a granola bar, some nuts, or a candy bar to give you some quick energy.

- Sweater or jacket
  - Don't be fooled by the outside temperature. If it's a warm spring day, the air conditioning in the test room could be cranked down to 65°, which is a little brisk for people who are going to be sitting quietly for more than 3 hours. If it's a cold December morning, the room could be 80° and in 20 minutes, you'll be sweltering. The best thing to do is to dress in layers and bring an extra sweater or light jacket. In winter, wear a short-sleeved or lightweight shirt, a heavier long-sleeved shirt over it, and also a sweater and bring a jacket. In warmer weather, wear a T-shirt and a lightweight shirt over it and bring a jacket.

The following are some "can't haves":

- Scratch paper
- You have to use your test booklet.
- Notecards, notebooks, textbooks, and dictionaries
- Since you can't have them, why carry them?
- Laptops or powerbooks
- Highlighter pens
- Calculators with paper tape or a power cord, pen input devices, or electronic writing pads—in other words, anything in which information could be stored

ABOUT TEST ETIQUETTE

- Don't wear jewelry that makes a noise every time you move. You could make the person at the desk next to you more than a little annoyed.
- Don't wear perfume. You might sit next to someone with allergies, and you don't want to set off a sneezing and coughing fit.
- Do turn off your cell phone.
- Do turn off your pager.
- Do turn off the alarm on your watch.

THE NIGHT BEFORE THE TEST

Once you've assembled all the things you'll need for test day, put them in a place where you *absolutely cannot* miss them on the way out the door to the test. There is always one student who arrives breathless at the test site because he or she left home without the admissions ticket and had to rush back and get it.

Once everything is in a safe place, decide what you can do for yourself to help you relax. Don't even think about cramming. Go to the movies. Visit friends. Watch TV. Surf the Web. But do get a good night's sleep and set the alarm for plenty of time to get up, get ready, and get out the door without rushing. Rushing starts the anxiety level building.

THE DAY OF THE TEST

When you choose the layers of clothes to wear for the test, be sure they are comfortable. If you have a lucky color or a lucky piece of clothing, wear it. Take along a lucky charm if you have one and it won't distract anyone. Remember what we said about clunky jewelry and perfume.

If you're not a breakfast eater, test day probably is not the day to start. It is a good idea, though, to eat something if you can.

If you feel yourself getting nervous as you wait for the proctor to read through the rules and the test to begin, think the following to yourself:

- I don't need to answer all the questions on the test.
- Guessing costs me nothing.
- I do know a set of proven test-taking strategies to help me.
- Take a deep breath!

Good luck!

APPENDIX

ACT Assessment Test-Taking Strategies Wrap-up

REVIEWING YOUR TEST-TAKING STRATEGIES

By now, the overall strategies for taking the ACT Assessment should come naturally to you if you practiced them as you took each test in this book. You should also be familiar with the test strategies for the individual tests. Here's a quick review of the overall strategies and the ones for the specific tests. If you aren't sure about any one of them, go back to the full explanation and read it again.

Ten General Strategies for the ACT Assessment

1. KNOW the directions.
2. SKIM the passages and PLAN the order in which to answer them.
3. PACE yourself.
4. Answer the EASY ITEMS first.
5. ELIMINATE first, and GUESS second.
6. FOCUS on the wording—in the questions and in the answers.

7. Answer the RIGHT QUESTION.
8. REFER to the passage or problem.
9. Be EFFICIENT in how you FILL in your answers.
10. FINISH EARLY AND CHECK.

ACT Assessment English Test Strategies

1. Figure out the ERROR ON YOUR OWN.
2. Look for COMMON ERRORS.
3. LISTEN for the error.
4. Don't create a NEW ERROR.
5. SUBSTITUTE your answer into the passage.
6. ADD ONLY relevant details.
7. ORDER sentences or paragraphs based on the MAIN IDEA.
8. SHORTER is better.

DON'T FORGET TO USE THE OVERALL STRATEGIES.

ACT Assessment Math Test Strategies

1. Read the ANSWER CHOICES before solving the problem.
2. Answer the RIGHT QUESTION.
3. ESTIMATE the answer.
4. Find the mathematical operation in WORD PROBLEMS.
5. Use NUMERICAL VALUES for variables.
6. SUBSTITUTE answer choices into the question.

ACT Assessment Reading Test Strategies

1. SKIM, READ, REVIEW.
2. Read for the BIG picture.
3. Read for the ORGANIZATION.
4. Read ALL the answer choices.
5. SUBSTITUTE vocabulary answers.

ACT Assessment Science Reasoning Strategies

1. SKIM, READ, REVIEW.
2. Read for the BIG picture.
3. Find DIFFERENCES.
4. Find CHANGES.
5. Read ALL the answer choices.

PRACTICE ANSWER SHEET

English Test

1 (A) (B) (C) (D)	20 (F) (G) (H) (J)	39 (A) (B) (C) (D)	58 (F) (G) (H) (J)
2 (F) (G) (H) (J)	21 (A) (B) (C) (D)	40 (F) (G) (H) (J)	59 (A) (B) (C) (D)
3 (A) (B) (C) (D)	22 (F) (G) (H) (J)	41 (A) (B) (C) (D)	60 (F) (G) (H) (J)
4 (F) (G) (H) (J)	23 (A) (B) (C) (D)	42 (F) (G) (H) (J)	61 (A) (B) (C) (D)
5 (A) (B) (C) (D)	24 (F) (G) (H) (J)	43 (A) (B) (C) (D)	62 (F) (G) (H) (J)
6 (F) (G) (H) (J)	25 (A) (B) (C) (D)	44 (F) (G) (H) (J)	63 (A) (B) (C) (D)
7 (A) (B) (C) (D)	26 (F) (G) (H) (J)	45 (A) (B) (C) (D)	64 (F) (G) (H) (J)
8 (F) (G) (H) (J)	27 (A) (B) (C) (D)	46 (F) (G) (H) (J)	65 (A) (B) (C) (D)
9 (A) (B) (C) (D)	28 (F) (G) (H) (J)	47 (A) (B) (C) (D)	66 (F) (G) (H) (J)
10 (F) (G) (H) (J)	29 (A) (B) (C) (D)	48 (F) (G) (H) (J)	67 (A) (B) (C) (D)
11 (A) (B) (C) (D)	30 (F) (G) (H) (J)	49 (A) (B) (C) (D)	68 (F) (G) (H) (J)
12 (F) (G) (H) (J)	31 (A) (B) (C) (D)	50 (F) (G) (H) (J)	69 (A) (B) (C) (D)
13 (A) (B) (C) (D)	32 (F) (G) (H) (J)	51 (A) (B) (C) (D)	70 (F) (G) (H) (J)
14 (F) (G) (H) (J)	33 (A) (B) (C) (D)	52 (F) (G) (H) (J)	71 (A) (B) (C) (D)
15 (A) (B) (C) (D)	34 (F) (G) (H) (J)	53 (A) (B) (C) (D)	72 (F) (G) (H) (J)
16 (F) (G) (H) (J)	35 (A) (B) (C) (D)	54 (F) (G) (H) (J)	73 (A) (B) (C) (D)
17 (A) (B) (C) (D)	36 (F) (G) (H) (J)	55 (A) (B) (C) (D)	74 (F) (G) (H) (J)
18 (F) (G) (H) (J)	37 (A) (B) (C) (D)	56 (F) (G) (H) (J)	75 (A) (B) (C) (D)
19 (A) (B) (C) (D)	38 (F) (G) (H) (J)	57 (A) (B) (C) (D)	

PRACTICE ANSWER SHEET

Math Test

1 Ⓐ Ⓑ Ⓒ Ⓓ Ⓔ	16 Ⓕ Ⓖ Ⓗ Ⓙ Ⓚ	31 Ⓐ Ⓑ Ⓒ Ⓓ Ⓔ	46 Ⓕ Ⓖ Ⓗ Ⓙ Ⓚ
2 Ⓕ Ⓖ Ⓗ Ⓙ Ⓚ	17 Ⓐ Ⓑ Ⓒ Ⓓ Ⓔ	32 Ⓕ Ⓖ Ⓗ Ⓙ Ⓚ	47 Ⓐ Ⓑ Ⓒ Ⓓ Ⓔ
3 Ⓐ Ⓑ Ⓒ Ⓓ Ⓔ	18 Ⓕ Ⓖ Ⓗ Ⓙ Ⓚ	33 Ⓐ Ⓑ Ⓒ Ⓓ Ⓔ	48 Ⓕ Ⓖ Ⓗ Ⓙ Ⓚ
4 Ⓕ Ⓖ Ⓗ Ⓙ Ⓚ	19 Ⓐ Ⓑ Ⓒ Ⓓ Ⓔ	34 Ⓕ Ⓖ Ⓗ Ⓙ Ⓚ	49 Ⓐ Ⓑ Ⓒ Ⓓ Ⓔ
5 Ⓐ Ⓑ Ⓒ Ⓓ Ⓔ	20 Ⓕ Ⓖ Ⓗ Ⓙ Ⓚ	35 Ⓐ Ⓑ Ⓒ Ⓓ Ⓔ	50 Ⓕ Ⓖ Ⓗ Ⓙ Ⓚ
6 Ⓕ Ⓖ Ⓗ Ⓙ Ⓚ	21 Ⓐ Ⓑ Ⓒ Ⓓ Ⓔ	36 Ⓕ Ⓖ Ⓗ Ⓙ Ⓚ	51 Ⓐ Ⓑ Ⓒ Ⓓ Ⓔ
7 Ⓐ Ⓑ Ⓒ Ⓓ Ⓔ	22 Ⓕ Ⓖ Ⓗ Ⓙ Ⓚ	37 Ⓐ Ⓑ Ⓒ Ⓓ Ⓔ	52 Ⓕ Ⓖ Ⓗ Ⓙ Ⓚ
8 Ⓕ Ⓖ Ⓗ Ⓙ Ⓚ	23 Ⓐ Ⓑ Ⓒ Ⓓ Ⓔ	38 Ⓕ Ⓖ Ⓗ Ⓙ Ⓚ	53 Ⓐ Ⓑ Ⓒ Ⓓ Ⓔ
9 Ⓐ Ⓑ Ⓒ Ⓓ Ⓔ	24 Ⓕ Ⓖ Ⓗ Ⓙ Ⓚ	39 Ⓐ Ⓑ Ⓒ Ⓓ Ⓔ	54 Ⓕ Ⓖ Ⓗ Ⓙ Ⓚ
10 Ⓕ Ⓖ Ⓗ Ⓙ Ⓚ	25 Ⓐ Ⓑ Ⓒ Ⓓ Ⓔ	40 Ⓕ Ⓖ Ⓗ Ⓙ Ⓚ	55 Ⓐ Ⓑ Ⓒ Ⓓ Ⓔ
11 Ⓐ Ⓑ Ⓒ Ⓓ Ⓔ	26 Ⓕ Ⓖ Ⓗ Ⓙ Ⓚ	41 Ⓐ Ⓑ Ⓒ Ⓓ Ⓔ	56 Ⓕ Ⓖ Ⓗ Ⓙ Ⓚ
12 Ⓕ Ⓖ Ⓗ Ⓙ Ⓚ	27 Ⓐ Ⓑ Ⓒ Ⓓ Ⓔ	42 Ⓕ Ⓖ Ⓗ Ⓙ Ⓚ	57 Ⓐ Ⓑ Ⓒ Ⓓ Ⓔ
13 Ⓐ Ⓑ Ⓒ Ⓓ Ⓔ	28 Ⓕ Ⓖ Ⓗ Ⓙ Ⓚ	43 Ⓐ Ⓑ Ⓒ Ⓓ Ⓔ	58 Ⓕ Ⓖ Ⓗ Ⓙ Ⓚ
14 Ⓕ Ⓖ Ⓗ Ⓙ Ⓚ	29 Ⓐ Ⓑ Ⓒ Ⓓ Ⓔ	44 Ⓕ Ⓖ Ⓗ Ⓙ Ⓚ	59 Ⓕ Ⓖ Ⓗ Ⓙ Ⓚ
15 Ⓐ Ⓑ Ⓒ Ⓓ Ⓔ	30 Ⓕ Ⓖ Ⓗ Ⓙ Ⓚ	45 Ⓐ Ⓑ Ⓒ Ⓓ Ⓔ	60 Ⓐ Ⓑ Ⓒ Ⓓ Ⓔ

PRACTICE ANSWER SHEET

Reading Test

1 (A) (B) (C) (D)	11 (A) (B) (C) (D)	21 (A) (B) (C) (D)	31 (A) (B) (C) (D)
2 (F) (G) (H) (J)	12 (F) (G) (H) (J)	22 (F) (G) (H) (J)	32 (F) (G) (H) (J)
3 (A) (B) (C) (D)	13 (A) (B) (C) (D)	23 (A) (B) (C) (D)	33 (A) (B) (C) (D)
4 (F) (G) (H) (J)	14 (F) (G) (H) (J)	24 (F) (G) (H) (J)	34 (F) (G) (H) (J)
5 (A) (B) (C) (D)	15 (A) (B) (C) (D)	25 (A) (B) (C) (D)	35 (A) (B) (C) (D)
6 (F) (G) (H) (J)	16 (F) (G) (H) (J)	26 (F) (G) (H) (J)	36 (F) (G) (H) (J)
7 (A) (B) (C) (D)	17 (A) (B) (C) (D)	27 (A) (B) (C) (D)	37 (A) (B) (C) (D)
8 (F) (G) (H) (J)	18 (F) (G) (H) (J)	28 (F) (G) (H) (J)	38 (F) (G) (H) (J)
9 (A) (B) (C) (D)	19 (A) (B) (C) (D)	29 (A) (B) (C) (D)	39 (A) (B) (C) (D)
10 (F) (G) (H) (J)	20 (F) (G) (H) (J)	30 (F) (G) (H) (J)	40 (F) (G) (H) (J)

PRACTICE ANSWER SHEET

Science Reasoning Test

1 Ⓐ Ⓑ Ⓒ Ⓓ	11 Ⓐ Ⓑ Ⓒ Ⓓ	21 Ⓐ Ⓑ Ⓒ Ⓓ	31 Ⓐ Ⓑ Ⓒ Ⓓ
2 Ⓕ Ⓖ Ⓗ Ⓙ	12 Ⓕ Ⓖ Ⓗ Ⓙ	22 Ⓕ Ⓖ Ⓗ Ⓙ	32 Ⓕ Ⓖ Ⓗ Ⓙ
3 Ⓐ Ⓑ Ⓒ Ⓓ	13 Ⓐ Ⓑ Ⓒ Ⓓ	23 Ⓐ Ⓑ Ⓒ Ⓓ	33 Ⓐ Ⓑ Ⓒ Ⓓ
4 Ⓕ Ⓖ Ⓗ Ⓙ	14 Ⓕ Ⓖ Ⓗ Ⓙ	24 Ⓕ Ⓖ Ⓗ Ⓙ	34 Ⓕ Ⓖ Ⓗ Ⓙ
5 Ⓐ Ⓑ Ⓒ Ⓓ	15 Ⓐ Ⓑ Ⓒ Ⓓ	25 Ⓐ Ⓑ Ⓒ Ⓓ	35 Ⓐ Ⓑ Ⓒ Ⓓ
6 Ⓕ Ⓖ Ⓗ Ⓙ	16 Ⓕ Ⓖ Ⓗ Ⓙ	26 Ⓕ Ⓖ Ⓗ Ⓙ	36 Ⓕ Ⓖ Ⓗ Ⓙ
7 Ⓐ Ⓑ Ⓒ Ⓓ	17 Ⓐ Ⓑ Ⓒ Ⓓ	27 Ⓐ Ⓑ Ⓒ Ⓓ	37 Ⓐ Ⓑ Ⓒ Ⓓ
8 Ⓕ Ⓖ Ⓗ Ⓙ	18 Ⓕ Ⓖ Ⓗ Ⓙ	28 Ⓕ Ⓖ Ⓗ Ⓙ	38 Ⓕ Ⓖ Ⓗ Ⓙ
9 Ⓐ Ⓑ Ⓒ Ⓓ	19 Ⓐ Ⓑ Ⓒ Ⓓ	29 Ⓐ Ⓑ Ⓒ Ⓓ	39 Ⓐ Ⓑ Ⓒ Ⓓ
10 Ⓕ Ⓖ Ⓗ Ⓙ	20 Ⓕ Ⓖ Ⓗ Ⓙ	30 Ⓕ Ⓖ Ⓗ Ⓙ	40 Ⓕ Ⓖ Ⓗ Ⓙ

Notes

Notes

Notes

Notes

Notes

Notes

Notes

Notes

Wondering how to pay for college?
Have we got a deal for you!

THOMSON
——————————*——— ™
PETERSON'S

At **BestCollegeDeals.com**, we don't have a bridge to sell you or a potion to make all of your problems go away. We've got the real deals. Financial aid gems—from tuition waivers and merit-based scholarships to prepayment plans and family discounts—that you've probably never heard of. And because every family's situation is different, we'll help you calculate how much you really have to pay for college. With skyrocketing tuition costs and a volatile stock market, you can't afford to pass up a deal like this. Now about that bridge…

Visit **www.bestcollegedeals.com** today
for the Internet's newest personalized financial aid planning tool!

IHBCD03